It's another Quality Book from CGP

This book is for anyone doing AQA Modular Science at GCSE.

It contains lots of tricky questions designed to make you sweat — because that's the only way you'll get any better.

It's also got some daft bits in to try and make the whole experience at least vaguely entertaining for you.

What CGP is all about

Our sole aim here at CGP is to produce the highest quality books — carefully written, immaculately presented and dangerously close to being funny.

Then we work our socks off to get them out to you — at the cheapest possible prices.

Contents

The Final Exam

Module Three — Environment

Module Four — Inheritance and Selection

Module Seven — Patterns of Chemical Change

(AQA Syllabus reference)

Contents

The Final Exam

Module Eight — Structures and Bonding

Module Eleven — Forces

Module Twelve — Waves and Radiation

(AQA Syllabus reference)

Contributors:

Charley Darbishire
Toby Langley
Simon Little
Pratheeban Nambyiah
Alison Palin
Sam Patterson
Claire Thompson
Suzanne Worthington

Based on original questions by:

Jane Cartwright
Chris Christofi
Bill Doling
Alex Kizildas
Nigel Saunders
Paddy Gannon

Published by Coordination Group Publications Ltd
ISBN 1 84146 938 6
Groovy Website: www.cgpbooks.co.uk

Printed by Elanders Hindson, Newcastle upon Tyne.
Clipart sources: CorelDRAW and VECTOR.

Proofreading by:
Deborah Dobson
Simon Cook
Iain Nash
Leila Cornah
Taissa Csáky

12.1

Population and Habitat

Plants and animals can live in very inhospitable environments, but to survive they have to adapt to their surroundings...

Q1 What do the words predator and prey mean? Give two examples of a predator and its prey.

Q2 Draw a table with the headings shown on the right.

In the "**factor**" column, list the things that can affect the size of a population of organisms. In the "**examples**" column, give an example of this factor at work.
One line has been done for you as an example.
(Think of plant examples as well as animal examples)

Factor	Examples
Competition for water	Weeds and wheat

Q3 The sidewinder is a snake which lives in deserts. It moves sideways across the sand by throwing its body into a series of S-shapes, always keeping a loop of the S-shape off the ground, with two other parts touching.

Explain why it does this.

Q4 Many desert animals, such as the kangaroo rat, spend the day in a burrow and come out at night.

What are the **advantages** and **disadvantages** of doing this?

Q5 Desert plants are adapted to survive in their environment.

Study each of these features carefully. For each feature, decide what **condition** in the environment the plant has adapted to, and **explain** how the adaptation helps the plant to survive in the desert.

a) The seeds of flowering desert plants can lie dormant in the soil for years until the rain allows them to germinate, grow and flower quickly.
b) Some plants have long roots which reach deep underground.
c) Some plants have shallow roots which spread just under the surface.
d) Succulent plants store water in their leaves, stems and roots.
e) Some plants drop their leaves during a dry spell. They usually have small leaves.
f) Some plants take in and store carbon dioxide at night. During the day their stomata are closed.
g) Many plants have modified leaves which form thorns, and photosynthesis occurs in the stems.

Q6 Lemmings are small rodents that live in the tundra. They have a rounded body about 12cm long. Their fur is light brown, and they have small ears that are hidden by fur. Lemmings live in burrows.

Explain how the lemming is adapted to life in the Arctic.

Q7 Copy and complete the paragraph below. Use the words in the box on the right.

In a community, the populations of predators and prey are __________ . The population of any species is usually limited by the amount of __________ available. An __________ in the population of prey in a community means there is more food available for its __________ . As a consequence, the population of the predators may increase. However, an increase in the population of the predators will mean that more __________ (prey) is needed, and so the population of the prey will __________ .

decrease
increase
food
predators
food
linked

12.1 Population and Place of Habitat

Q1 The graph below shows the average daytime temperature (line) and rainfall (bars) in the Arctic. The temperature can fall to –80°C and the wind can blow at over 300 km/h. It's dark all the time in winter but in the summer, the sun never sets.

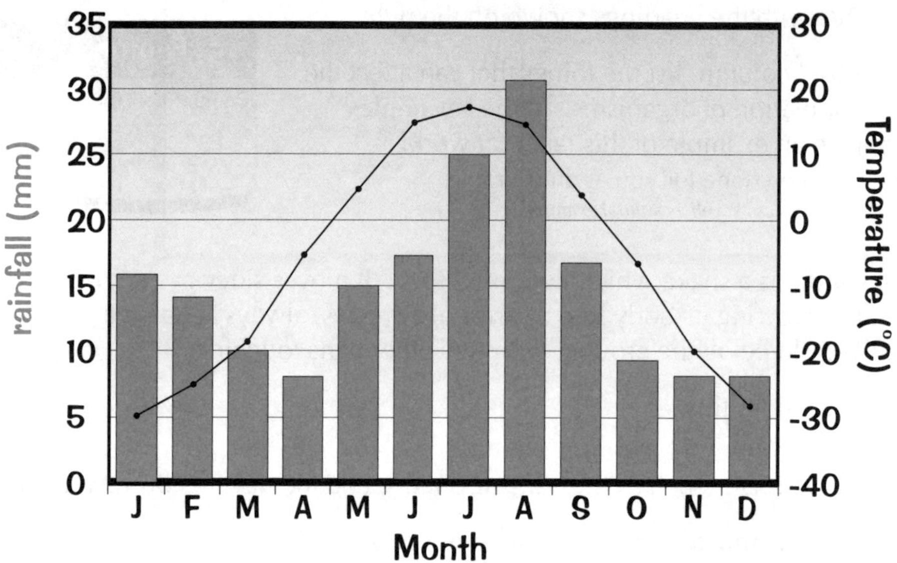

a) From this information, **suggest** what the environment is like in the Arctic.

b) It's not all sea and ice in the Arctic. There is a lot of barren land too, known as the tundra. The plants there often grow very close to the ground, and have small leaves. **Suggest** a reason why the plants grow in this way.

c) **What problems** will animals face living in the Arctic? **Suggest** some adaptations that would allow animals to live successfully in the Arctic.

Q2 The camel lives in the desert — a dry, hot environment. To help it survive, it's **adapted** to its environment in several ways.

Explain how each of these features helps the camel survive in the desert.

a) It has a large surface area.
b) It can drink up to 20 gallons of water at once and store it easily.
c) It produces little urine and even less sweat.
d) It is a sandy colour.
e) It has large feet.
f) It has a hump where it stores all its fat, so there is no layer of body fat.
g) It can tolerate big changes in its body temperature.

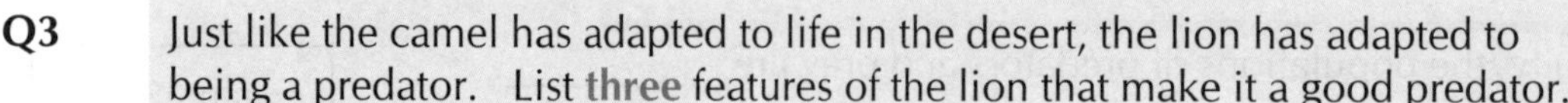

Q3 Just like the camel has adapted to life in the desert, the lion has adapted to being a predator. List **three** features of the lion that make it a good predator.

Q4 List **three physical** factors which may affect an organism's ability to live, grow and reproduce.

Population and Place of Habitat

12.1

Q1 **Copy and complete** the table to show what things plants and animals compete for.
(Hint — two of these are the same for both plants and animals.)

Plants	Animals
1)	1)
2)	2)
3)	3)

Q2 Answer the following questions about how rabbits are adapted to life as prey.

- **a)** Describe how the way a rabbit moves helps it survive.
- **b)** How does the colour of the rabbit's fur help it to avoid capture?
- **c)** Rabbits' eyes are on either side of their head.
  How does this help them spot predators?
- **d)** Why does the rabbit have big ears?
- **e)** How does a rabbit's tail alert other rabbits of danger?

Q2 Complete the following paragraph about the polar bear using the words from the box. Each word can be used only once.

white *insulation* *reduces* *prey*
thick *sheds* *prevent* *minimum*
powerful *camouflage* *runner*

The polar bear's surface area is kept to a _________ compared to its body weight. This _________ heat loss. It has a _____ layer of blubber for _________. Its fur is greasy so it _____ water after swimming to _______ cooling due to evaporation. It has _____ fur for _________ and is a _____ _____ which helps it catch _____ on land.

A bear adapted to 4000° C? — must be a solar bear.

Top-tips: You may get a <u>different plant or animal</u> to the ones in this section in your exam. But apply the <u>same techniques</u> as you did when answering these questions and it'll be a piece of cake.

12.2 Food Chains and Pyramids

Food chains and pyramids. What does fast-food have to do with the ancient Egyptians and how does that come into GCSE Science...

Q1 What does the food chain **grass → cow → person** mean in words?

Q2 **Connect** these food chains to form a food web for these woodland plants and animals.

trees → butterfly → robin → sparrowhawk

trees → aphids → ladybird → robin

trees → mouse → owl

grass → mouse → owl

grass → rabbit → owl

Q3 Pyramids of number are useful for displaying information.

a) What **information** does a pyramid of number give?

b) In the food chain, carrot → rabbit → fox **which row** in the table on the right represents the most likely numbers of each organism?

c) What do you notice about the **size** of the organism as you look from left to right along this food chain?

d) Which pyramid of number below most closely matches the correct answer to part **b)**?

e) What do you notice about the size of the organism and the width of its bar on the pyramid of number in the correct answer to part **d)**?

	Carrots	Rabbits	Foxes
A	1	100	4000
B	1	4000	100
C	100	1	4000
D	100	4000	1
E	4000	1	100
F	4000	100	1

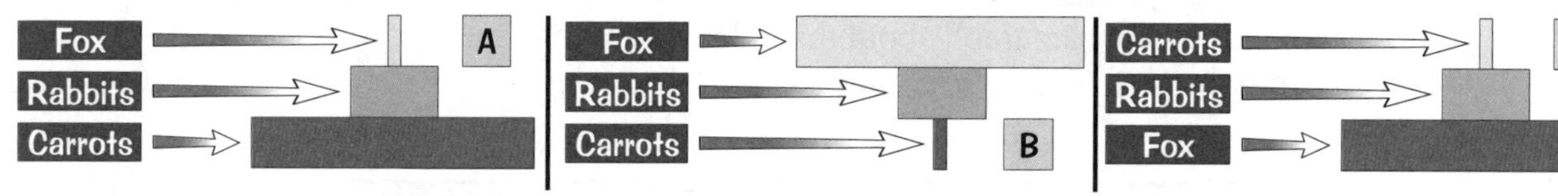

Q4 **Draw** pyramids of number for the food chains in **a)** and **b)**. Make sure you **label** each step with the name of the organism and how many of them there are.

a) Microscopic water plants (1 million) → water fleas (100,000) → trout (50) → kingfisher (1)

b) Oak tree (1) → caterpillars (500) → birds (5)

c) Ideally, the width of each bar would be drawn to scale, so that the trout bar in part **a)** would be fifty times wider than the kingfisher bar. This is usually not possible. **Explain why**.

d) If you have done part **b)** correctly, it will not look very pyramid-shaped. **Why** can a pyramid of number have an unusual shape like this?

e) **Draw** a pyramid to show the following short food chain: wheat → human. **Decide** on a suitable width for the wheat bar *(Hint: thousands of plants might be needed to feed one person)*.

f) In tropical countries, a disease called schistosomiasis can be a big problem. It's caused by a parasitic worm, about 1cm long, which lives in the blood vessels and feeds on blood. A person might be infected by dozens of these worms. **Add** a labelled bar for the worm to your pyramid of numbers. **Explain why** this pyramid is not pyramid-shaped.

g) Think of another food chain that will produce a pyramid of number that is **not** pyramid-shaped. **Draw** and **label** the pyramid, and write down the food chain along side it. **Explain** why your pyramid has its unusual shape.

Food Chains and Pyramids

12.2

Q1 Explain what is meant by the word **biomass**.
What information does a pyramid of biomass give?

Q2 One of the food chains in the North Sea is: **phytoplankton → zooplankton → small fish → cod**

The biomass of each of the organisms in the food chain was estimated from samples and experiments. It was found that for every 1kg of cod, there were 100kg of phytoplankton, 80kg of zooplankton and 10kg of small fish. In each case, the masses are dry masses.

a) **Draw** a pyramid of biomass for this food chain. Draw it **to scale**, and make sure that you label each bar with the name of the organism and its biomass in kg.

b) In some pyramids of number and biomass, the top bar can be shown as a vertical line. **Explain** why this is sometimes necessary.

c) Between which two organisms in this food chain is the **most** mass lost? **How much** mass?

d) Between which two organisms in this food chain is the **greatest proportion** of mass lost?

e) Suggest reasons why the biomass is **less** at each level than the one before it.

f) The wet mass of a small fish averages about 1.5kg, and that of adult cod averages about 7.5kg. Assuming that both types of fish have the same proportion of water in their bodies, **how many** small fish feed one cod?

Q3 Look at these pyramids:

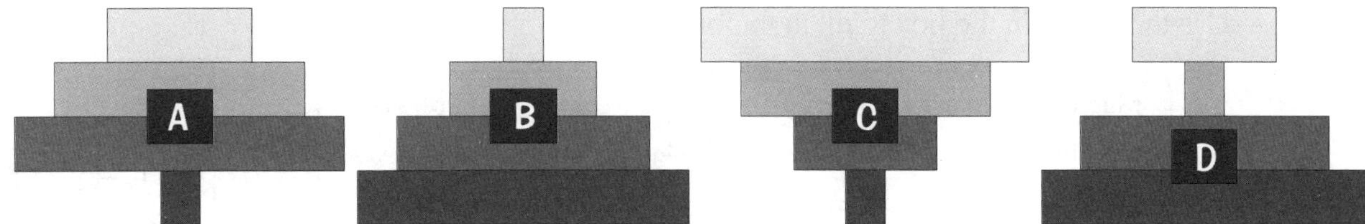

Explain which of the pyramids above could **represent**:

a) The pyramid of number for a community that relies on a large producer.
b) The pyramid of biomass for a woodland community.
c) The pyramid of number for a food chain that ends with parasites such as fleas.
d) The pyramid of number for a marine community in which the producers are tiny algae.

Q4 Fill in the blanks in the following paragraph, using the words in the box.

The mass of living material at each stage in a food chain is ________ than it was at the stage below. This means pyramids of ________ get ________ the higher you go. This is not always the case with pyramids of ________.

number
less
narrower
biomass

It's a cod eat small fish eat zooplankton world out there...

Remember it takes a lot of food from the level below to keep one animal alive. Pyramids of biomass always get narrower the higher you go, but pyramids of number can be any shape — all the fleas on one mangy dog still weigh less than the dog itself. (Unless it's got them *really really* bad...)

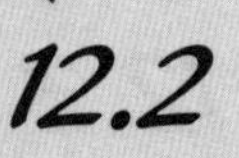

Food Chains and Pyramids

Q1 **Algae → slugs → frogs → heron** ...is an example of a food chain found in a pond.

For every heron, there are 80 kg of frogs, and for every kg of frogs there are 20 kg of algae.
If there are 400 kg of frogs in the lake how many herons are there?
How much algae is there?

Q2 **Answer** these questions about how energy is transferred through food chains:

a) **What** sort of organism is always at the start of any food chain?
b) **How** does this sort of organism bring energy into the chain?
c) **What** happens to the amount of energy and material present as you move up a food chain?

Q3 Farmer Giles likes to be efficient. He wants to produce as much food as possible from his land.

He has two options:

1) Use the land for grazing cattle and sheep
2) Grow vegetables, wheat and other crops than can be eaten by humans.

Which option should he choose for maximum efficiency? **Explain** your answer.

Q4 Energy and material are lost at each stage in a food chain. It doesn't disappear – it's used up.

a) Explain how energy and material is lost at each stage in a food chain.
b) Use the words in the box to fill in the blanks.

Much of the energy loss in ________ occurs as ______ loss to the environment. This loss is _____ high in mammals and birds. Their bodies must be kept at a ________ temperature which is usually ________ than that of their environment.

higher
very
heat
respiration
constant

c) Explain why a pet goldfish requires much less food than a pet gerbil.
Bear in mind the last part of the question.
d) Suppose that a cow gets 250 kJ of energy from eating some grass, uses 75 kJ for respiration and loses 150 kJ through excretion. What percentage of the energy is retained by the cow?

Q5 Like any business, the efficiency of food production is very important.

a) Battery farmed chickens have their **ability to move restricted** and are kept in conditions close to their own body temperature.
How does this method of farming increase the efficiency of **food production**?
b) **Describe** how hormones are used to increase the efficiency of **fruit growing**.
c) **What** are the **advantages** and **disadvantages** of these two methods of food production?

All this eating is tiring me out...

Energy and material is **lost** at each stage in a food chain. So the efficiency of food production can be **improved** by reducing the number of stages in food chains. You can also **minimise** the energy loss at each stage, but this can have some **disadvantages**. For us that is, not to mention the poor chickens.

Waste Materials and The Cycles

12.3

Q1 Material is constantly being removed from, and returned to the environment.

a) **Why** do living things **remove materials** from the environment?

b) **How** are the materials **returned** to the environment?

c) **Why** is it **important** that the materials are returned?

Q2 Bacteria and fungi can break down solid waste materials from animals.

They can also break down materials in dead animals and plants.
This is known as decomposition or decay.

a) **What general word** is used to describe bacteria and fungi that break down dead material?

b) **What is the benefit** to the bacteria and fungi of **digesting** these materials?

c) **What carbon compound** will be returned to the atmosphere as a result of their activities?

d) **What substances** will they release into the soil?

e) **Why** are bacteria and fungi important for the **recycling** of carbon in the carbon cycle?

Q3 Microorganisms digest materials best under certain conditions.

In each of the following statements about the conditons,
pick the correct word from each pair.

a) Microorganisms digest material faster in **warm** / **cold** conditions.

b) They digest faster if the conditions are **dry** / **moist** .

c) Many microorganisms are also more active if there is **plenty of** / **not a lot of** oxygen.

Q4 Humans sometimes use microorganisms to decompose materials.

a) **Why** are decomposing microorganisms **added** to waste at a sewage works?

b) **Why** must the waste in a compost heap be **exposed to air**?

c) **How** do plants **benefit** from having compost put on them?

Q5 For a stable community of organisms, processes which remove substances from the environment should be balanced with what?

Top-tips: **Without microorganisms decomposing animal waste and dead plant and animal material, plants would have <u>no nutrients</u> to grow with. Then animals, like us, would have no food, and die, die, die...**

12.3 The Carbon Cycle

The Carbon Cycle describes how carbon is removed from the environment, used by plants and animals and then returned to the environment. The Spin Cycle removes water from your clothes.

Q1 Green plants remove carbon from the environment.

a) What process in plants removes carbon dioxide from the atmosphere?

b) What process in plants returns some of this carbon dioxide to the atmosphere?

c) Copy and complete the diagram opposite using the words below. **Light** boxes are spaces for substances. **Dark** ones are spaces for processes.

photosynthesis	*carbon dioxide*
respiration	*carbon*

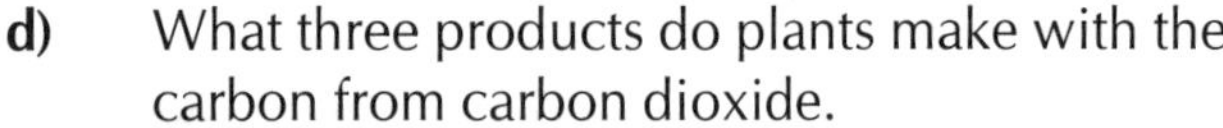

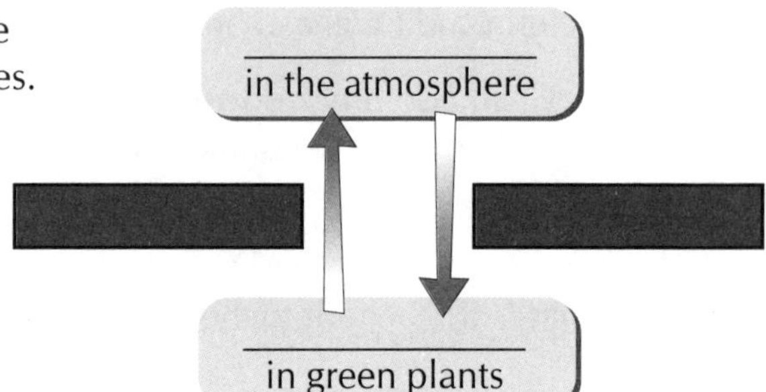

d) What three products do plants make with the carbon from carbon dioxide.

Q2 Animals also need carbon to survive — they get it by eating green plants.

a) What happens to the carbon present in plants when they are eaten by animals?

b) What process in animals returns carbon dioxide to the atmosphere?

Q3 Explain how the carbon present in dead plant and animal material is returned to the atmosphere.

Q4 Fill in the blanks in the paragraph about the carbon cycle below, using the words in the box.

fats	microorganisms	dioxide	carbohydrates
respire	carbon	eating	proteins
respiration	green	decomposed	

_______ _______ is removed from the atmosphere by _______ plants for photosynthesis. Some is returned by _______ . The carbon is used to make _______ , _______ and _______ which make up the body of the plants. Animals get carbon by _______ plants, and return some carbon dioxide to the atmosphere when they respire. Dead plant and animal material is _______ by _______ . More carbon dioxide is returned to the environment when they _______ .

The Nitrogen Cycle

12.3

It's no surprise that the nitrogen cycle tells us about the constant cycling of nitrogen in the environment. It's a bit more complicated than the carbon cycle though — make sure you can do all these questions.

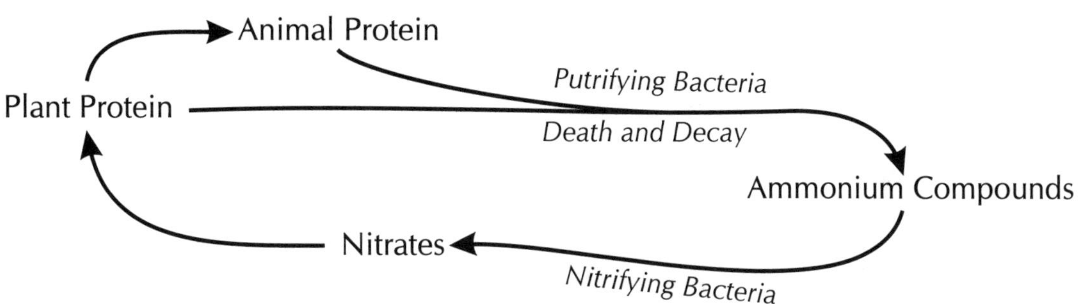

Q1 As in the carbon cycle, it's green plants that **remove** nitrogen from the environment.

a) How do green plants get nitrogen from the environment?

b) What do the plants need nitrogen for?

c) Why do animals need nitrogen?

d) How do they get the nitrogen that they need?

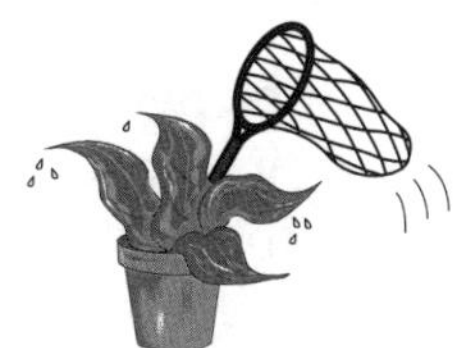

Q2 Nitrogen is **returned** to the environment when plant and animal material decomposes.

a) What sort of bacteria break down animal waste and dead plant and animal material?

b) What is produced by this process?

c) Explain how the product is converted to nitrates in the soil.

Q3 What happens to the **energy** present in the nitrates originally absorbed by the plants?

Q4 **Label** the following statements true or false.

a) Green plants absorb nitrogen from the air around them.

b) Plants and animals return nitrogen to the atmosphere when they respire.

c) Green plants absorb nitrates from the soil.

d) Animals get nitrogen by eating green plants.

e) Plants and animals need nitrogen to make fats in their bodies.

f) Nitrifying bacteria convert animal waste and dead plant and animal material into ammonium compounds.

g) Nitrifying bacteria convert ammonium compounds to nitrates.

h) Animals can absorb nitrogen directly from the air.

12.3 Waste Materials and The Cycles

Q1 Complete this diagram of the **nitrogen cycle**, using the labels on the right.

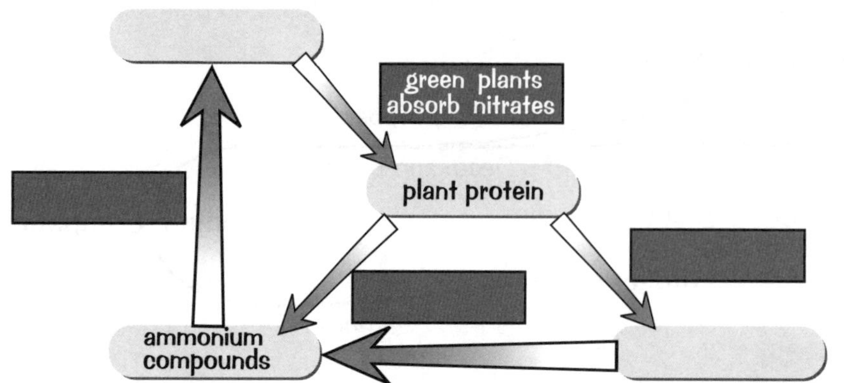

Q2 Draw up a table like the one shown on the right. Complete your table to show the processes that convert **nitrates** in the soil to **ammonium compounds**, and those that convert ammonium compounds back to nitrates in the soil.

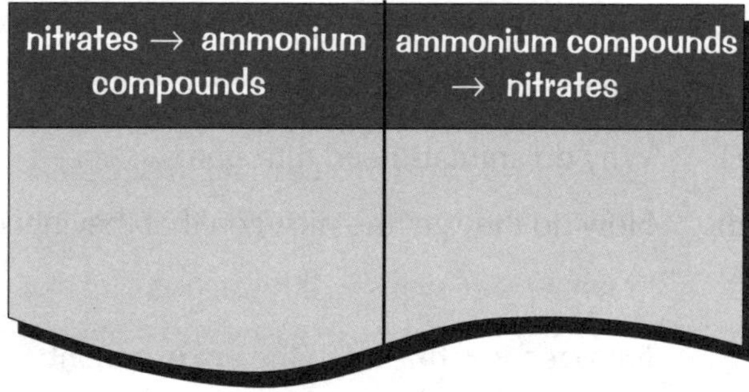

nitrates → ammonium compounds	ammonium compounds → nitrates

Q3 You've reached the last question of this huge section. Here's a quick test to see if you really know everything. Go on, you know you want to.

a) Name **two** places where humans use decomposing microorganisms.

b) Will materials decompose quicker in cold or warm temperatures?

c) Name **two** sorts of material in plants that are made from carbon.

d) Which **process** in green plants removes carbon dioxide from the atmosphere?

e) How does the **decomposition** of plant and animal material replace carbon dioxide in the atmosphere?

f) What sort of bacteria convert ammonium compounds to **nitrates** in the soil?

g) What sort of chemical in plants and animals requires **nitrogen**?

Learn — learn like you've never learnt before...

The nitrogen cycle goes on and on forever, but you only have to care about it until your exam is over. So learn all those different stages, and smile about your swotting. Go on ... who's to know...?

Our Effect on the Environment

12.4

For a supposedly intelligent species, humans have done some pretty dumb stuff to this planet. It's no wonder none of the animals will talk to us...

Q1 With so many people in the world, we take up a lot of the room. **List four** ways that humans reduce the amount of land available for other animals and plants.

Q2 For each of the following **pollutants** produced by the human race, decide whether they affect air, land or water and put them in the appropriate column. Some pollutants may fit in more than one column.

sulphur dioxide, pesticides, nitrogen oxides, sewage, carbon dioxide, herbicides, fertiliser

air	land	water

Q3 Mr M^c^Doodah owns a highly successful global fast food business. There is such demand for his burgers and hot dogs that he needs **more land** to farm his cows. He decides to buy some land in the Amazon rainforest, cut down the trees and graze cattle on it.

In what **three** ways will his actions increase the amount of greenhouse gases in the atmosphere.

Q4 As you can see from the graph opposite, the world population is growing exponentially. **Answer** these questions about how this affects the environment.

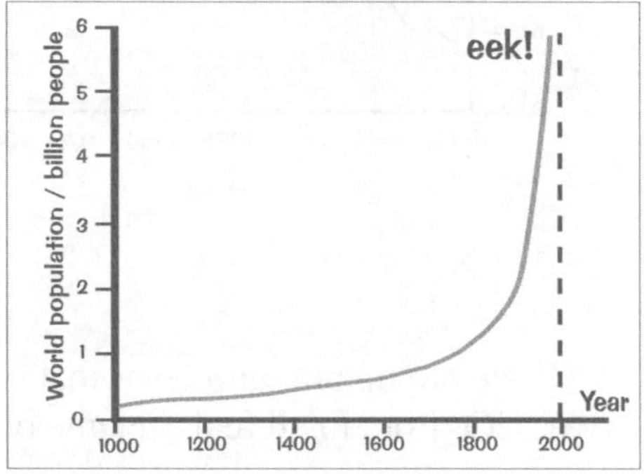

a) **How** does this affect the rate of use of raw materials?

b) **What** could this mean for supplies of non-renewable energy sources such as coal, oil and gas?

c) Are the effects of human activity **larger** or **smaller** than they were 200 years ago?

d) **Explain** why the proper handling of waste has never been more important than it is now.

Q5 Most of the world's energy is produced by **burning fossil fuels** such as coal, oil and natural gas. This method of energy production has several environmental drawbacks.

a) **Name** the greenhouse gas produced by burning fossil fuels.

b) **Why** has large scale deforestation increased the amount of this gas in the atmosphere?

c) Some fossil fuels contain sulphur or nitrogen impurities.
Explain why burning these fuels produces acid rain.

d) **Suggest** another reason why being overly reliant on fossil fuels is not a good idea.

(Hint — look at the last question.)

12.4

The Greenhouse Effect

The Greenhouse Effect — it does exactly what it says on the tin. If only everything in life could be that simple.

Q1 Only some of the gases in the atmosphere, called **greenhouse gases**, are good at absorbing heat energy. These include carbon dioxide and methane, which both occur naturally in the atmosphere.

a) Name a **natural source** of carbon dioxide.

b) The graph on the right shows the amount of carbon released from burning fossil fuels since 1850. **Describe** the graph — how has the release of carbon from fossil fuels changed? **Suggest** why this change happened.

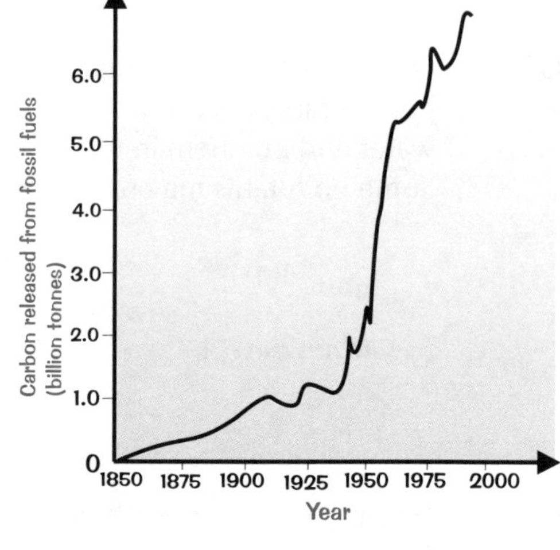

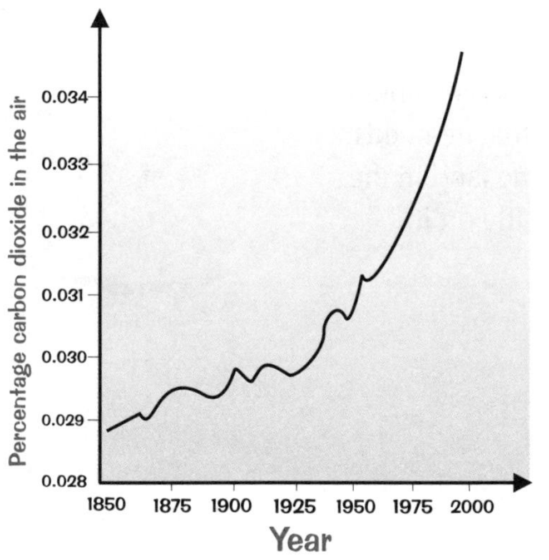

c) The graph on the left shows the amount of CO_2 in the atmosphere since 1850. **Describe** the graph — how has the amount of CO_2 in the atmosphere changed? **Suggest** why this change happened.

d) **Work out** approximately how many times more carbon was released in 1975 compared to 1875.

e) **Work out** approximately how many times more CO_2 there was in the atmosphere in 1975 compared with 1875.

f) There are natural processes that can absorb the carbon released as CO_2 from fossil fuels. Name one of these processes.

g) Explain what the changes in the amount of CO_2 in the atmosphere could do to the temperature of the Earth.

Q2 It's not just burning fossil fuels that increases the level of greenhouse gases in the atmosphere. Methane is produced by some sorts of **farming**.

a) How do cows produce methane?

b) Rice is grown in paddy fields which are covered by water. How does this produce methane?

c) The human population is growing very quickly. What **effect** will this have on the amount of methane produced by these two sources?

The Greenhouse Effect

12.4

Q1 Look at the graphs on the **right**. The first one shows the changes in the amount of CO_2 in the atmosphere since 1850. The second shows changes in average global temperature per year in °C since 1880.

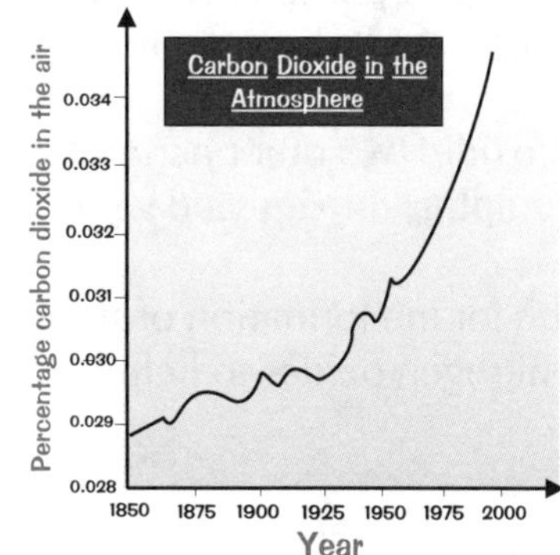

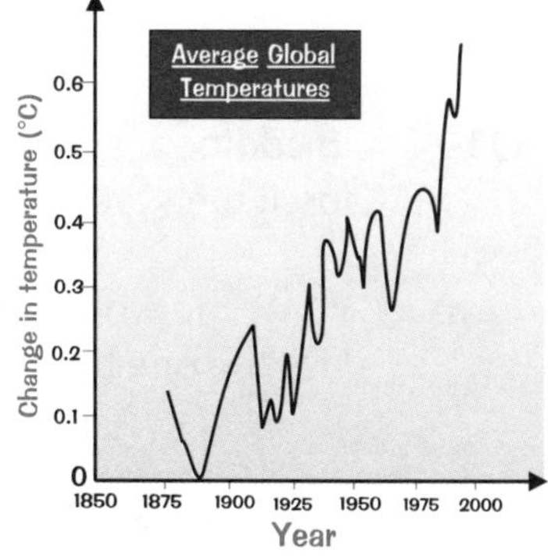

a) Describe the changes in average **temperature**.

b) Is it possible to say that the temperature changes are caused by the changes in the amount of CO_2 in the atmosphere?

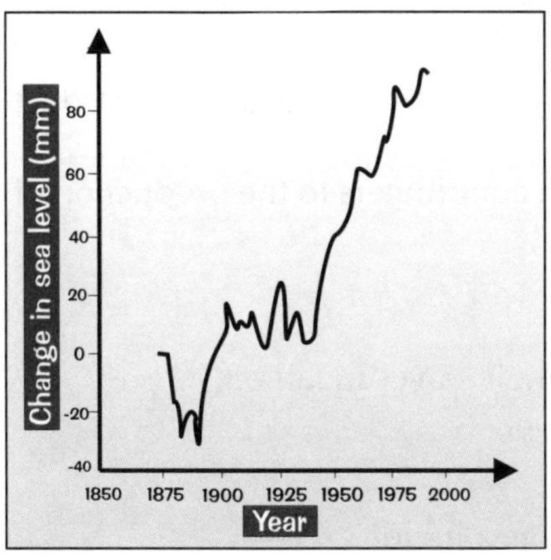

The graph on the left shows the changes in **sea level**. Compare this graph with the one showing changes in temperature.

c) **Suggest** how changes in the Earth's temperature ("Global Warming") could cause a change in sea level.

d) What do you think could happen to **low-lying** areas of the world if the amount of carbon dioxide in the atmosphere continues to rise?

Q2 The Dodo Treaty is a pact between countries — they agree to **limit** CO_2 emissions. President Mush has decided to abandon it.

a) The President said he wasn't convinced that carbon dioxide emissions were causing global warming. Using the graphs above, **explain** whether you agree or disagree with him.

b) He also said that limiting CO_2 emissions would be bad for **industry**. **Why** is this true?

c) **Suggest** a way to **reduce** the amount of CO_2 in the atmosphere that doesn't involve limiting the amount produced.

Q3 The Greenhouse Effect is caused by an **insulating** layer of gases in the atmosphere.

a) **Explain** how the layer of carbon dioxide and methane in the atmosphere keeps the Earth warmer than it would be if the layer was not there.

b) **What** would Earth's climate be like if there was **no** insulating layer at all?

Is it getting warmer in here — or is it just me?

The examiners love this topic — they get to test your ability to make reasoned arguments. So no waffling, just state the facts and make sure you read any graphs they give you very carefully. Unlike Mr Mush.

12.4

Acid Rain

Acid rain is pretty bad — especially if you're a tree or a fish. And whose fault is it? Well ours actually...

Q1 In addition to carbon dioxide, two other harmful gases are released when fossil fuels are burned: **sulphur dioxide** and various **nitrogen oxides**.

a) **Write** the word equation for the formation of sulphur dioxide from sulphur and oxygen. Use the one below for nitrogen oxides to help you.

nitrogen + oxygen —heat→ nitrogen oxides

When non-metal oxides dissolve in water, they produce acidic solutions. Sulphur dioxide and nitrogen oxides are all very soluble.

b) Using the information in the pink box above, **explain** how burning fossil fuels produces acid rain.

c) Power stations burn lots of fossil fuels so they are big contributers to the production of acid rain. **Suggest** another source of acid-rain producing gases.

Q2 Trees are damaged by acid rain, mainly as it causes their leaves to fall off.

a) How will a tree be affected if its leaves fall off?

b) Aluminium in the soil is harmful to trees, but usually insoluble. Acid rain dissolves aluminium, how will this harm trees?

c) The roots of trees in acid soils can grow poorly. What effects will this have on these trees?

Q3 As acid rain falls into rivers and lakes, they become increasingly acidic. Water flowing off the land contains high levels of aluminium and mercury released by the acid rain.

a) What will happen to the water plants in acidified lakes and rivers?

b) Small crustaceans at the bottom of the aquatic food chain die if the pH falls below about 6. **What** will happen eventually to the other animals in the lake if the pH falls below 6?

c) The soluble aluminium can react with sulphuric acid to make aluminium sulphate. This clogs the gills of fish with sticky mucus. **Suggest** the likely effect of this on the fish.

Acid rain? I must be seeing things...

There's not much to know about acid rain, so make sure you know it all really well. Remember which gases cause it and how they are produced. Oh, and make sure you know all about its effects too.

Pollution

12.4

Q1 The Examiners' favourite phrase this year is "**sustainable development**"

a) **What** is sustainable development? (Proper definition please.)

b) **Why** is it important?

Q2 The efficiency of farming has been greatly increased by the introduction of chemicals such as fertilisers.

a) How do fertilisers aid the growth of crops?

b) A farmer accidently sprays his field next to a river with too much fertiliser. It rains soon after he finishes. What will happen to the excess fertiliser?

c) What is the name of the damage fertilisers cause to lakes and rivers? (Make sure you spell it correctly.)

Q3 The sentences below are about a lake becoming polluted with fertilisers. They are muddled up.

a) Rewrite them in the correct order.

- **Fish and other aquatic animals die because of a lack of oxygen.**
- **The microbes take more oxygen from the water for their respiration.**
- **Excess fertilisers leach from the soil and are washed into the lake.**
- **The number of microbes that feed on dead organisms increases.**
- **There is increased competition between the plants, and some die as a result.**
- **Water plants in the lake start to grow rapidly.**

b) In the corrected sequence, **why** should water plants grow **more quickly**?

c) **What resources** are the water plants **competing** for? **Which resource** is probably in excess?

d) If there are more plants in the lake, you might expect more oxygen to be produced by photosynthesis. **Why** does the oxygen content of the water go **down** instead?

e) Normally, the action of decomposers such as bacteria is welcomed. It allows scarce nutrients to be recycled so other organisms in the community can use them (eg: in the nitrogen cycle). **Why** is the action of decomposers such a **problem** in the case of a eutrophic lake?

Q4 Raw sewage can also sometimes find its way into rivers and lakes.

a) **What resource** does raw sewage provide for microorganisms in water?

b) **Explain** why the introduction of raw sewage to water also causes eutrophication.

Top-tips: **The thing to remember about eutrophication is that the pollution isn't directly harming anything. Whether it's fertiliser or sewage, the problem is that it provides lots of food for microorganisms. They then steal the oxygen from everything else. Got it? ...of course you have.**

13.1

Variation

You and your mates don't look the same.
Your characteristics are "both inherited and due to environmental factors".

Q1 Identical twins have the same genes, so they are genetically identical. The table shows four people, identified by the letters a, b, c and d.

Characteristic	Person a	b	c	d
Have a sun tan	✔	✔		
They are male	✔	✔	✔	
They are female				✔
Can tongue roll	✔		✔	
Normal hair colour is brown	✔	✔	✔	✔
Have bleached white hair			✔	✔
Have brown eyes	✔	✔	✔	

a) i) **Use** the information in the table to identify which two people are identical twins.
ii) **Explain** your answer.

b) Give **one characteristic** which shows:
i) Continuous variation.
ii) Discontinuous variation.

Note — tongue rolling has a direct genetic cause.

Q2 People belong to one of these four blood groups: A, B, AB and O.

Copy and complete the paragraph below using the words in the box.

discontinuous	*environmental*	*inherited*	*range*

Blood groups show ________________ variation. Here, there is not a wide ________________ of characteristics. Our blood group is ________________ and is not altered by ________________ conditions.

Q3 Use the following words to complete the blanks: *asexual, exact, gametes, parent, two.*

Mitosis is a process used during growth and ________________ reproduction. Each chromosome in the original cell makes an ____________ copy of itself. When this type of division is complete, ____________ daughter cells are produced, each having the same chromosome number as the ____________ cell. Meiosis is a reduction division — this means that the number of chromosomes in the original cell is reduced (halved). This process is used in the production of male and female ____________. Meiosis involves some jumbling of genetic material, so producing variation.

Q4 Copy this table. Then fill in the missing information.

Organism	Number of chromosomes in a body cell	Number of pairs of chromosomes	Number of chromosomes in each gamete
Fruit Fly	8		
Kangaroo	12		
Rye Plant	20		
Chicken	36		
Mouse	40		
Humans	46		
Crayfish	200		

Variation

13.1

Q1 Copy and complete the passage below by using each of the following words once.

exactly	*sexual*	*parent*	*produce*	*without*	*mixing*
clones	*reproduction*	*copies*	*two*		
offspring	*parent*	*less*	*genes*	*asexually*	

Many plants can reproduce ______. This means they can ______ exact ______ of themselves ______ the need for another plant. The ______ of the ______ plant are ______, they have ______ the same ______ as the ______ plant. Asexual ______ produces ______ variation in the offspring than ______ reproduction which involves the ______ of genetic information from ______ parents.

Q2 Try these questions about genes and different characteristics.

a) **Where** are chromosomes found in the body?
b) **How many pairs** of human chromosomes are there?
c) Which of the characteristics in the box below are **totally inherited**? That is, which are determined **only** by the alleles you inherit from your parents?

body weight, hair colour, academic ability, blood group, inherited diseases, eye colour, skin colour.

The other characteristics on the list may be affected by something else.

d) What else might they be affected by?

Q3 Genes, chromosomes and DNA are important things you need to know about.

a) **Draw** simple diagrams of the following items listed in the box below.

cell, nucleus, chromosome, gene, DNA

b) **Humans show lots of variation**, in eye colour, hair colour etc. Explain how **genes** give rise to this variation.
c) **Copy and complete** the following sentences using each word from the box below once.

new	divide	growth
multiply	replace	
divide	identical	replicating

Body cells ____________ to produce ______ cells that are ______________ to the original cell. The new cells continue to ____________ and _______________ by ___________________ themselves. The cells produced are used for ____________ and also to _____________ old cells.

13.1

Mitosis and Meiosis

Q1 Put these descriptions in the right columns of a copy of the table below.

Male and female gametes join

No joining of sex cells needed

Offspring are not genetically identical to parents

Only one parent is needed

Offspring are clones of parent

Two parents are needed

Asexual Reproduction	Sexual Reproduction

Q2 Describe what's happening at each of the numbered stages in the diagrams below.

Diagram *A* – the stages involved in cell reproduction by ***mitosis***.

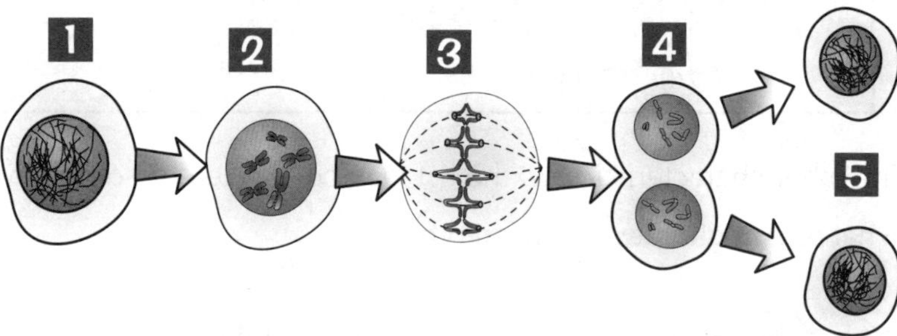

Diagram *B* – the stages involved in cell reproduction by ***meiosis***.

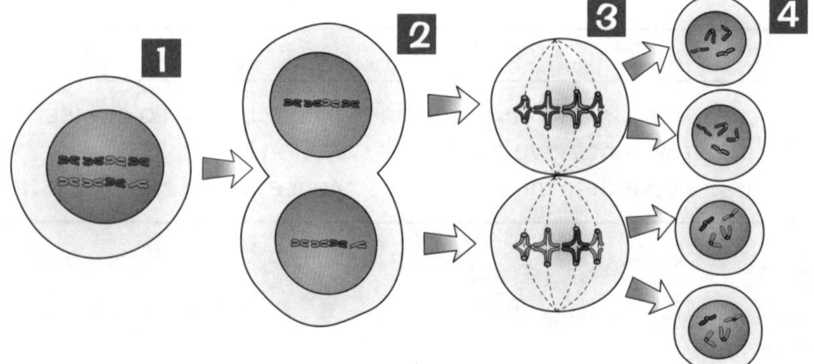

Biscuits show variation too — ginger nut, digestive...

It's not just about the genes you "inherit" from your parents — environment and lifestyle can have a lot to do with it as well. I'd look loads different if I'd grown up in Florida. I'd have a great tan, for a start...

Selective Breeding

13.2

Manky moggies don't win cat shows — breeders look for the best characteristics to produce the purrfect champion...

Q1 Use the following words to complete the blanks in the paragraph below:

alleles *breed* *characteristics* *colours* *milk* *people* *selective* *variety* *varieties*

Artificial selection is when _______________ choose what characteristics to breed into living things. This can be used to produce new _______________ and breeds of organisms. We choose the individuals which have _______________ which are useful to us. We then _________ from these individuals. We choose individuals from their offspring which have the features useful to us, and breed from them. We repeat this over and over again. This is called _______________ breeding. A use for this in agriculture is the production of varieties of plants and breeds of animal that produce greater yields or other desired characteristics. Examples of selective breeding in animals include the Fresian cow that produces greater _________ yields and dogs like the Basset hound that has droopy ears. Plants like wheat have been bred to grow bigger 'ears' with more grain. Also, new varieties of roses now exist with a wide range of flower _______________ and shapes. Selective breeding, though, greatly reduces the number of _______________ in a population (the gene pool) and therefore reduces _______________.

Q2 People have produced new breeds of dogs to achieve either a particular look or temperament in the dog. Some of the features we have bred in dogs, though, are not advantageous to the dog.

Shar-pei

Basset hound

Bedlington

Bulldog

a) **All dogs** have been bred from **wolf** ancestors. Give **two features** of wolves that are no longer found in some modern breeds of dogs.

b) Why are mongrels (random crossbreeds) often **healthier** than pedigree dogs?

Bulldogs have narrow hips. Often these dogs can only give birth if they are assisted by people.

c) What would **happen** to this breed of dog if people **stopped assisting them** to give birth?

Q3 Choose the correct word from inside the brackets to complete each of the sentences below.

a) The process of breeding animals for the best characteristics is called (**artificial** / **natural**) selection.

b) Selective breeding (**increases** / **decreases**) the number of alleles in a population.

c) Farmers often selectively breed to (**decrease** / **increase**) yields of food produced.

d) Selective breeding involves (**asexual** / **sexual**) reproduction.

e) Breeding characteristics like floppy ears into dogs is *(***advantageous** /**disadvantageous***)* to the dog.

13.2

Cloning

Q1 The UK exports date-palms to Iran and oil-palms to Malaysia. The reason we can do this is because Britain has advanced technology in tissue culturing. The diagram shows how tissue culturing works.

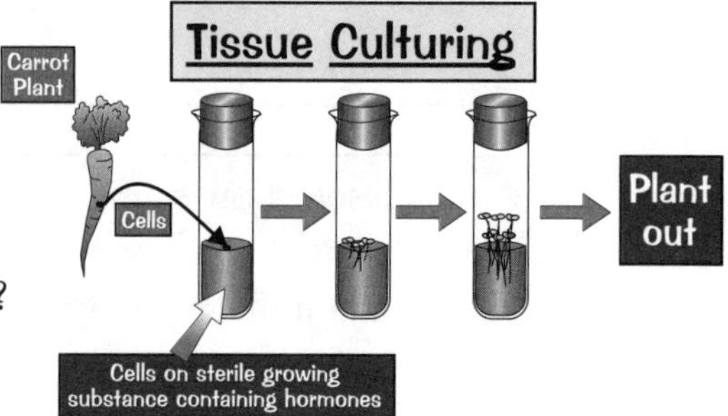

a) What type of **reproduction** is this?

b) i) Why are all the plants produced **identical**?

ii) What name is given to **identical** offspring?

c) i) What are the **advantages** of using tissue cultures?

ii) What are the **disadvantages** of using tissue cultures?

d) What **other** technique produces identical plants?

Q2 When we grow parts of plants into new plants, we call these cuttings.

a) **What type** of reproduction is shown here?

b) **How** do the plants on the right of the diagram **compare genetically** with the plants that the cuttings were taken from?

c) **How** do seeds from these plants **compare genetically** with the parent plants?

d) i) **What** is the **advantage** of taking cuttings?

ii) **What** is the **disadvantage** of taking cuttings?

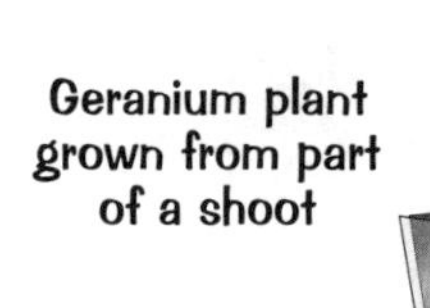

Q3 Choose the correct word from inside the brackets to complete the sentences.

a) Plants produced from cuttings grow into new plants by (***meiotic*** / ***mitotic***) cell division.

b) Tissue cultures are a useful way of producing large numbers of (***different*** / ***identical***) plants from a small number of cells.

c) Genetically identical plants are produced by (***asexual*** / ***sexual***) reproduction.

d) Growing plants from tissue cultures (***decreases*** / ***increases***) the gene pool.

e) Cloning techniques are also used in producing identical animals by splitting embryo cells (***after*** / ***before***) they specialise.

Top-tips: Plants — don't say much, don't listen to what you say, don't even take exams. They do some cool stuff though. Imagine if you could cut off your finger and it would grow into a whole new person. Then there'd be two yous. So you'd only have to do half the work, half the revision. Imagine...

Cloning

13.2

Q1 Use the following words to complete the blanks:

asexual *cells* *cuttings* *embryo* *genetically* *host* *identical* *mitosis* *naturally* *splitting* *tissue*
Clones are ____________ identical organisms. These are produced in plants during ____________ reproduction when ____________ takes place. In plants, examples include reproduction by bulbs, stem tubers and runners, as well as ____________. Using ____________ cultures also results in genetically ____________ offspring, plants or clones. This technique involves growing new plants from small groups of ____________ from part of a plant. Cloning techniques are also used in producing identical cells in agriculture. This is done by ____________ embryo cells (before they become specialised) from a developing animal ____________ and then transplanting the identical embryos into a ____________ mother. Clones are also produced ____________ as in the case of identical twins.

Q2 The diagram shows how animal clones, like cattle, are produced in agriculture. (That's not how that Dolly the sheep was made, by the way).

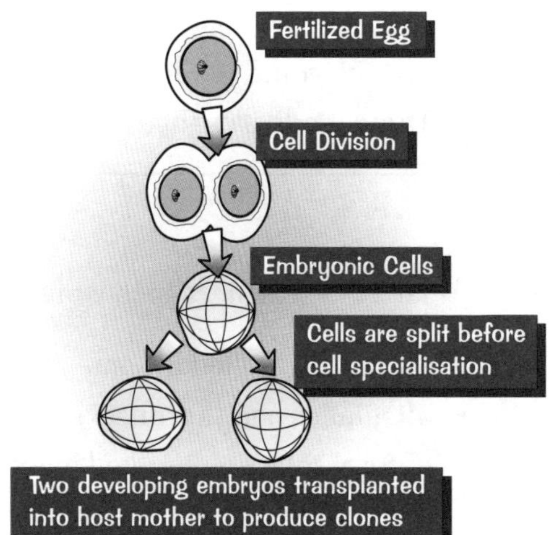

a) By what **process** does the fertilised egg divide?

b) Why are the two offspring produced called **clones**?

c) **i)** What are the **advantages** of using this technique?

ii) What are the **disadvantages** of using this technique?

d) A farmer has a sheep with an excellent coat for making wool. The farmer wants to increase the number of sheep like this he has.

i) Should he use **breeding** or **cloning** techniques?

ii) Give a **reason** for your answer.

Q3 Choose the correct word from inside the brackets to complete the sentences.

a) Genes from chromosomes within cells from humans can be removed using **enzymes / alcohol**.

b) The gene removed from the **human / bacteria** cell will continue to make the same **protein / carbohydrate**.

c) In the pharmaceutical industry, large numbers of bacteria are cultured in this way to produce proteins for drugs and hormones, for example **insulin / asprin**.

Hello — haven't we met somewhere before...

Cloning. A scary sci-fi topic if ever I saw one... Remember — clones are genetically identical organisms. You need to be able to describe how plants are cloned naturally and artificially... and list the advantages and disadvantages of producing crops and livestock that are clones.

13.3

Evolution

This section is about how plants and animals change and adapt over millions of years. You could try looking for fossils in your garden. You wouldn't find any, but it'd pass the time.

Q1 Use the following words to complete the blanks:

adaptations characteristics changed Darwin degenerate environment food evolution existence extinct fittest nature organisms survival natural

Evolution is about how living things have ____________ over millions of years. Lamarck and ______________ had different ideas about how this happened. Lamarck believed that new structures appeared when there was a need for them and those that are not used __________.

He also proposed that changes acquired in the lifetime of organisms were then passed on to the offspring. Darwin on the other hand proposed that organisms with the best ___________ to their ______________ survive and have offspring which inherit those adaptations.

Useful characteristics become more common. Less well adapted organisms die out. All ________________ over-reproduce, so individual organisms have to compete, particularly for _________________. Disease and predation cause large numbers of organisms to die. This is called the struggle for ______________. This struggle leads to the _______________ surviving. In other words, those individuals with the most suitable __________ are the most likely to survive. So, ______________ selects the characteristics that are going to aid ______________. This is called ____________________ selection. These gradual changes are the mechanism by which ________________ occurs.

Q2 Place the sentences below in the right order to explain the evolution of the giraffe.

~ **mutation** resulted in some giraffes having longer necks than others.
~ **all** giraffes had **short** necks.
~ **natural selection** resulted in longer necked offspring surviving.
~ the giraffe population had individuals whose necks **varied** in length.
~ only **long** necked giraffes **survived** the competition for food.

Q3 The diagram shows the earliest occurrence and abundance of fossil vertebrates.

a) What were the **first vertebrates** to evolve?
b) Which were the **last vertebrates** to evolve?
c) How do fossils help us to **understand** evolution?
d) Although the diagram shows evolution as being continuous, there are missing links in the fossil record of many animals.
e) How can we **explain** these missing links?

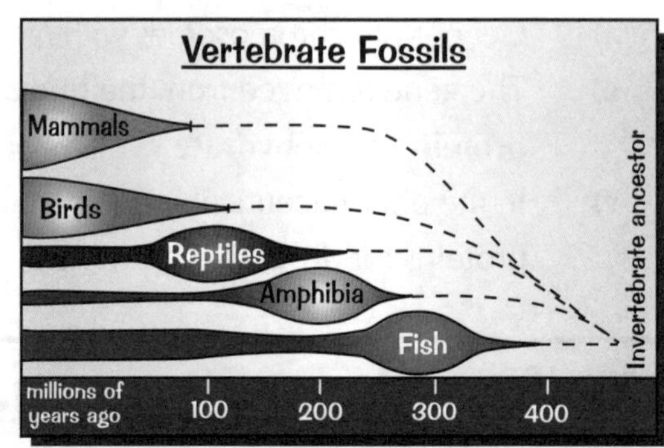

the width of each bar shows the amount of fossils of that age

Natural Selection

13.3

Q1 Use the following words to fill in the blanks:

alleles *disease* *environment* *favourable* *offspring*
natural *die* *species* *survive* *variation*

There is a wide range of ____________ within particular ____________ because of differences in their genes. Predation, ____________ and competition (often for food) cause large numbers of individuals to ____________. Individuals that survive are those that are most suited to their ________________. Those individuals that survive pass on their genes (and therefore their characteristics) to their ____________. This process is known as ____________ selection. Natural selection can alter the frequency of particular ____________ in a population. Alleles determining ____________ characteristics increase in frequency. This is because alleles which enable individuals to ________________ are passed on to the next generation.

Q2 The peppered moth is normally light in colour. Occasionally, a black variety appears. Insect-eating birds like the thrush prey on these moths.

a) i) **Why** does a **black** moth appear in a population of **light** coloured moths?
ii) **How** is the population of these moths kept **constant**?

In 1848 the first black variety was noticed in Manchester. By 1895, 98% of the moth population of Manchester was black. During this time, the local tree bark also became darker as a result of increasing pollution.

Peppered Moth

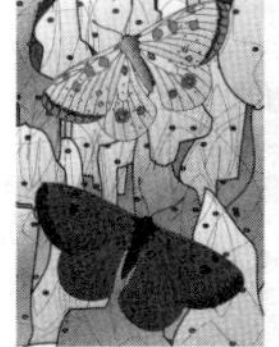

White and Black peppered moths on tree bark in unpolluted area

White and Black peppered moths on tree bark in polluted area

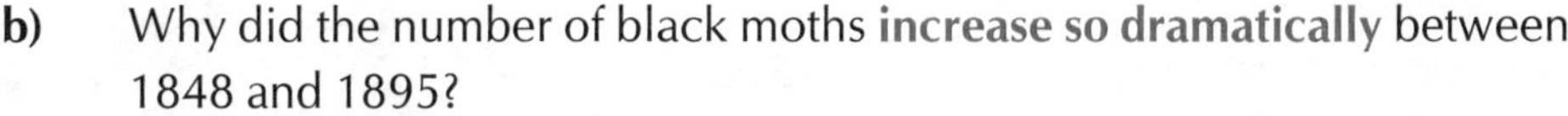

b) Why did the number of black moths **increase so dramatically** between 1848 and 1895?

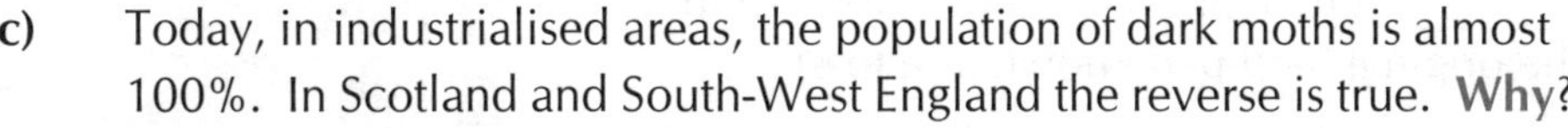

c) Today, in industrialised areas, the population of dark moths is almost 100%. In Scotland and South-West England the reverse is true. **Why**?

d) **Why** is the black variety **not** a new species?

e) **What** is the name for the **process** that determines the survival features of a population?

Q3 Complete the sentences by choosing the correct words from inside the brackets.

a) The frequency of alleles which determine useful characteristics **decreases** / **increases** in a population.

b) Diseases cause a population to **decrease** / **increase**.

c) Organisms that are the best survivors are those that are **best suited to their environment** / **strongest**.

d) Survivors pass their genes on to their **offspring** / **partner**.

e) Natural selection is the process by which **evolution** / **mutation** takes place.

f) In order for changes to occur in the characteristics of a population, **mutation** / **predation** must take place.

Q4 Mutations can occur naturally or be caused by other factors such as exposure to radiation.

a) **What problems** might occur if a mutation appeared in a **reproductive cell**?

b) **What problems** can occur if a mutation appears in **body cells**? What is the name for this **condition**?

c) **Write down** an **example** of a mutation that is **neutral** (does not affect chances of survival).

d) **Write down** an **example** of a mutation that is **advantageous** (increases chances of survival).

13.3

Evolution and Fossils

Q1 Which of these statements are true and which are false? Correct the false ones.

a) Lamarck and Darwin shared the same ideas about how evolution occurs.

b) Lamarck believed that new characteristics appeared only when they were needed.

c) Darwin's theory of evolution suggested useful characteristics become more common as they are transferred from parent to offspring.

d) Organisms that adapt well to their environment tend to become extinct.

e) Darwin's theory of evolution was difficult to accept by many groups of people due to their religious beliefs.

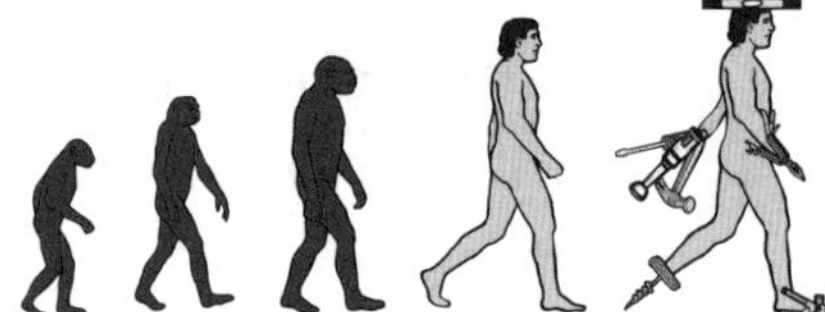

Q2 There are different ways that fossils can be formed.

a) Most fossils form from the hardest parts of animals. **Fill in** the missing words in each of the sentences below then match them up to the stages in the diagram.

i) When they die, hard parts of animals don't _______ easily. _______________ collects around the dead animals and they become buried.

ii) The sediment surrounding the ____________ remains also turns to rock, but the fossil stays distinct inside the rock.

iii) Over a long period of time the hard parts __________ and are replaced by ____________. A rock like substance is formed in the same shape as the original hard part known as a fossil.

iv) Fossils formed in this way usually develop from hard parts of animals such as __________ , __________ and ____________ .

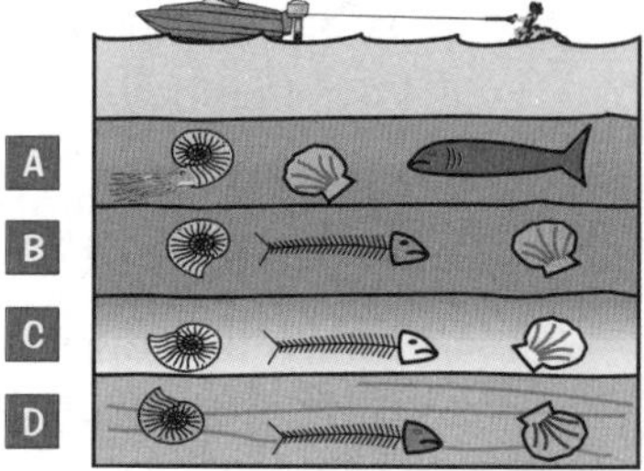

In the film Jurassic Park, scientists were able to find fully **preserved** mosquitoes that had been trapped in **amber** for **millions** of years.

b) i) What prevented them from decaying?

ii) Give two other examples of conditions that would prevent decay of dead plants and animals?

c) Sometimes the soft material of a plant or animal decays slowly and is replaced by **minerals**. Complete these sentences by choosing the correct word from the brackets.

i) This process doesn't occur very often as decay is normally very **fast / slow**.

ii) For fossils to form in this way (known as 'petrification') a plant or animal usually has to fall into a **swamp / swimming pool** and be covered.

iii) The slow decay of the plant or animal is due to a lack of **oxygen / carbon**.

Survivor — but luckily no John Leslie this time...

The environment selects characteristics that make individuals survivors. Survivors pass on their genes to their children, who pass them on to theirs, and so on and so on... That's how evolution works.

Mutations

13.3

Q1 Complete the blanks by using the following words:

antibiotics	beneficial	carcinogens	divide
genetic	sex	harmful	ionising
mitosis	mutagens	mutations	naturally
neutral	chromosome	nucleus	replication

A mutation is a change in a gene or a ______________. New genes can arise from such a change. Mutations can occur ______________________ when DNA is incorrectly copied during _____________. Gene mutations may start in a single ____________ of one cell. As the cells ____________ to produce more cells, the number of cells carrying the new form increases. The chance of ____________ occurring can be increased by exposure to _____________ radiation, X-rays, ultra-violet light and also certain chemicals. The greater the dose, the greater the chance of mutations occurring. Chemicals that cause mutations are called ________________ and include substances found in cigarette smoke. Such substances are called ______________ because they can increase the chance of people having cancer. Most mutations are ________________. If mutations occur in ________________ cells, the children may develop abnormally. This can result in early death. Mutations that occur in body cells can cause uncontrollable cell division, resulting in cancer. Some mutations are ______________ in their effects, causing no apparent harm or benefit to the individual. On rare occasions, a mutation can be ________________, increasing an organism's chances of survival. Bacteria mutating has definitely benefited them by giving them resistance to the ____________ we use against them. Mutation is the source of ________________ variation. Changing by acquiring new forms of old genes is how living things have evolved by natural selection.

Q2 In our everyday lives we are subject to different mutation-causing influences.

a) **Why** do doctors recommend that you use suncream when sunbathing?
b) **What precautions** must a radiographer take when taking an X-ray of you and why?
c) **Why** is carbon tetrachloride no longer used as a cleaning agent by dry cleaners?

Earlier this century radioactive paints were used when making watches and clocks to make the numbers glow in the dark.

d) **Why** do you think many workers who made these clocks later developed throat and mouth cancer?

Top Tips: Eeek — nasty stuff. If only they'd known then what we know now... Remember — mutations can be pretty horrible, but they aren't always bad — think of those moths.

13.4

Cystic Fibrosis

Inheritance is why you don't look like your chums — but you do look like your mam and dad.

Q1 Use these words to complete the blanks.

allele	*both*	*carriers*	*genetic*
	membranes	*recessive*	

Cystic fibrosis is a __________ disease. One in twenty people in this country carry the recessive allele. Sufferers must have two __________ alleles. Cystic fibrosis is a disorder of cell __________. In the lungs, the membranes produce thick sticky mucus which makes breathing more difficult and causes more infections to the lungs Infections are treated with antibiotics. The mucus can be removed by regular physiotherapy and massage. Excess mucus is also produced in the pancreas, causing digestive problems. Sufferers have a shortened life. Since the disease is caused by a recessive __________, it must be inherited from ____________ parents. Parents who have the recessive allele are ____________ of the disorder. Carriers have no ill-effects themselves.

Q2 Match the genotypes with the correct description.

carrier of cystic fibrosis

normal

sufferer of cystic fibrosis

CC

cc

Cc

Q3 The diagram below shows a cross between two people who are unaffected by cystic fibrosis.

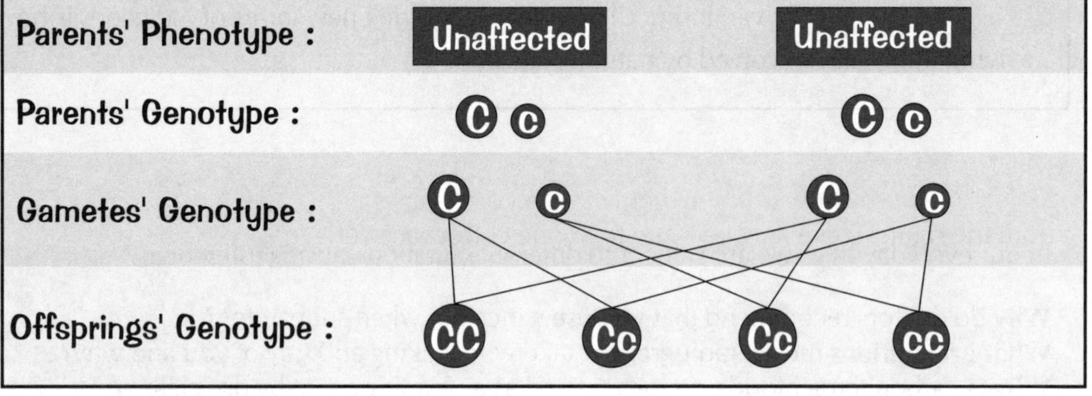

a) From the **diagram**, which individuals are:

i) carriers?

ii) sufferers?

iii) homozygous?

iv) heterozygous?

b) What do we mean by **carriers**?

c) **Draw this diagram** in the form of a checkerboard.

Cystic Fibrosis

Q1 Complete the sentences by choosing the right word or words from inside the brackets.

a) Cystic fibrosis is an (**infectious** / **inherited**) disease.
b) Cystic fibrosis is caused by a (**dominant** / **recessive**) allele.
c) Children can inherit the cystic fibrosis disease when (**both**/**one**) of their parents have the recessive allele.

Q2 The diagram shows a family who have been tested for the cystic fibrosis allele.

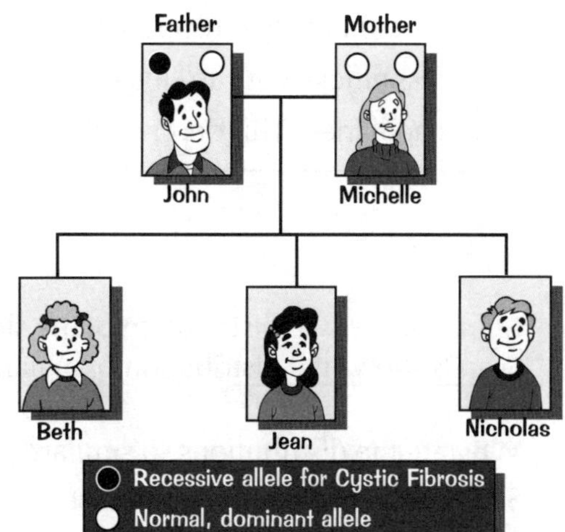

a) Using appropriate letters, give the **genotypes** of the mother and father.
b) Will any of the children be **sufferers**?
c) i) Can you say **which children** will carry a recessive allele?
ii) **Explain** your answer.
d) What is the **chance** of Beth being a carrier?
e) What **proportion** of their children are likely to be **normal**?
f) i) From the **diagram**, can we tell whether both of the father's parents were **carriers**?
ii) **Explain** your answer.

Q3 If two carriers have children, there is a 1 in 4 chance of each child having the disease.

a) **Show** how this proportion is derived with a genetic diagram.
b) **Can** children suffer from the disease if only **one** parent has a **recessive allele**?

One in twenty people carry the allele for cystic fibrosis in this country.

c) What does "**carrying**" the allele **mean**?

Q4 Match up the statements on the left with the correct answers from the right. There may be more than one correct answer.

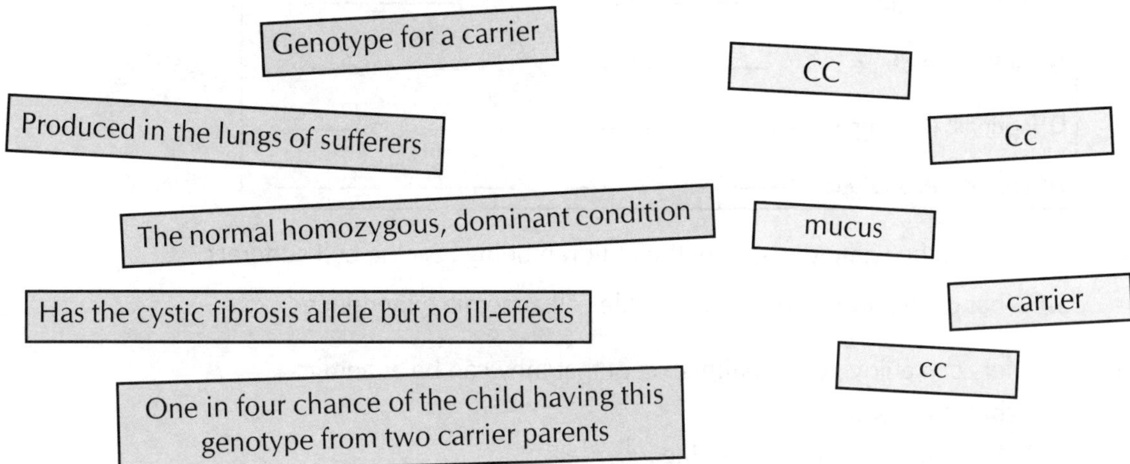

13.4 Genetic Diseases

Q1 Use the following words to complete the blanks:

alleles	*carrier*	*malaria*	*oxygen*	*protected*	*recessive*	*red*

Sickle cell anaemia is a disorder of ______________ blood cells. It is caused by a ______________ allele. Being a ______________ of this disorder can be an advantage in countries where ______________ is prevalent. Carriers are ______________ from malaria. The disease gets its name from the shape of the red blood cells. Children who inherit two recessive ______________ from their parents have red cells which are less efficient at carrying oxygen. The red blood cells also stick together in the blood capillaries. This deprives the body cells of ______________.

Q2 Map A shows the distribution of the sickle cell allele in Africa.
Map B shows the distribution of malaria in the same geographical region.

a) **Why** are the distributions so similar?

b) Sickle cell anaemia is a **killer** disease.

i) What is an **advantage** for people who are **carriers** of the disease?

ii) What is a **disadvantage** for people who are **carriers** of the disease?

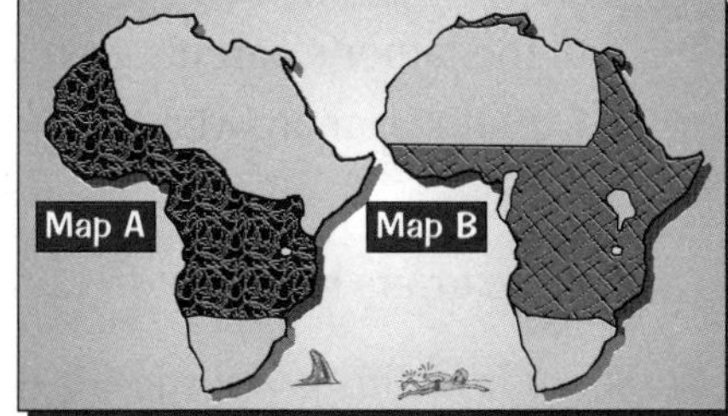

Q3 Two carriers of sickle-cell anaemia marry and have three children.

a) **Complete** the spaces in this diagram.

Parents' Phenotype :	________		________	
Parents' Genotype :	________		________	
Gametes' Genotype :	___	___	___	___
Offsprings' Genotype :	____	____	____	____
Offsprings' Phenotype :	______	______	______	______

b) **i)** What is the **chance** of one of the children being a sickle cell sufferer?

ii) What **problems** do sufferers of sickle cell anaemia experience?

c) Carriers can enjoy good health, except that they can be anaemic.

i) What is **anaemia**?

ii) What is the **advantage** of being a carrier?

Genetic Diseases

13.4

Q1 Use the following words to fill in the blanks.

allele ***dominant*** ***nervous*** ***one***
Huntingdon's Chorea is caused by a ________________ allele. This means that ________________ parent can pass on the disorder. A child has a 50% chance of inheriting the condition from one parent with a single dominant ____________________. This disease affects the _______________ system. Symptoms often develop when the person who has inherited the allele is over 35-40 years of age. The disease causes involuntary movements and mental deterioration. There is no cure and the condition progressively worsens.

Q2 A man who is heterozygous for Huntingdon's Chorea marries a normal woman.

a) What is the **chance** of their **first child** having the disease?

Diseases caused by a dominant allele are often expected to disappear.

b) **i)** **Explain** why.

ii) Why is Huntington's Chorea **not disappearing**?

Q3 The table shows the prevalence of Huntingdon's Chorea in a number of places. Tasmania has a small community, yet has the highest number of cases.

Suggest a possible **reason** why the number of cases of Huntington's Chorea is **highest** in Tasmania.

The prevalence of Huntington's Disease (per million of the population)	
Cornwall	50
Tasmania	170
Victoria	45
USA	50

Q4 Use the diagram on the right to answer these questions on Huntingdon's Chorea:

a) **Fill in** the spaces to show a cross between a heterozygous man and a woman who is homozygous recessive.

b) What **proportion** of offspring from this cross are sufferers?

	Father		Mother	
Parents' Phenotype :	________		________	
Parents' Genotype :	________		________	
Gametes' Genotype :	___	___	___	___
Offspring's Genotype :	_____	_____	_____	_____
Offspring's Phenotype :	______	______	______	______

Oh my, Grandma — what big ears you have...

The important thing about Huntington's Chorea is that it's caused by a <u>dominant allele</u>. Sickle-cell anaemia is caused by two recessive alleles. But remember — if you've got just one recessive allele, you'll be a carrier, but won't <u>get</u> the disease — and you'll be protected from malaria to boot. Bizarre.

13.5 Menstrual Cycle Hormones

Q1 "The combined Pill" is a contraceptive taken by women that works by controlling egg production.

a) Which **two** hormones does the pill contain?
b) What do you think the effect of taking the pill **regularly** would be on the level of oestrogen in the body?

Maintaining oestrogen at this level inhibits production of FSH.

c) After a period of time, **what effect** would this have on **egg production**?
d) Would you expect the egg production of someone on the pill to **return to normal** after they stopped taking it? **Why**?

Q2 In total, four hormones control menstruation.

a) **Name the two places** where they are produced.
b) **Copy the diagram** on the right and indicate where the two hormone-producing locations are in the body.

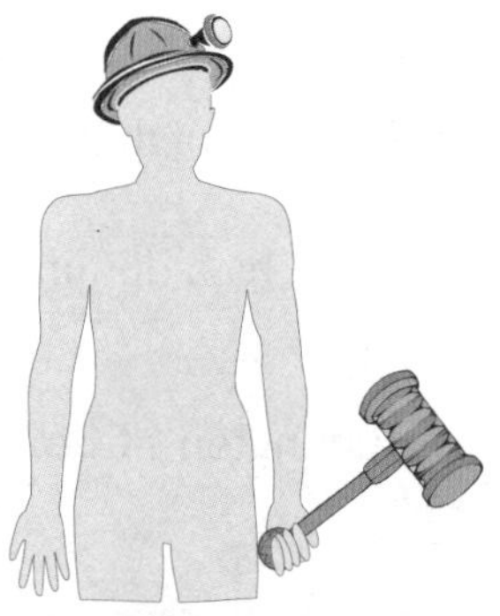

Q3 Women's fertility can be altered with the introduction of particular hormones.

a) Which hormone would be given to **increase** the fertility of a woman with low fertility?
b) **Explain** how this hormone has the required effect.

Q4 Match each of the four hormones in the grey boxes on the left with their matching descriptions.

Oestrogen

Progesterone

LH

FSH

Stops production of FSH, causes the lining of the uterus to thicken and stimulates LH production around day 14.

Maintains the lining of the uterus. When the level of progesterone falls, the lining breaks down.

Causes an egg to develop in one of the ovaries and stimulates them to produce oestrogen.

Stimulates the release of an egg after 14 days.

Menstrual Cycle Hormones

13.5

Q1 The diagram below shows what happens at different stages of the **menstrual cycle** and during **pregnancy**.

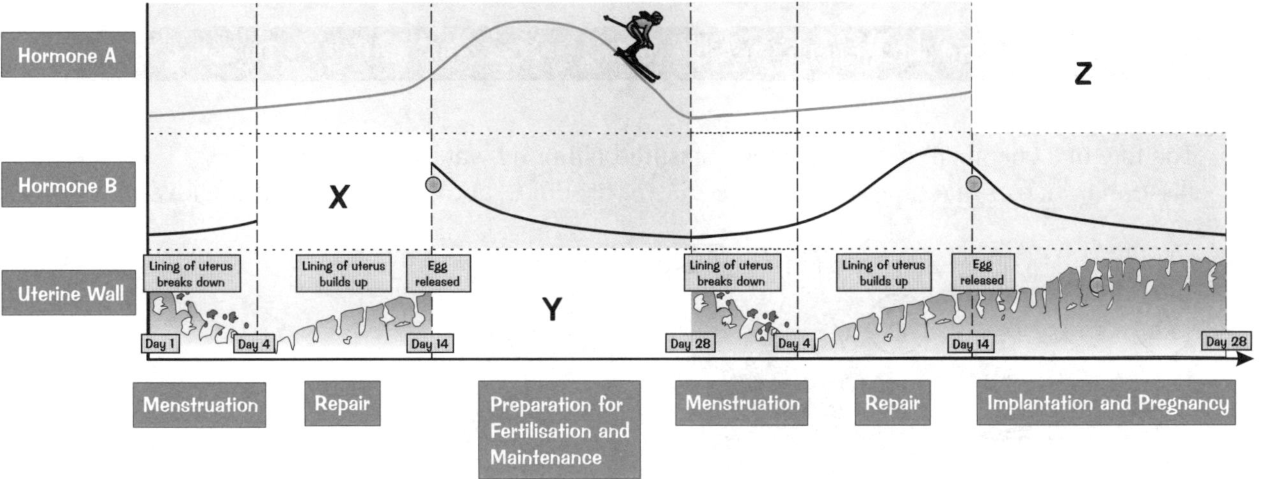

a) **Name** hormones **A** and **B**.

b) Three sections of the diagram (**X**, **Y** and **Z**) have been left incomplete. **Draw** what you would expect to see.

c) **Which hormone**, not shown on the diagram above, **directly** causes **egg release**?

d) **Which hormone**, again not shown above, causes **oestrogen stimulation**?

Q2 With the help of that diagram above, answer the following questions:

a) Name the **hormone** that brings about the **repair and thickening** of the uterus lining.

b) Name the **hormone** that **maintains** the uterus lining and prepares the body for pregnancy.

Q3 What does "target organ" mean if we're talking about the menstrual cycle?

Q4 The period of pregnancy also stimulates the production of a particular hormone.

a) Which hormone **remains** in production throughout pregnancy?

b) **Explain** why this needs to happen.

Q5 Fertility treatment can be used by couples who are having problems conceiving. Part of this treatment can involve stimulating egg production.

a) Which hormone would be taken to stimulate **egg development**?

b) Which hormone is then produced by the ovaries to stimulate **egg release**?

c) Give **two** examples of problems with this treatment.

Progesterone — sounds like a new type of pasta...

Hormones can be pretty tricky — but you've got to know about them. For each hormone you need to know what controls it and what it controls. Draw a graph of all the hormone levels. It'll help you get it all straight in your brain — and it's the sort of graph that tends to appear in the Exams.

Rates of Reaction

16.1

Reactions don't just happen — they sometimes need a little something to set them off. What you need to know is how long different reactions take.

Q1 Place these chemical reactions **in order** of their speed, starting with the fastest reaction:

Frying an egg | Striking a match | A car rusting | Concrete setting | Digesting food

Q2 The rate of a chemical reaction can be measured either by watching for the **disappearance of reactant** or the **appearance of product**. Look at the apparatus below.

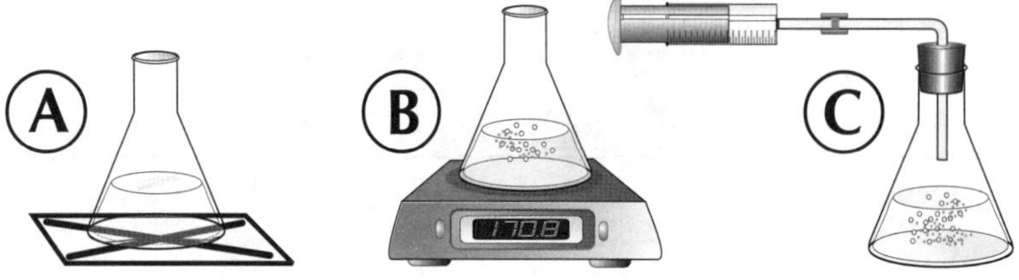

For each reaction below, say which of the apparatus above could be used.

a) Marble chips with hydrochloric acid

b) Magnesium and sulphuric acid

c) Sodium thiosulphate and hydrochloric acid

Q3 Which of the statements below are **true** and which are **false**?

	True	False
Catalysts are used up in reactions		
Catalysts are specific to certain reactions		
Enzymes are biological catalysts		
Reactions slow if catalysts are used		
Enzymes increase the activation energy		
Reactions will speed up if they are heated		
Reactions slow down if they are diluted		
Increasing concentration increases the rate of reaction		
Pressure increases the rates of gaseous reactions		
Reactions are fast at the start		

Q4 The following changes may speed up the rate of a chemical reaction between an **acid** and **magnesium**.

Put a tick in the box next to each one that will **SPEED UP** the reaction (assume that there is initially an excess of acid).

- [ ] HEATING THE ACID.
- [ ] USING MORE CONCENTRATED ACID.
- [ ] USING POWDERED METAL, NOT RIBBON.
- [ ] USING TWICE THE VOLUME OF ACID.
- [ ] USING A SUITABLE CATALYST.
- [ ] ADDING MORE MAGNESIUM.

Q5 **Describe** a simple reaction that could be studied by monitoring the rate at which the **product** is formed.

Q6 Reactions can be monitored by looking at how the mass of reactants decreases.

Describe a simple reaction that could be studied in this manner.

16.1

Rates of Reaction

Q1 Products are produced at a rate shown by a **rate curve**.

a) Copy the graph opposite then draw a **typical rate curve**.

b) Add the labels on the right to the curve you've drawn:

Fast

Slowing

Stopped

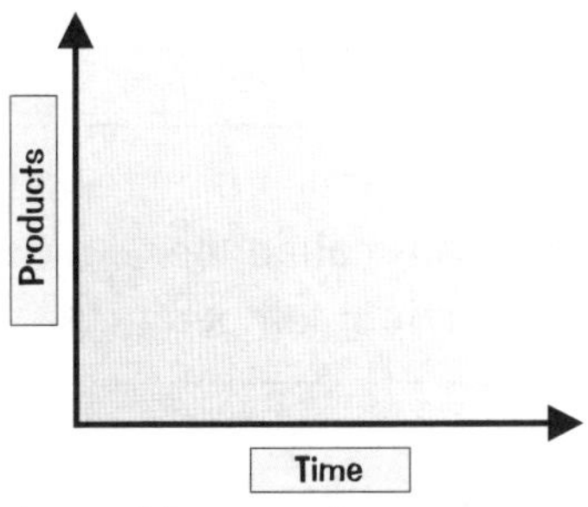

c) For a reaction to occur reacting particles must bump into each other with enough energy.

Imagine a reaction where two chemicals  and  collide to react.

The product would be 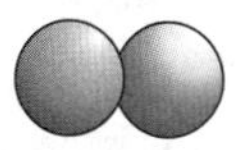

The reaction would therefore be: 

Look at the stages of a reaction below — these ones, just here...

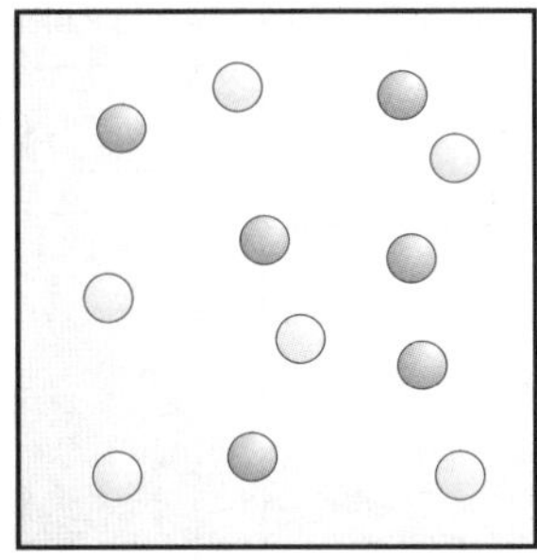

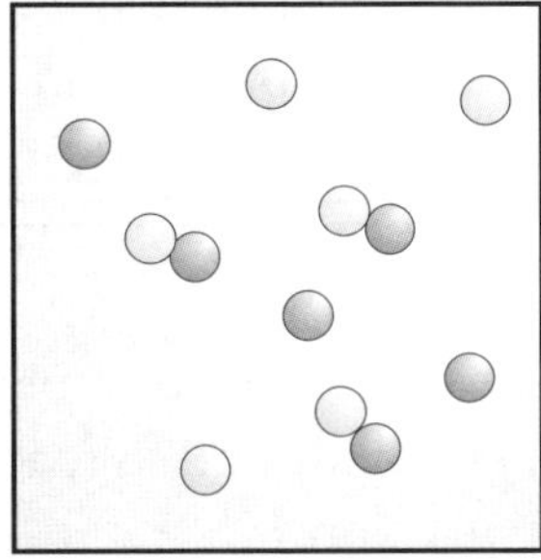

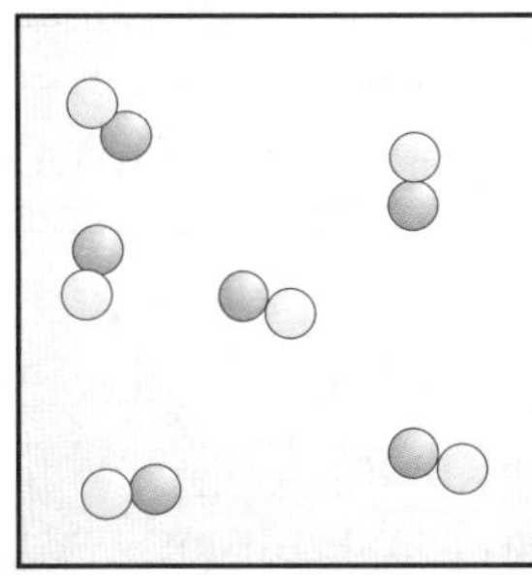

Reaction			
Speed		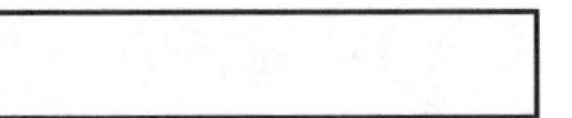	

Complete the diagrams by placing the labels below under the correct pictures.

END MIDDLE START

STOPPED FORWARD FAST

Q2 Reacting particles don't always collide **properly** or **effectively**. Sometimes they miss or collide as shown on the right.

Complete the diagram to show what might be happening to the particles in each case.

Particles miss each other	A glancing collision	A head-on collision

Test this page first — if you react badly seek a doctor...

Well, there're four things that affect the rates of reactions — learning your collision theory should take care of that. Then it's just a case of learning the three ways of monitoring reaction rates. Just be sure you can explain them — and can draw a graph of the results against time for each of them.

Collision Theory

16.1

Q1 **Fill in** the blanks below using each word once.

energy collide catalyst concentration collision theory

Particles can only react if they ______ with enough ______ for the reaction to take place. This is called the ______ ______. There are four factors that can change the rate of a reaction; temperature, ______, surface area and the use of a suitable ______.

Q2 **Fill in** the blanks in the text and complete the diagrams below using each word once.

moderate collision faster energy surface area faster catalyst fast slow particles faster faster more often collision successful slow fast faster low concentration catalyst present high concentration large surface area

TEMPERATURE

Increasing the temperature will cause the particles to move ______ with more energy. They will therefore collide ______ ______ and with greater ______. These two things mean there are more successful collisions per second and therefore a ______ rate of reaction.

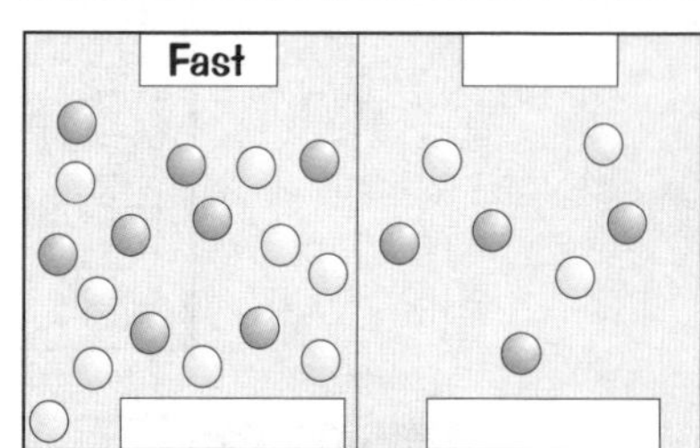

CONCENTRATION

Increasing the concentration of a reactant simply means there are more ______ which may collide and so react. More collisions means a ______ reaction.

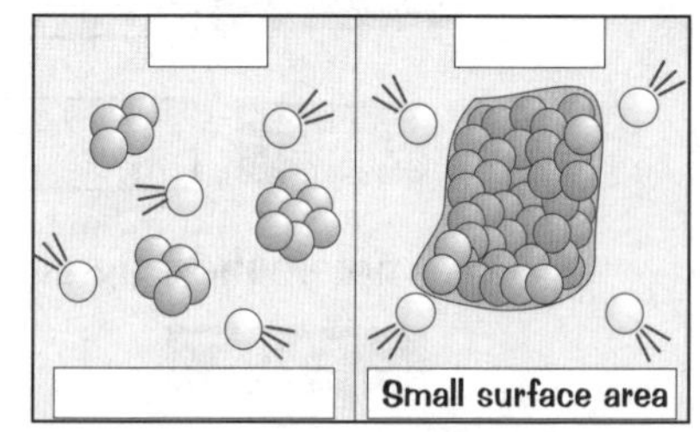

SURFACE AREA

Using a powder instead of a lump means the ______ ______ is greater, which means a greater area of reactant is exposed and so available for a collision. More collisions means a ______ reaction.

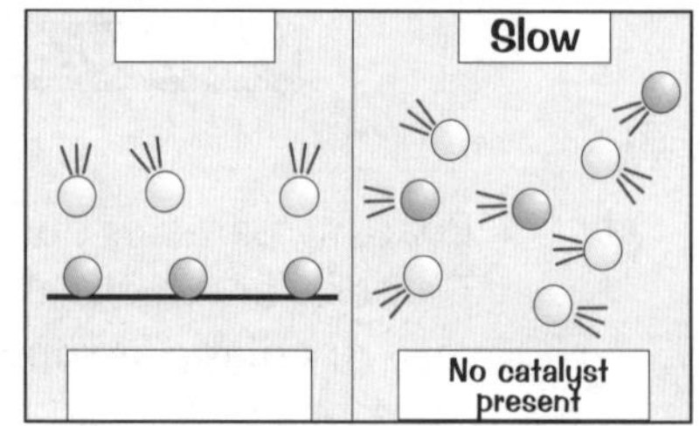

CATALYSTS

Use of a suitable catalyst means that the particles may react even if they collide with only ______ energy. This means more ______ collisions are likely. Some catalysts work because one of the particles is fixed to a surface. This makes the chance of a __________ more likely. More collisions means a ______ reaction.

Slow

No catalyst present

Q3 Choose the sentence that **best describes** the collision theory:

- Particles collide at random and always react.
- Collisions between particles often result in a reaction.
- Reacting particles must collide with enough energy in order to react.
- Collisions between molecules are sometimes needed before a reaction occurs.

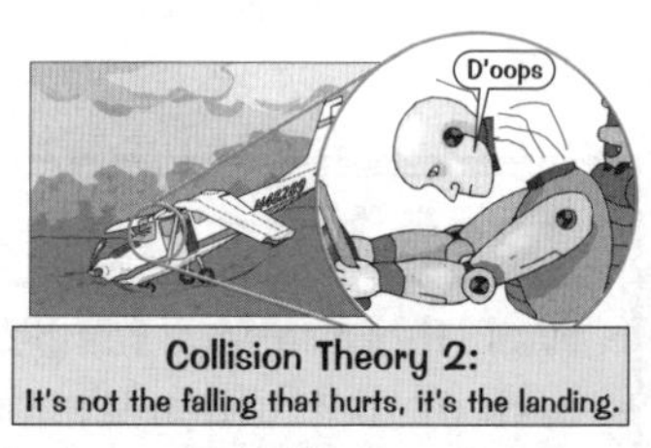

Collision Theory 2:
It's not the falling that hurts, it's the landing.

16.1 Experiments on Rates of Reaction

Q1 The reaction between sodium thiosulphate and hydrochloric acid produces a yellow precipitate of solid sulphur. This makes the solution cloudy and stops us seeing clearly through it. The cross below the flask in the diagram will slowly disappear as more precipitate is produced.

In an experiment to investigate rates of reaction, the time taken for the cross to disappear was measured.

50cm³ of sodium thiosulphate solution was used and 10cm³ of hydrochloric acid was added.

The experiment was repeated at different temperatures.

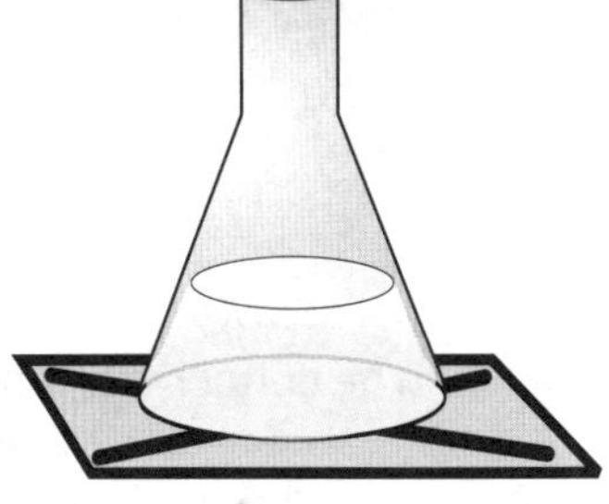

Temperature (°C)	20	30	40	50	60	70
Time taken (s)	163	87	43	23	11	5

a) **Copy the graph** on the right and use the results above to plot a line showing the relationship between temperature and time taken.

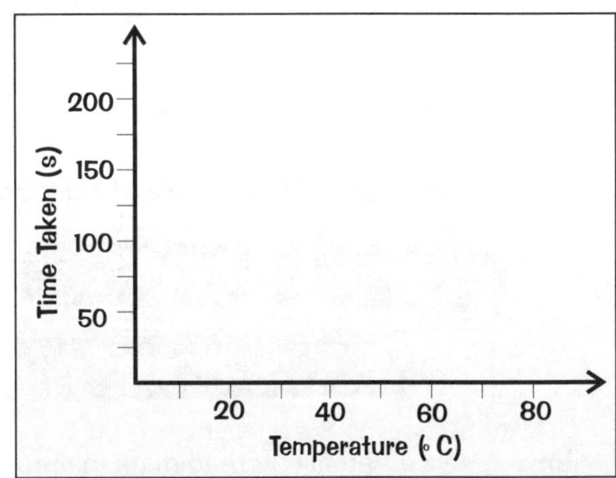

b) **Use the graph** to draw a simple conclusion about the effect of temperature on the time taken for the reaction to finish.

c) The rate of a reaction may be found by dividing 1 by the time taken (1/t). **Copy the table** above and add a row with the reaction rate at each temperature.

d) **Plot a graph** of rate against temperature. (If the actual numbers for the rate value are too small to plot, use 'Rate x1000' on the vertical axis).

e) **From the graph** work out how temperature affects the **rate** of a chemical reaction.

f) Use your knowledge of the collision theory to **explain** your conclusion.

Q2 The same reaction can be used to investigate the effect of **concentration** on the rate of a reaction. When changing the concentration, it is important to keep the total volume used exactly the same.

Volume of sodium thiosulphate (cm³)	50	40	30	20	10
Volume of water (cm³)	0				
Time taken (s)	80	101	137	162	191
Rate (1/t)					

a) **Complete** the table above, adding the volume of water and calculating the rate of the reaction (to four decimal places).

b) **Copy** the axes on the right. Then, using data from the table, show how the volume of sodium thiosulphate used affects the time taken and rate of the reaction.

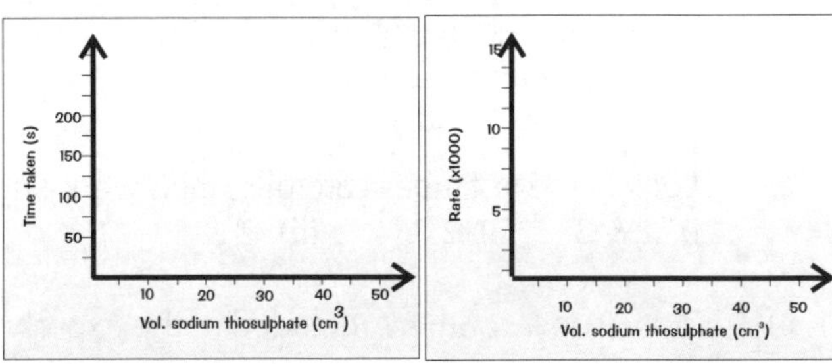

c) Use these graphs to draw a **simple conclusion** about the effect of concentration on reaction rate.

d) **Explain** your conclusion in terms of particles and the collision theory.

Catalysts

16.1

Q1 The diagrams to the right show how 0.5g of zinc and 0.5g of copper react with dilute sulphuric acid.

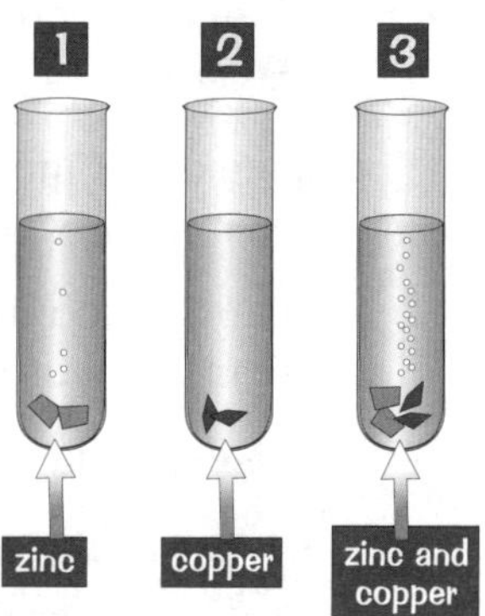

a) Does the **copper metal** react with dilute sulphuric acid?

b) Does **zinc** react with dilute sulphuric acid?

c) How do **zinc and copper** together react with dilute sulphuric acid?

d) **Describe** what copper does to the reaction in tube 3.

Tube 3 was left for several hours until the reaction was finished. The copper was removed, dried and weighed. Its mass was 0.5g.

e) What does this tell you about the **action** of copper in speeding up the reaction between zinc and dilute sulphuric acid?

Q2 The graph shows an energy profile for a typical **exothermic** reaction.

a) **Make a copy** of the graph and mark on:

the reactants | the products | the activation energy | the energy change of the reaction

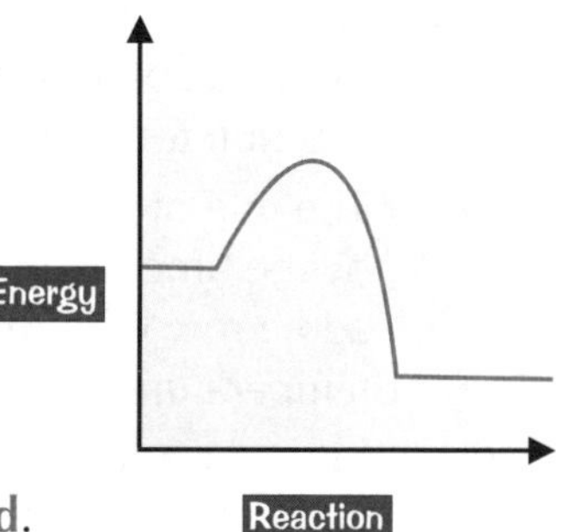

b) Use a different colour to mark the profile of the reaction when **catalysed**.

Q3 What are the **advantages** of using catalysts in the industrial manufacture of chemicals?

Q4 The experiment below can be used to investigate enzyme activity.

Trypsin is an enzyme which acts as a catalyst to the breakdown of protein. Photographic film has a protein layer that holds the silver compounds in place (these appear black). Different films use different proteins. If the protein is destroyed this black layer falls off leaving a clear plastic film.

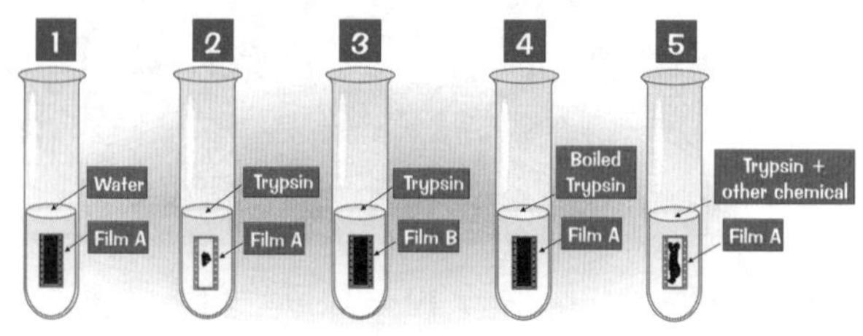

a) Look at the test tubes carefully, then work out what **you** can say about the following test tube pairs:
i) 2 & 3 **ii)** 2 & 4 **iii)** 2 & 5

b) Why was **test tube 1** included in the experiment?

16.1 Hazards

Q1 Link up the hazchem (hazardous chemical) symbols with their description. Give an example of each:

Highly Flammable
Catches fire easily.

Toxic
Can cause death either by swallowing, breathing in or absorption through the skin.

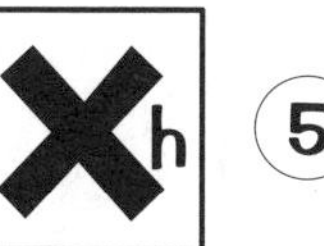

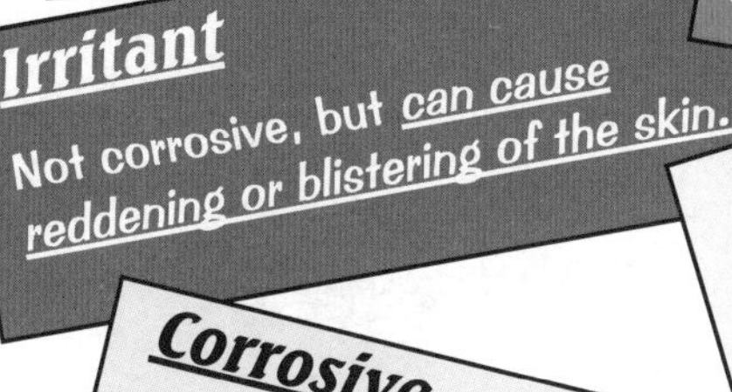

Irritant
Not corrosive, but can cause reddening or blistering of the skin.

Harmful
Similar to toxic but not quite as dangerous.

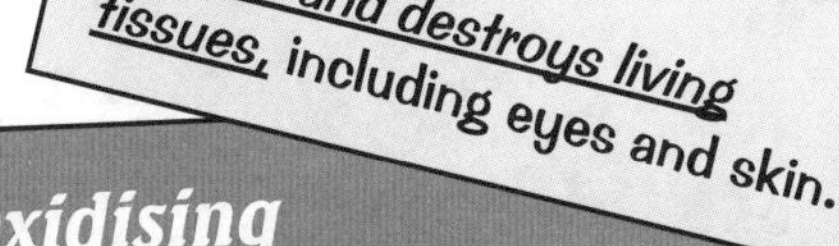

Corrosive
Attacks and destroys living tissues, including eyes and skin.

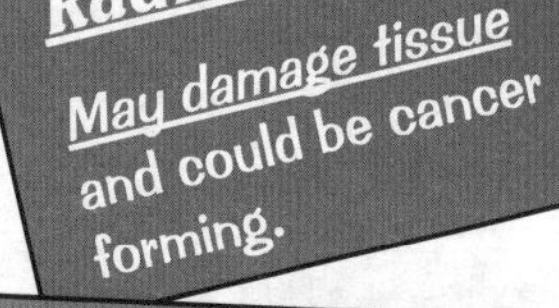

Radioactive
May damage tissue and could be cancer forming.

Oxidising
Provides oxygen which allows other materials to burn more fiercely.

Explosive
Can explode in the presence of a naked flame.

8

Q2 Why do we have a system of hazchem symbols? Why are they pictures, not just words?

Q3 How you would handle a "corrosive chemical"?

Q4 Look at the following information from the side of a chemical tanker.

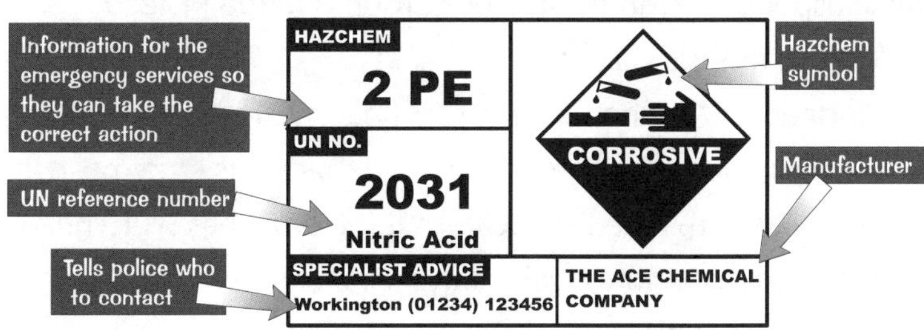

a) Why does the information have a **hazchem symbol**?

b) Why might the emergency services require **more** information than just the hazchem symbol?

c) Why is a **phone number** always included?

d) A tanker overturns in a crowded shopping area, but doesn't crack open. The Hazchem label tells the emergency services that its contents are corrosive, requiring full body protection when handled, but that they can be washed down the drains. Write a **short summary** of the important steps a fire officer handling this tanker should take.

Enzymes

16.2

Q1 Cheese goes mouldy after a while.

a) What causes cheese and other foods to go off?

b) Why does cheese stay fresh for longer if kept in a fridge?

c) **Explain** why meat or vegetables in a freezer can stay fresh for months.

Q2 Suggest what part enzymes might play in the following pictures. Use the headings to help you.

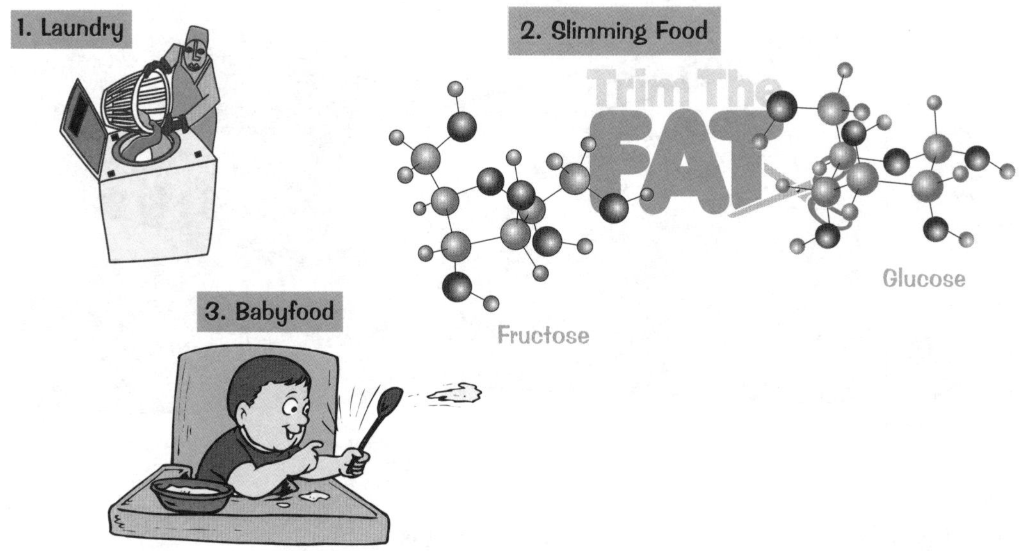

Q3 Professor Slashenburn, a megalomaniac, has decided to set up a factory in the middle of the Sahara (he lives in Cumbria, and would quite enjoy a bit of sun for a change). Rumours quickly spread that he is up to no good. Some claim that he's shipping in exotic bacteria for his experiments. In addition, his factory soon begins spewing out large quantities of smoke.

a) The local superhero, Sultanaman, suspects the fumes may be carbon dioxide instead. Name a simple test he could perform to test his suspicion.

b) The test shows that the fumes are indeed CO_2. The locals are not happy. They also want Prof. Slashenburn to justify the use of the nasty bacteria from which he extracts his enzymes. If you were the professor, how would you try to convince the locals that the enzymes were necessary?

c) Sultanaman suggests he find a way to use non-biological catalysts instead. Why might Prof. Slashenburn resist this suggestion?

d) How could Sultanaman convince him otherwise?

16.2 Enzymes

Q1 The enzymes in yeast help to produce energy from sugar. They can do this by breaking down glucose into carbon dioxide and ethanol.

a) Write a **balanced equation** for this reaction. The experiment was repeated at different temperatures and the volume of CO_2 recorded every 30 minutes. The results are shown in the table below.

b) Use the results to **plot eight graphs** on the same axes. Set the axes out as below. (For easy comparison, use different colours for each temperature).

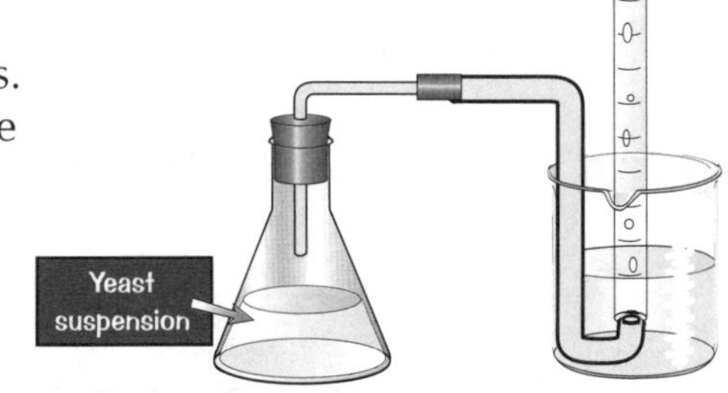

Time (s)	Volume of CO_2 collected (cm^3) at temperature (°C)							
	20	25	30	35	40	45	50	55
0	0	0	0	0	0	0	0	0
30	0	0	1	3	3	1	1	0
60	0	0	2	6	6	2	2	0
90	0	1	3	9	9	3	3	0
120	1	1	5	13	13	4	3	0
150	1	2	7	18	18	6	4	0
180	2	3	10	25	25	8	5	0
210	3	5	14	35	35	10	6	0
240	4	7	18	45	45	12	7	0

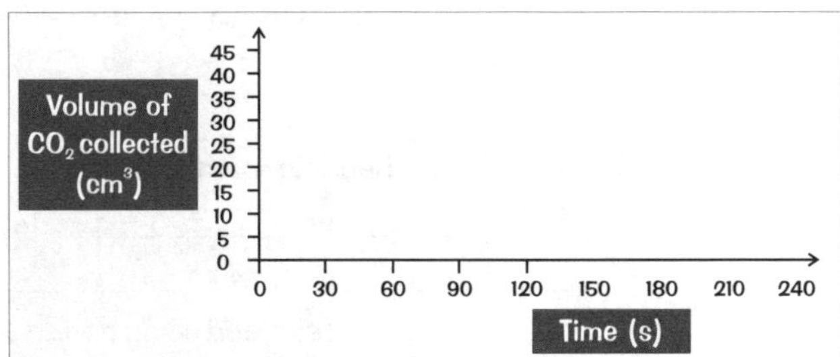

c) From your graphs, which temperature(s) appear to be the **best working temperature(s)** for this enzyme?

d) **Explain** what happens to the enzyme at temperatures **above** these optimum temperatures.

e) The process of fermentation is very important. Name two major products that depend on fermentation.

Q2 Bacteria are used in the food industry as well as yeast.

a) Milk is the starting material for which **two** foods?

b) Why is pasteurised milk normally used instead of fresh milk?

c) For one of the foods in your answer to **a)**, **describe** how it is made and the importance of the fermentation process.

Enzyme — new fast acting formula includes bacteria...

Enzymes are made of protein — that's all they are. And it all depends on their shape — so the enzymes that catalyse the browning of apples won't make you any yoghurt. Learn one or two examples, and don't forget how temperature and pH affect their efficiency — make sure you can draw graphs of these. And that's all there is to it. It's not like a foreign language or anything.

Energy Transfer in Reactions

16.3

Q1 **Fill in the blanks** in the following passage (the words can be used more than once):

energy	exothermic	endothermic	cold	taken in
hot	given out	negative	ΔH	energy
break	made			

a) A reaction that gives out ______ is called an ______ reaction.
A reaction that takes in ______ is called an ______ reaction.

b) ______ reactions can feel ______ as energy is ______ ______. ______ reactions can feel ______ as energy is ______ ______.

c) The energy change of a reaction is often given the symbol ______.
For ______ reactions the energy change is positive, i.e. heat is needed.
A ______ energy change indicates an exothermic reaction, i.e. heat is released.

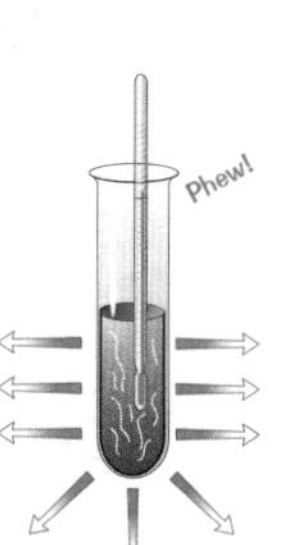

d) Virtually all chemical reactions involve ______ changes. Whether they are ______ or ______ depends on the balance between the ______ needed to ______ bonds in the reactant, and the ______ released when bonds are ______ in the products.

Q2 **Classify these reactions** or changes as **exothermic** or **endothermic**:

a) Burning a fuel.
b) Neutralising an acid.
c) Thermal decomposition of calcium carbonate.
d) Rapid oxidation of iron.
e) Rapid dissolving of ammonium nitrate.

Q3 Here are some more bond energies (kJ/mol): N≡N = 945; H-H = 435; N-H = 389

a) How much energy is needed to **break** the N≡N bond?
b) How much energy is needed to **break** the H-H bond?
c) How much energy is **released** when the N-H bonds are formed?
d) Write out the equation below using **structural** formulae for the molecules.

$$N_{2\,(g)} + 3H_{2\,(g)} \rightleftharpoons 2NH_{3\,(g)}$$

e) **Calculate** the energy needed to break all the reactant bonds.
f) Work out the **energy released** when the products are formed.
g) Calculate the **overall energy change** (that's **the net energy transfer**) for the reaction.
Is it an **exothermic** or **endothermic** reaction?

16.3 Energy Transfer in Reactions

Q1 Burning ethanol can be represented by the following equation:

$$C_2H_5OH + 3O_2 \rightarrow 2CO_2 + 3H_2O$$

You'll need this table of bond energies for questions 1 and 2

Bond Energies (kJ/mol)
C—C = 346
C—H = 413
C=O = 740
C—O = 360
O—H = 463
O=O = 497

a) Write out the equation using **structural** formulae for the molecules.

b) **What is** the energy needed to break all the reactant bonds?

c) **Work out** the energy released when all the product bonds are formed.

d) **Calculate** the overall energy change, ΔH. Is it **positive** or **negative**?

e) **State** whether the reaction is **exothermic** or **endothermic**.

Q2 Consider the following reaction, and **calculate:**

$$CH_4 + 2O_2 \rightarrow CO_2 + 2H_2O$$

a) The total energy needed to **break all** of the bonds of the reactants.

b) The total energy **released** in making the bonds of the products.

c) The total **energy change** (i.e. the **net energy transfer**) for this reaction.

d) On the energy profile opposite, mark on:

- **i)** The reactants ($CH_4 + 2O_2$).
- **ii)** The products ($CO_2 + 2H_2O$).
- **iii)** ΔH (overall energy change).
- **iv)** The activation energy.

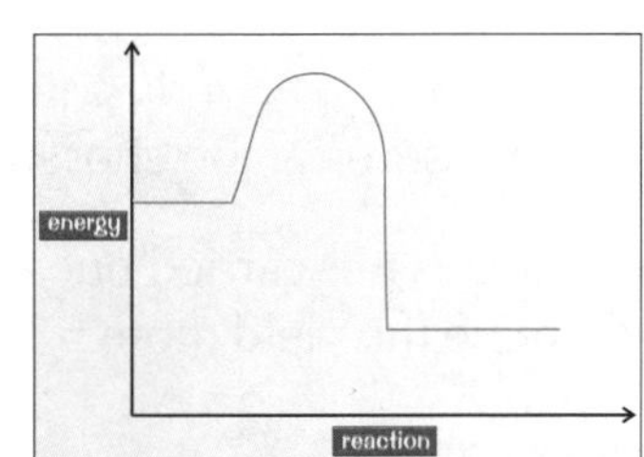

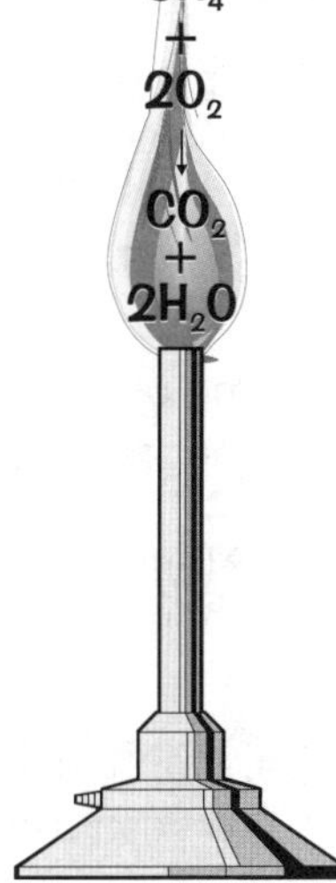

e) Is this an **exothermic** or **endothermic** reaction?

Q3 In the **Contact Process** for making sulphuric acid, sulphur dioxide is catalytically converted to sulphur trioxide:

a) **Mark** on the profile:

- **i)** The reactants.
- **ii)** The products.
- **iii)** ΔH (overall energy change).
- **iv)** The activation energy.

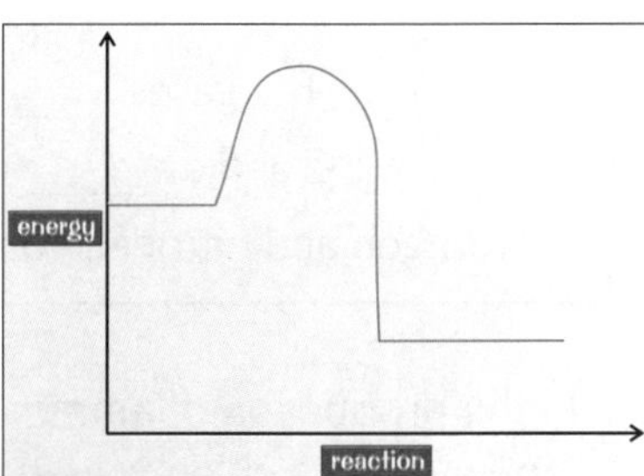

b) **Mark** on the diagram the profile you would expect for a reaction catalysed by vanadium (V) oxide.

Top Tips: This sort of thing's difficult at first — but once it's clicked, you'll remember it. Don't forget that pulling things apart takes energy — so breaking bonds is endothermic, while making them is exothermic. Make sure you can calculate the total energy change of a reaction (ΔH) from bond energies.

Ammonia and Fertilisers

16.4

Q1 Why is the Haber Process **so important**?

Q2 The two gases used to make ammonia in the Haber Process are hydrogen and nitrogen.

a) **Where** does the nitrogen come from?
b) **Where** does the hydrogen come from?

Q3 Look at the diagram opposite.

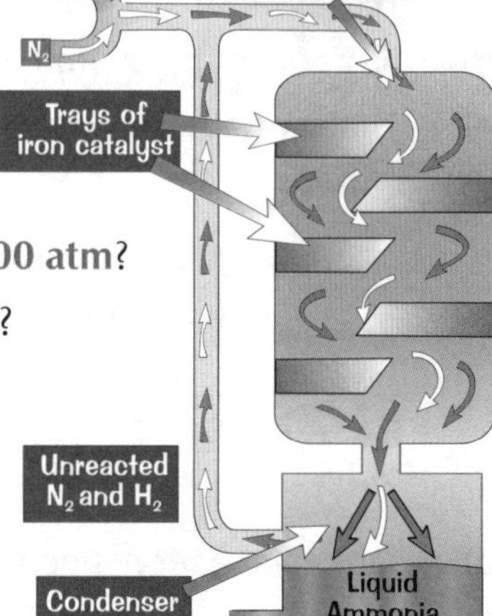

Pressure 200 atmospheres
Temperature 450 °C
Catalyst iron

a) Why is the iron catalyst on **large trays**?
b) How does this **affect** the reaction?
c) What is the **function** of the condenser?
d) Why is the reaction at a temperature of **450°C** and a pressure of **200 atm**?
e) How would a **very low temperature** affect the rate of this reaction?
f) Nitrogen + Hydrogen $\rightleftharpoons$ Ammonia.
   i) Write this equation in **symbols** and balance it.
   ii) What does the symbol " $\rightleftharpoons$ " mean?
g) Not all the nitrogen and hydrogen end up as ammonia. **Why** is this and **how** is it compensated for?

Q4 The production of ammonia on an industrial scale needs to be economical. The temperature and pressure can be chosen to maximise the yield.

Explain why the reaction is **not** carried out at even **higher pressures** when this would increase the yield more.

Q5 **Complete** the following paragraphs by filling in the missing words from the list below. You can use the words once, more than once or not at all.

450 1000 ammonia molecule hydrogen nitrogen molecules 200 fertilisers unreacted Haber Process recycled pressure

_______ is manufactured by the _______ _______. One use for ammonia is in the making of _______. The gases _______ and _______ are brought together under the special conditions of _______ °C and a _______ of _______ atm. Nothing is wasted — any _______ gas is _______. Hydrogen and nitrogen combine in a ratio of 3 _______ of _______ to 1 _______ of _______.

Q6 In the production of ammonia, the yield increases as the pressure is increased. However, at a given pressure, the lower the temperature the greater the yield.

a) Using the data given in the table, plot a **graph** of the variation of yield with pressure when the temperature is kept at 450°C.
b) On the graph, **sketch a second line** showing the yields of ammonia you would expect at 350°C.
c) Why is a **lower temperature** not used in ammonia production?

Pressure of reaction	*Approx. yield of ammonia*
100	10
200	25
300	40
400	45

16.4 Ammonia and Fertilisers

Q1 The reaction that produces ammonia is shown below:

Nitrogen + Hydrogen $\rightleftharpoons$ Ammonia

$$N_2 + 3H_2 \rightleftharpoons 2NH_3$$

a) This reaction is **exothermic**. What does this mean?

b) If you **increase the pressure**, what will happen to the yield of ammonia?

c) If the temperature is raised, the yield of ammonia is decreased, but the rate of reaction is much higher. **Why is this**?

d) The yield at a lower temperature is higher yet the temperature chosen for this process is high. **Explain** why such a high temperature is chosen.

e) A high pressure will give an increased yield and an increase in the rate of reaction. **Explain** this statement in terms of particles, gases and the collision theory.

f) Iron is the catalyst used in this reaction. Why is it so **important** to have a catalyst?

Q2 Ammonia is made into fertilisers in three main stages. Firstly, the ammonia needs to be converted into nitric acid.

Step 1

$$NH_{3(g)} + 5O_{2(g)} \xrightarrow{Pt} 4NO_{(g)} + H_2O_{(l)}$$

a) **Balance** this equation and state the **products** made in the reaction.

b) Ammonia reacts with oxygen as shown in this equation above. What conditions are needed?

$$NO_{(g)} + 3O_{2\,(g)} + H_2O_{(g)} \rightarrow HNO_{3(aq)}$$

c) **Balance** the equation.

d) Name the product formed in this reaction.

Step 3

Nitric acid then needs to be converted into ammonium nitrate.

e) What **type** of reaction is this?

f) **Write** a word equation and a balanced symbol equation for this reaction.

g) Ammonium nitrate is a fertiliser. Which **element** in ammonium nitrate is particularly useful for plants?

h) What do plants **use** this element for?

Top Tips: You need to know the factors that improve the rate of reaction and the yield. Don't forget, yield and rate of reaction are favoured by different factors, so the industrial conditions are a compromise. The equations on this page can be boring, but you do need to know them.

Ammonia and Fertilisers

Q1 If the Haber Process ceased and ammonium compounds were not made, what effect would this have on:

- **a)** The production of **fertilisers**?
- **b)** The production of **crops**?

Q2 Ammonia compounds make good inorganic fertilisers.

Name an **inorganic fertiliser** and state how they differ from **organic fertilisers**.

Q3 **Complete** the following passage about the production of fertilisers, using the words given.

neutralised	ammonium nitrate	oxidised	cooled	fertilisers	nitrogen monoxide
oxygen	nitric acid	water	nitric acid	ammonia	

Ammonia is __________ to form nitric acid. In the first stage in the production of __________, __________________ is formed and needs to be __________ before it goes into the next stage.
The nitrogen monoxide reacts with __________ and __________ to form ____________________.
The ______________________ is then __________ with __________ to form __________________________ fertiliser.

Q4 What **property** of ammonium nitrate makes it useful as a fertiliser?

Why can this property be a problem from time to time?

Q5 Nitrates are vital for plants. However, large quantities of nitrates in streams can cause algae and plants to grow out of control, which can eventually starve the stream, leading to death and decay.

- **a)** What **microbes** are needed for decay to occur?
- **b)** What **element** in the river does the decay process use up, and how will this affect the fish?
- **c)** What is the **name** given to this whole process?
- **d)** In your own words **explain why** nitrates cause the plants and algae to grow and why eventually this causes death.
- **e)** How can **farmers** help to prevent all this happening?

Fertilise your mind — with this page...

Fertilisers are needed to provide important nutrients for plants, particularly food crops. Don't forget the ways that nitrate fertilisers can pollute the water, and what farmers can do to reduce this problem.

Simple Reversible Reactions

Q1 Look at the two diagrams opposite.

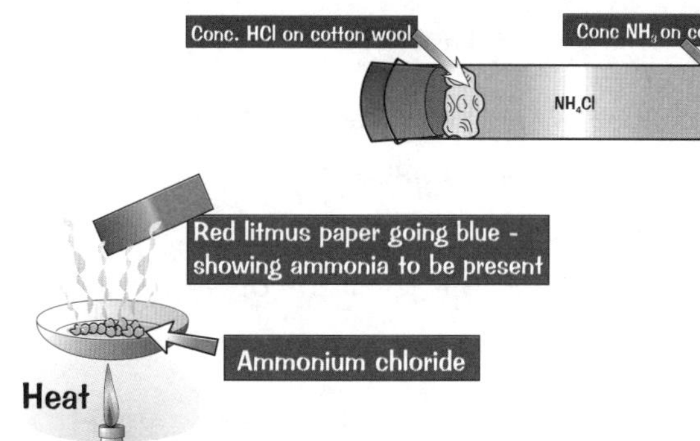

a) Write **balanced equations** for both the reactions in the diagrams.

b) What does the **symbol** "⇌" mean?

c) Use this symbol to rewrite your answer to part **a)** as a **single** equation.

Q2 Copper sulphate can be either blue crystals or a white powder.

a) How can you change the **blue crystals** to a **white powder**?
b) How can you **reverse** the process?
c) Write a fully **balanced equation** to describe this change.

Q3 Study pictures **A**, **B** and **C** carefully.

a) **Complete** the following passage using the words given in the box above the passage. Use each word once only.

equilibrium	open	up	down	dynamic	balanced
activity	change	static	closed	equilibrium	dynamic

Picture **A** shows a see-saw which is perfectly _____ and not moving. It is in _____. This type of _____ is said to be _____. Picture **B** shows a different type of equilibrium. The escalator is moving _____, whilst the man is trying to walk _____. There is constant _____, but no _____ in overall position. This is _____ equilibrium. All reversible reactions are examples of _____ equilibrium. Dynamic equilibria always occur in _____ systems, where nothing can escape or get into the system. An _____ system is like a jar with the lid off — things can escape.

b) Picture **C** shows a bottle of pop. **What type** of equilibrium exists between the carbon dioxide dissolved in the drink and that in the air above it?

c) What **type of system** does **C** represent?

d) If the top were removed, what **type of system** would you have? What would happen to the equilibrium?

Q4 Look at the graph opposite.

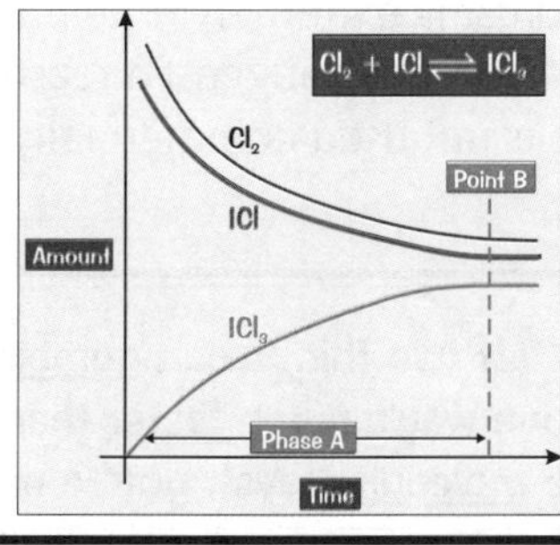

a) What is happening to the reactants during **phase A**?

b) What is happening at **point B**?

c) What type of **equilibrium** is this?

Simple Reversible Reactions

16.4

Q1 Consider the reaction: $N_2O_{4\,(g)} \rightleftharpoons 2NO_{2\,(g)}$

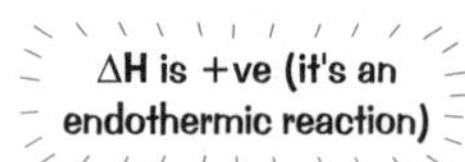

Suggest what would happen to the equilibrium if you:

a) increased the **temperature**.

b) increased the **pressure**.

c) doubled the **concentration** of N_2O_4.

Q2 The equation $N_2 + 3H_2 \rightleftharpoons 2NH_3$ describes the Haber process.

ΔH is -ve (it's an exothermic reaction)

Suggest what would happen to the position of equilibrium if you:

a) increased the **pressure**.

b) increased the **temperature**.

c) added more **nitrogen**.

d) removed the **ammonia**.

Q3 The diagram opposite shows the Haber Process.

a) **Write** a fully balanced equation for the reaction, including state symbols.

b) What **catalyst** is used?

c) What is the **function** of the catalyst?

d) Why are **fine pellets** used?

e) **Use the information** on the graph to suggest the optimum conditions for ammonia production.

f) **Explain** why high pressures are used.

g) The actual conditions are often 450°C and 200 atm pressure. **Explain** why these conditions are used.

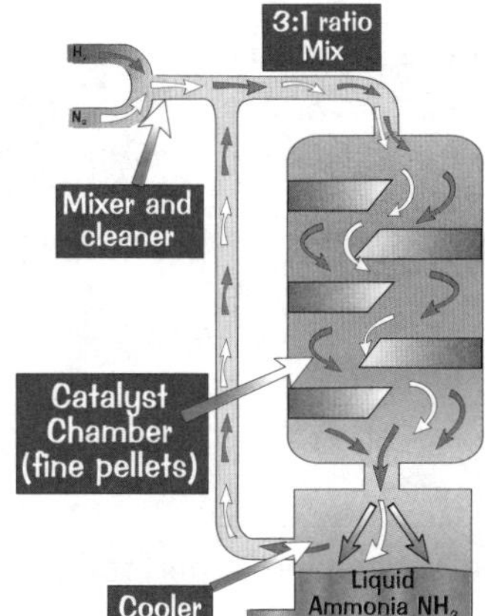

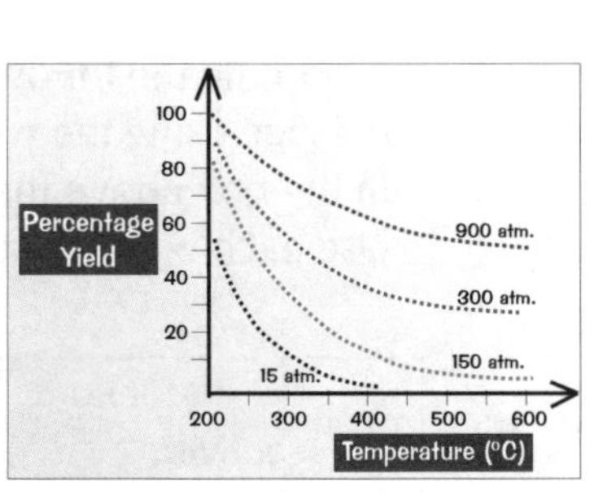

Q4 The equation $2SO_{2\,(g)} + O_{2\,(g)} \rightleftharpoons 2SO_{3\,(g)}$ describes tha Contact Process for making sulphuric acid.

ΔH is -ve (it's exothermic)

a) What is the effect on the position of equilibrium of increasing: (i) **temperature** (ii) **pressure**?

b) **Suggest** the optimum conditions that could be used for a high yield.

c) The actual operating temperature is around 450°C, despite a poor yield (see graph). **Explain** why such a high temperature is used.

d) In this process 100% conversion could be achieved using extremely high pressures of around 1000 atm. Suggest a reason why this pressure is **not** used commercially.

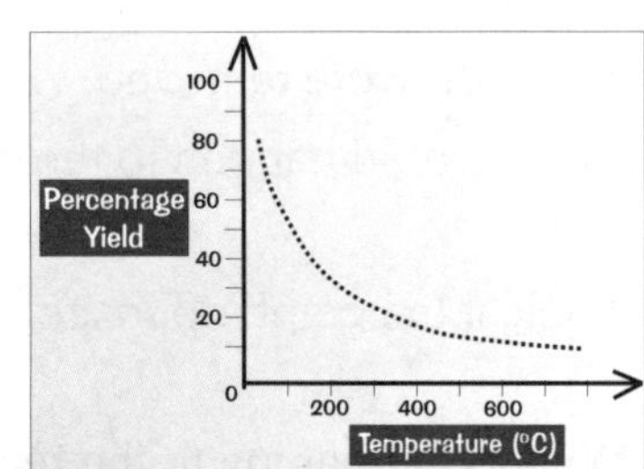

Top-tips: If two things can combine, they can separate — any reaction's basically reversible. Usually though one way's much faster than the other, so you don't notice. If you can picture what's happening at the molecular level, you're much more likely to remember it... probably.

16.5 Relative Formula Mass

Example: Find the **relative atomic mass** of zinc.
(Which is basically the same as asking...."**Find the Mass of One Mole of Zinc**")

Look on the Periodic Table (at the front of the book) for the relative atomic mass of zinc, which is 65,
(add a "g" for grams if it asked for a mole)
Answer = 65g

Q1 Find the **relative atomic mass** of...

a) Calcium (Ca) **b)** Sodium (Na) **c)** Iron (Fe)
d) Chlorine (Cl) **e)** Aluminium (Al) **f)** Mercury (Hg)

Example: Find the **relative formula mass** of zinc oxide.
(Which is basically the same as asking..,"find the mass of one mole of zinc oxide")

Add up the relative atomic masses of zinc and oxygen (65 + 16).
(Then put a "g" for grams if it asked for a mole)

Zinc oxide has a formula ZnO. Which contains: **(1 x Zn) + (1 x O)**
= (1 x 65) + (1 x 16)
= 65 + 16
= 81g

Q2 Find the **relative formula mass** of ...

a) Hydrogen molecules (H_2) **b)** Oxygen molecules (O_2) **c)** Chlorine molecules (Cl_2)
d) Bromine molecules (Br_2) **e)** Nitrogen molecules (N_2) **f)** Fluorine molecules (F_2)

Q3 Calculate the **relative formula mass** of the following compounds:

a) Copper oxide (CuO) **b)** Hydrogen chloride (HCl) **c)** Sodium chloride (NaCl)
d) Carbon monoxide (CO) **e)** Sodium bromide (NaBr) **f)** Lithium iodide (LiI)

Q4 Calculate the **relative formula mass** of these more complex compounds:

a) Carbon dioxide (CO_2) **b)** Water (H_2O) **c)** Ethene (C_2H_4)
d) Barium sulphate ($BaSO_4$) **e)** Lead iodide (PbI_2) **f)** Aluminium oxide (Al_2O_3)

Q5 And finally these **hideously** complex compounds:

a) Potassium manganate (VII) ($KMnO_4$) **b)** Tetrachloromethane (CCl_4) **c)** Citric acid ($C_6H_8O_7$)
d) Calcium hydroxide ($Ca(OH)_2$) **e)** Potassium dichromate ($K_2Cr_2O_7$) **f)** Lead nitrate ($Pb(NO_3)_2$)

Percentage Element in a Compound

16.5

Calculations = loads of easy marks once you've got them sussed. Read on to find out how...

Remember this formula:

$$\text{\% Mass of an element in a compound} = \frac{A_r \times \text{No. of atoms (of that element)}}{M_r \text{ (of whole compound)}}$$

Here is an example worked out for you:

Find the % sodium in Na_2SO_4

$$\frac{A_r \times n}{M_r} \times 100 \qquad \frac{23 \times 2}{142} \times 100$$

$$= \underline{32.4\%}$$

(Remember A_r = Relative Atomic Mass; M_r = Relative Molecular Mass)

Q1 Using the Periodic Table at the front of this book, find the following:

a) the % carbon in CO_2
b) the % carbon in CO
c) the % potassium in KCl
d) the % sodium in NaF
e) the % copper in CuO
f) the % sulphur in SO_2
g) the % oxygen in SO_2
h) the % sulphur in SO_3
i) the % oxygen in SO_3
j) the % hydrogen in H_2O
k) the % nitrogen in NH_3
l) the % sodium in $NaOH$
m) the % water in $CuSO_4.5H_2O$
n) the % aluminium in Al_2O_3
o) the % copper in $CuCO_3$
p) the % copper in $CuSO_4$
q) the % potassium in KNO_3
r) the % phosphorus in $(NH_4)_3PO_4$
s) the % nitrogen in NH_4NO_3
t) the % nitrogen in $(NH_4)_2SO_4$

Q2 Which has the greater proportion of carbon?
Show how you **calculated** your answer.

a) CH_4 **b)** C_6H_6 **c)** C_2H_5OH

Q3 Which has the greater proportion of aluminium?

a) Al_2O_3 **b)** Na_3AlF_6

Q4 Which of these iron ores has the most iron in it by **percentage** mass?

a) Siderite ($FeCO_3$) **b)** Haematite (Fe_2O_3) **c)** Magnetite (Fe_3O_4) **d)** Iron pyrite (FeS_2)

Q5 Calculate the **proportion** of metal in:

a) NaCl **b)** $MgCO_3$ **c)** Zn **d)** KOH

Q6 The molar mass of haemoglobin is about 33939g.

If each molecule contains two iron atoms, what percentage of the molecule is iron?

16.5 Empirical Formulas

To find out the empirical formula for a compound, you've got to find the amount of each element and then work out the simplest whole number ratio of the amounts.

Look at the example below:

A compound is 75% carbon and 25% hydrogen. What is its empirical formula?

Assume sample weighs 100g

This'll turn it into an easy ratio for the formula.

		Carbon		Hydrogen
% Element	=	75	=	25
Mass (g)	=	75	=	25
Divide by A_r for each element	=	$\frac{75}{12}$ = 6.25	=	$\frac{25}{1}$ = 25
$\frac{\text{Amount}}{\text{Smallest amount}}$	=	$\frac{6.25}{6.25}$	=	$\frac{25}{6.25}$
Ratio of amount	=	1	:	4

C_1H_4 or, better, CH_4

This is the empirical formula

Q1 Find the empirical formula of the following:

a) A hydrocarbon of 80% carbon, 20% hydrogen.

b) Cryolite, (an aluminium ore used in the extraction of aluminium from bauxite), containing 33% sodium, 13% aluminium, and 54% fluorine.

c) A compound of 82% nitrogen, 18% hydrogen.

d) Nitram (an ammonium fertilizer containing 35% nitrogen, 5% hydrogen and 60% oxygen

Q2 The method above uses the % of an element in a compound — but the same method can be used if the mass of an element is given.

a) 2.70g of aluminium is combined with 10.65g of chlorine. What is the empirical formula?

b) 1.6g of sulphur was heated in oxygen. Its mass increased to 4.0g. What is the **name** of this oxide of sulphur?

c) 1.48g of a calcium compound contains 0.8g of calcium, 0.64g of oxygen and 0.04g of hydrogen. **Name** the compound.

d) Copper sulphate crystals contain **water of crystallisation** (water in its crystal structure) and have the formula $CuSO_4.xH_2O$, where x is a number. 49.9g of a sample of copper sulphate was found to have 18g of water of crystallisation. **Calculate** x.

Empirical — my Dear Watson...

Empirical formulae are not the same thing as real (molecular) formulae — you've got to cancel those numbers. So, ethene's molecular formula is C_2H_4, but its empirical formula is CH_2 — you're writing the ratio of the numbers of moles in its simplest form.

Reacting Amount Calculations

16.5

Q1 Answer the following questions about this equation: $Fe + S \rightarrow FeS$

a) **Work out** the mass of **iron sulphide** produced when 5.6g of iron completely reacts with excess sulphur.

b) **Calculate** the mass of **iron sulphide** produced when 320g of sulphur is reacted with excess iron.

c) **Calculate** the mass of iron required to make 8.8g of **iron sulphide** by reacting iron with sulphur.

Q2 Answer the following questions about this equation: $CaCO_3 \rightarrow CaO + CO_2$

Calculate the mass of carbon dioxide that is released when 20g of calcium carbonate **decomposes** on heating.

Q3 Answer the following question about this equation:
$Fe_2O_3 + 3CO \rightarrow 2Fe + 3CO_2$

What **mass** of iron would be obtained from 160 tonnes of iron(III) oxide?

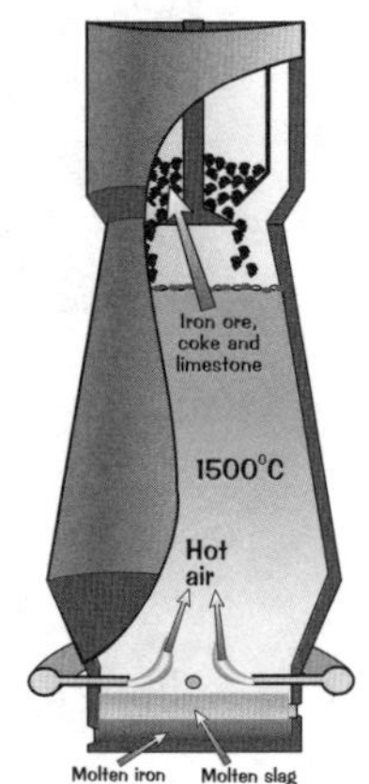

Q4 Which has the **greater number** of atoms:

230g of sodium or 230g of potassium?

Q5 How much **anhydrous** $CuSO_4$ is produced when 22.4g of **hydrated** copper sulphate ($CuSO_4.5H_2O$) is gently heated?

Q6 Answer the following question about this equation: $2Al_2O_3 \rightarrow 4Al + 3O_2$

How much aluminium oxide would be needed to make the following **amounts** of aluminium?

a) 1kg **b)** 2kg **c)** 4.5kg **d)** 1 tonne (1 tonne = 1000kg)

Q7 Copper oxide can be **reduced** to copper using methane.
The reaction follows the equation: $4CuO + CH_4 \rightarrow 4Cu + CO_2 + 2H_2O$
How much copper oxide would be needed to make 19.2g of copper?

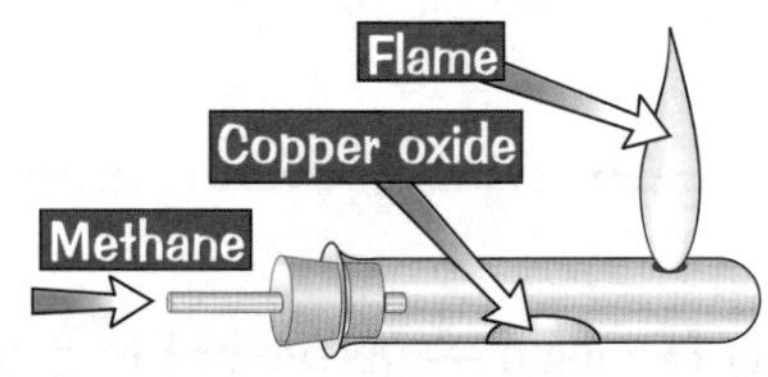

21st century mole

16.5

Calculating Volumes

To answer these questions, you need to know that a mass of M_r in grams ,of any gas, will always occupy 24 litres (that's 24,000 cm³) at room temperature and pressure (RTP)

$$\frac{\text{Volume of gas (in cm}^3\text{)}}{24{,}000} = \frac{\text{Mass of gas}}{M_r \text{ of gas}}$$

RTP is...

25°C
1 atmosphere pressure.

Example: What is the volume of 0.2g of H_2?

$$\frac{\text{Vol. of gas}}{24{,}000} = \frac{0.2}{2} \qquad \text{Vol. of gas} = \frac{0.2 \times 24{,}000}{2} = 2{,}400\text{cm}^3$$

Q1 Find the **volume at RTP** of the following:

a) 8g of helium (He) in litres

b) 4g of argon (Ar) in litres

c) 8.4g of krypton (Kr) in litres

d) 2.6g of xenon (Xe) in cm³

e) 11g of CO_2 in litres

f) 40g of CH_4 in litres

g) 8g of SO_3 in cm³

h) 131.75g of CH_3NH_2 in cm³

Q2 Find the **mass** of the following volumes of gas (they're at RTP):

a) 24 litres of He

b) 3 litres of He

c) 18 litres O_2

d) 2000 cm³ of O_3

e) 24 litres of C_2H_4

f) 30 litres of NH_3

g) 6200 cm³ SO_2

h) 9600 cm³ of CH_3NH_2

Not just a load of hot air... Volume doesn't depend on the type of gas. Temperature and pressure affect it, but they'll be constant in exam questions — probably RTP (make sure you can define this). Don't think you can forget tricky stuff like this, 5% of the Exam could be on it — pretty much a grade... so keep practising, until you get them ALL right each time, every single one...

17.1 Atoms and Molecules

Atoms may be dead small, but they govern how elements react — so they're pretty important...

Q1 From the diagrams, choose the letter of the pictures that best describe:

a) A **pure** element.
b) A **pure** compound.
c) A **mixture** of elements.
d) A **mixture** of compounds.
e) An example of molecules made from just **two elements**.
f) An example of molecules made from **three elements**.
g) Which example could be **water**?

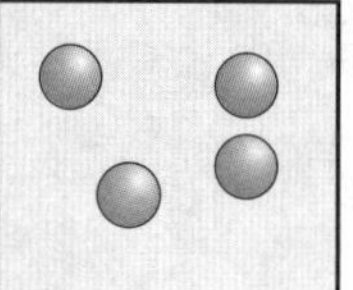

A

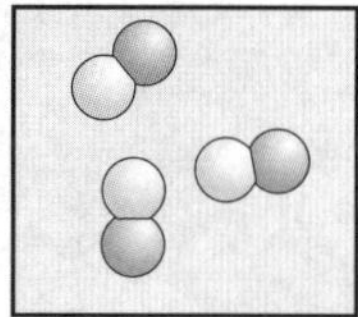
B

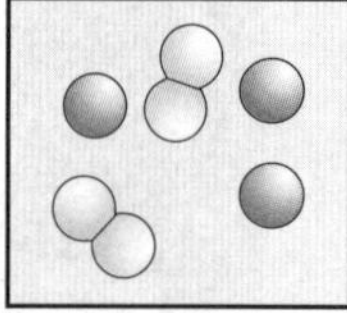
C

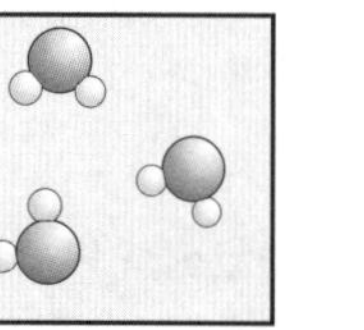
D

E

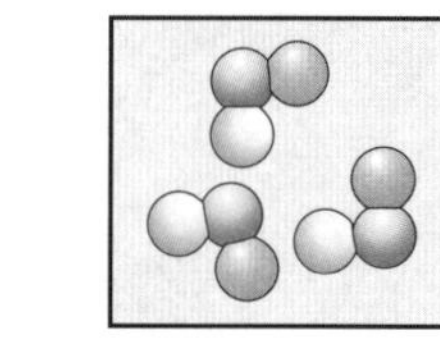
F

Q2 Who re-introduced the idea of the atom around 200 years ago?

Q3 Methane can be represented in the following ways:

Molecular formula: CH_4

Structural formula:

```
   H
   |
H- C -H
   |
   H
```

Molecular model:

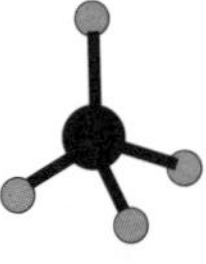

Complete the table for the following named substances:

Name	Molecular formula	Structural formula	Molecular model
Water		H–O–H (bent: O with H and H)	
Ammonia	NH_3		
Ethane		H–C–C–H with H above and below each C	
Carbon dioxide			

Q4 Use the following words to label A, B and C on this molecular model of silicon dioxide (sand).

silicon   oxygen   covalent bond

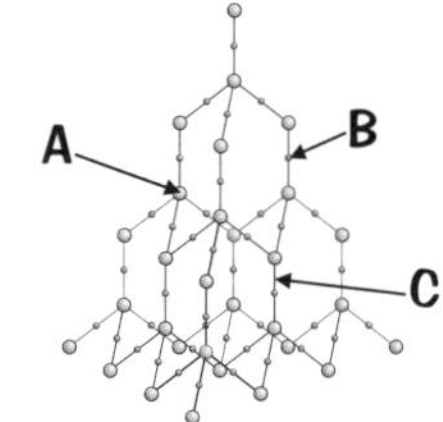

Let's stick together guys...

Atoms join up to make molecules. The "join" is a chemical bond and the arrangement of atoms is shown in a molecular model. You can show a molecule as a molecular formula or a structural formula or even build a three dimensional model with little balls and sticks, which is more fun.

Atoms

17.1

Q1 Answer these questions on atoms:

a) What is an **atom**?
b) **How many** different types of subatomic particles make up an atom?
c) What are their **names**?
d) What is a **nucleus**?
e) What is an **electron shell**?

Q2 Copy the diagram opposite, and complete the labels A, B and C.

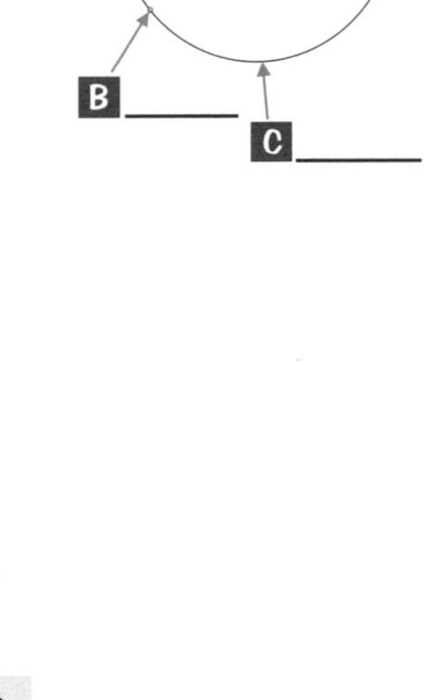

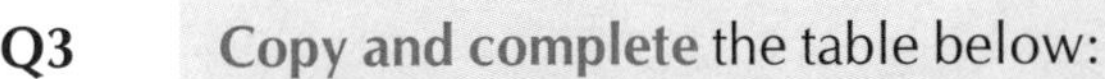

Q3 **Copy and complete** the table below:

Particle	Mass	Charge	Where it is found
Proton	1		
Electron		-1	
Neutron			In the nucleus

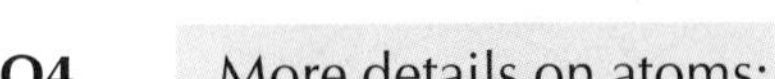

Q4 More details on atoms:

a) **Where** is most of the mass in an atom concentrated?
b) **What** is in between the **nucleus** and the **electrons**?

Q5 Nuclear reactions affect the nucleus. What do **chemical reactions** affect?

Q6 All atoms are neutral. If an atom has seven electrons then **how many** protons does it have?

Q7 Answer these questions on the atomic number and mass number of an element:

a) What does the **atomic number** tell us?
b) What does the **mass number** tell us?
c) **What** do the letters **A** and **Z** in the diagram stand for? What is **A - Z**?
d) **How many** protons are there in an atom of lithium?
e) **How many** electrons are there in an atom of lithium?
f) **How many** neutrons are there in an atom of lithium?
g) **Which number** *(mass or atomic)* determines what element an atom is?

A → 7, Z → 3, $^{7}_{3}\mathrm{Li}$

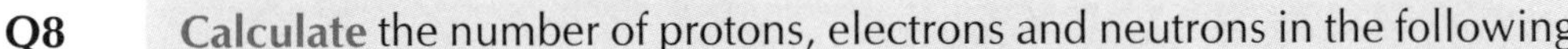

Q8 **Calculate** the number of protons, electrons and neutrons in the following:

a) Carbon ($^{12}_{6}\mathrm{C}$) **b)** Potassium ($^{39}_{19}\mathrm{K}$) **c)** Hydrogen ($^{1}_{1}\mathrm{H}$).

Q9 Some questions on isotopes:

a) What are **isotopes**?
b) **Give an example** of an isotope used in dating old objects.
c) Uranium 235 and Uranium 238 are isotopes. Are they chemically different? **Explain** why.

Top-tips: Some tricky new terms here — that's science for you. Make sure you know the difference between atomic number and mass number. Come the exam it'll be easy marks...

17.1

Electron Arrangement

Electron arrangement is easy. In fact it's very easy. All you need to remember is that the first shell can hold two and all others can hold eight. Then just fill 'em up...

Q1 Copy out the diagrams below. Complete them using crosses to show the **full electronic arrangement** — and write it down in numbers too. The first three have been done for you.

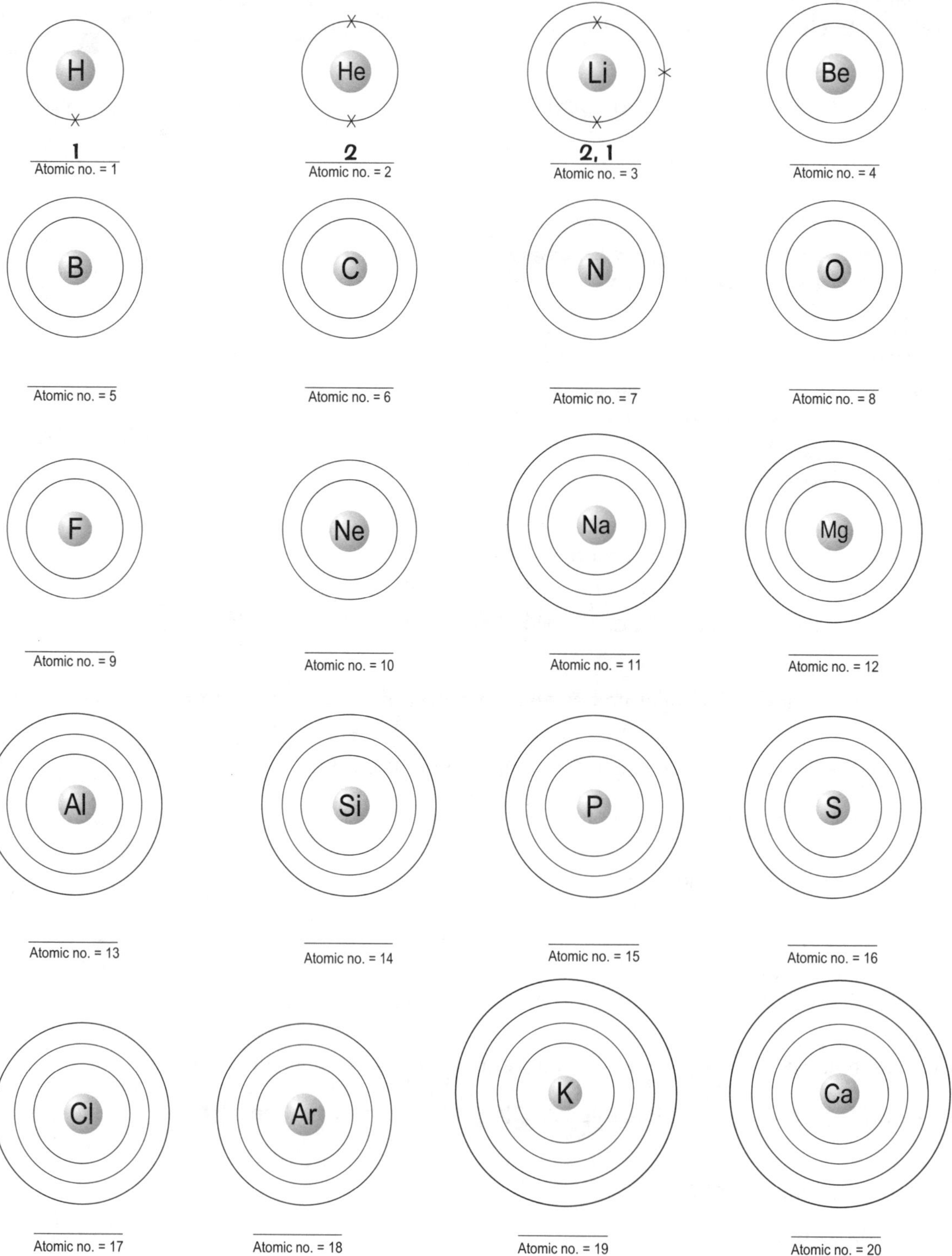

Top-tips: In Exams they're always asking you to draw out electronic arrangements, or "configurations". Make sure you can work them out from atomic numbers or the Periodic Table. If you're lucky, they might only ask you to draw the outer shell — easy or what. Bet you can't wait...

Covalent Bonding

17.1

Atoms join up to make molecules. They do this by forming chemical bonds. A chemical bond always involves electrons. A covalent bond is one where atoms share one or more pairs of electrons. This means that both the atoms can effectively have a full shell.

A full shell is a more stable arrangement of electrons, like in noble gases. Noble gases are inert and very stable. In summary, atoms undergo chemical reactions to attain a full shell, which makes them more stable — and that's why atoms react to make compounds...

When you've got all that you can answer these:

Q1 What is a **molecule**?

Q2 Give **another** name for the joining of two atoms together.

Q3 A covalent bond involves two atoms sharing what?

Q4 **Copy** these circles opposite. **Draw** two crosses on them to show the electrons in a single covalent bond:

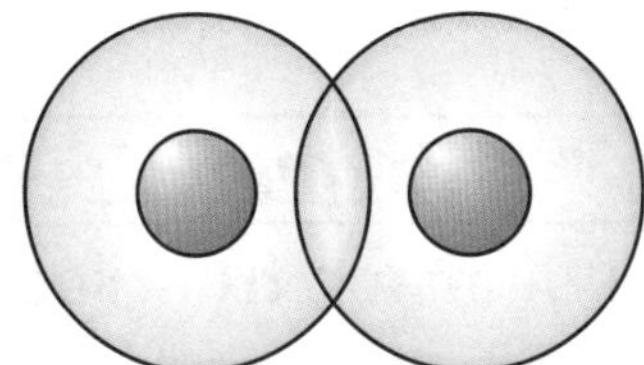

Q5 Why do atoms **share** electrons?

Q6 **Draw out** the dot and cross diagrams of the following molecules — showing the outer shells only (use the Periodic Table on the inside cover if needed).	**a)** Hydrogen (H_2): 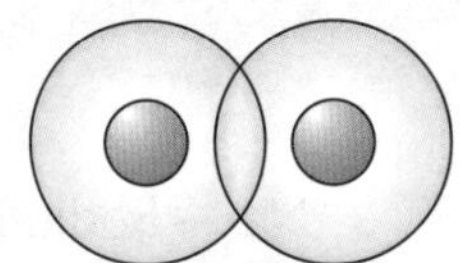
b) Water (H_2O): 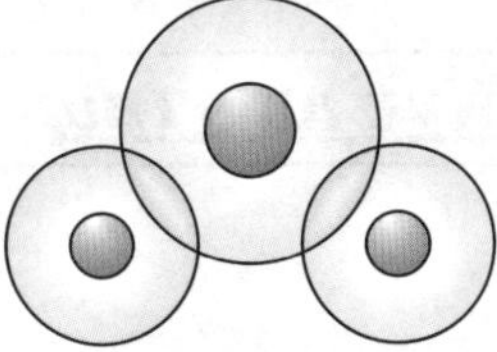	**c)** Ammonia (NH_3): 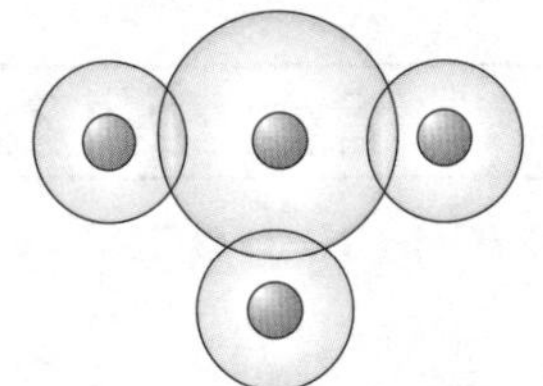
d) Methane (CH_4): 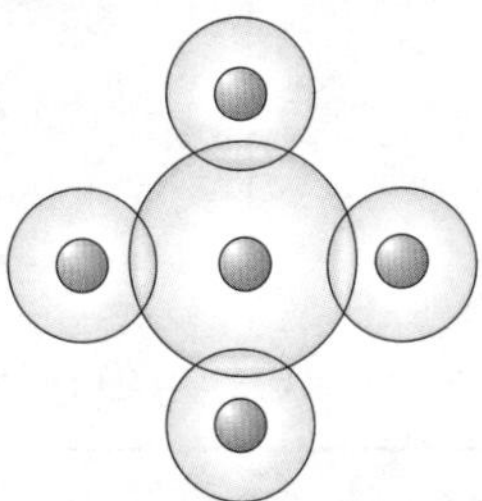	**e)** Chlorine (Cl_2): 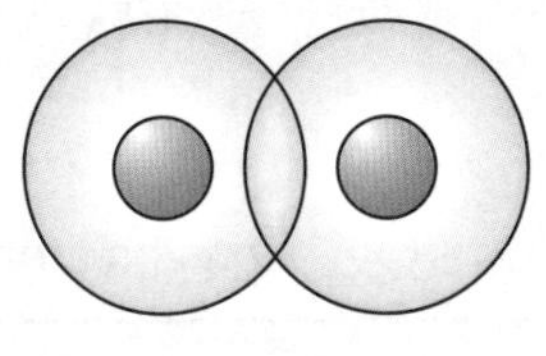

Q7 A single covalent bond involves sharing a pair of electrons. What does a **double covalent bond** involve?

Q8 Oxygen can attain a full shell by forming a double bond with itself.

Using dots and crosses show a double bond on the molecule to the right and label it. Then fill in the other electrons.

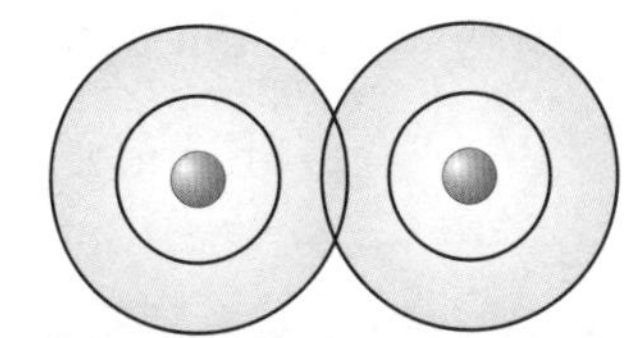

Oh hydrogen, you make me feel so complete...

Remember that atoms like to have a full outer shell, so some atoms will share electrons so that they feel they've got one. It's all so romantic, isn't it. Brings a tear to my eye... It really does...

17.1

Ions

Q1 Questions about ions here. Whoop-de-doo.

a) What is an **ion**?
b) Give **two** examples of ions made from single atoms.
c) Give **two** examples of ions made from several atoms.
d) **Complete** this paragraph using the words provided:

-ve protons negatively charged neutral positively charged
Atoms are electrically _______ because they have equal numbers of _______ (+ve) and electrons (____). If electrons are taken away from an atom, then it becomes ______ ______ because it has less electrons than protons. If electrons are added to an atom, it becomes ______ ______ because it then has more electrons than protons.

Example 1: Positive Ions (metals and hydrogen)

sodium ion from sodium

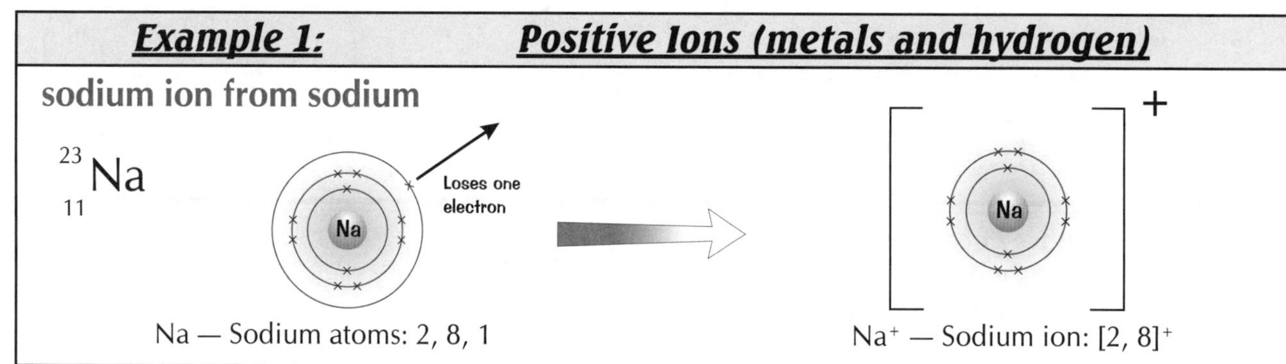

Na — Sodium atoms: 2, 8, 1

Na^+ — Sodium ion: $[2, 8]^+$

Example 2: Negative Ions (non-metals)

oxide ion from oxygen

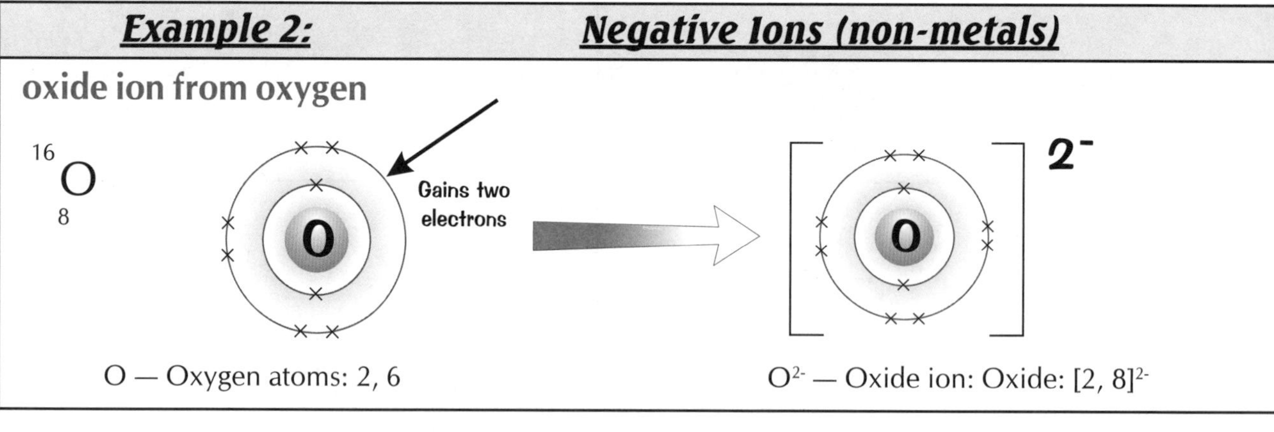

O — Oxygen atoms: 2, 6

O^{2-} — Oxide ion: Oxide: $[2, 8]^{2-}$

Q2 **Draw out** these ions exactly like those above. *__Remember__ Group 1 make 1^+ ions and Group 2 make 2^+*

a) Potassium. **b)** Magnesium. **c)** Calcium. **d)** Aluminium.

Q3 **Draw out** these ions exactly like those above. *__Remember__ Group 7 make 1^- ions and Group 6 make 2^-*

a) Fluoride. **b)** Chloride. **c)** Sulphide. **d)** Oxide.

Q4 What will be the **charge** on a **metal or hydrogen** ion? (e.g. Groups 1, 2 and 3)

Q5 What will be the charge on a **non-metal** ion? (e.g. Groups 6 and 7)

Ions

Q1 Answer these questions, covering all the basics of ionic bonding:

a) **What** is an ionic bond?
b) If an atom gains an electron, **what charge** does it have?
c) If an atom loses an electron, **what charge** does it have?
d) **Why** do sodium ions have a 1^+ charge?
e) **Why** do chloride ions have a 1^- charge?
f) **What charge** would you find on a Group 2 ion?
g) **What charge** would you find on a Group 6 ion?
h) **Why** is it rare to find a 4^+ ion of carbon?
i) **What** is a cation and what is an anion?

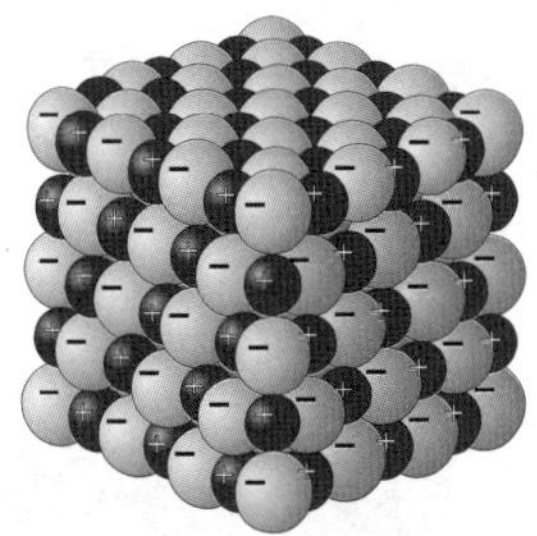

Ionic substances are tough but brittle — don't push them too far.

Q2 **Draw** an electron configuration diagram to show what happens in the following reactions.

a) A lithium atom reacting with a chlorine atom. **Name** the compound formed.
b) A magnesium atom reacting with two chlorine atoms.

Q3 **Why** is sodium chloride **neutral**?

Q4 **Draw** a picture to show the positions of sodium and chloride ions in a sodium chloride crystal.

Q5 **Name** the following ions:

a) Na^+ **b)** Cl^- **c)** S^{2-} **d)** NO_3^- **e)** SO_4^{2-} **f)** I^- **g)** F^- **h)** K^+ **i)** Ca^{2+} **j)** Mg^{2+} **k)** PO_4^{3-} **l)** H^+ **m)** Ba^{2+}

Q6 Give the **formulae** of magnesium oxide, sodium fluoride, sodium oxide, magnesium sulphate and sodium sulphate. Use the ions in the last question to help you.

Q7 Select from the list below:

SO_4^{2-} Mg^{2+} Kr MgO CO_2

a) An example of a gas consisting of **single atoms**.
b) An example of a substance made from **ions**.
c) An example of a substance made from **molecules**.
d) An example of a **compound**.
e) An example of an **ion**.
f) An example of a **molecular ion** (compound ion).

Q8 Which in the following list are **general** properties of an ionically bonded compound?

a) High boiling point
b) Usually dissolve in water
c) Conductor when solid
d) Non-conductor when melted
e) Weak forces hold molecules together
f) Non-crystalline

Please sir, spare an electron sir...

Ionic compounds are formed when electrons are <u>swapped</u> between one atom and another. Remember they contain a metal or hydrogen and a non-metal — and don't forget which ions are <u>positive</u> and which <u>negative</u>.

17.1 Structures

Q1 Using the words below, **complete the table** to summarise the properties of different types of structure.

High Low Poor Good

Bonding	Structure	Melting point	Boiling point	Conductivity		
				Solid	Liquid	Aqueous solution
Ionic	Giant					
Covalent	Giant					
Covalent	Molecular					
Metallic	Giant					Not applicable

Q2 "Substances have physical properties because of their chemical properties".

Explain what this means and state whether or not you agree with it.

Q3 **Why** are ionic substances generally brittle?

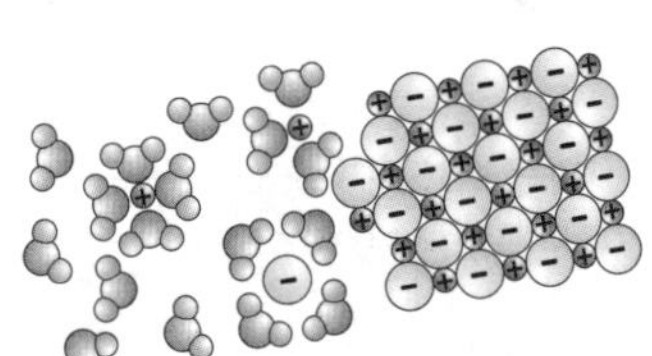

Q4 Why do ionic substances only **conduct electricity** when molten or when dissolved in water?

Q5 Referring to the diagram opposite, **explain** why ionic crystals dissolve in water.

Q6 **Describe** how an atom of iron joins up to other atoms in an iron bar.

Q7 Metals have "giant structures of atoms". What is a **giant structure**?

Q8 What are "**free electrons**", and where do they originate?

Q9 How do a metal's free electrons affect its **properties**?

Q10 Answer these questions about substances changing state:

a) Heating a substance supplies its particles with what?
b) What do the particles of a solid do when supplied with energy?
c) Describe how a solid melts.
d) What does the melting point of a solid mean?
e) What do the particles of a liquid do when supplied with energy ?
f) What happens to its particles when water boils?

How Structure Affects Properties

Q1 This question is about **simple molecular compounds**. Answer each and every bit.

a) What sort of substances are **simple molecular compound**?

b) Name three **simple molecular compounds**.

c) Do **simple molecular compounds** have high or low melting and boiling points?

d) Do they **conduct electricity**?

e) What features of their **structure** give them these **properties**?

Q2 Complete the paragraphs below using the word list.

covalently intermolecular slip weak easy low no water
diamond oxygen bonded atoms graphite large forces
high diamond don't graphite methane diamond carbon
four three layers rigid no strong one graphite

Simple molecular compounds consist of millions of molecules held together by __________ _____. The covalent bonds within the molecules are _____ but the intermolecular forces are _____. This makes it _____ to pull the the molecules away from each other, so simple molecular compounds have _____ melting and boiling points.

Giant covalent structures consist of millions of _____ which are held together by covalent bonds. Due to the _____ number of covalent bonds in their structures, they have __________ melting and boiling points. __________ and __________are both giant covalent structures made from __________. In diamond each carbon atom forms _____ covalent bonds which leads to a _____ structure. In graphite each carbon atom forms _____ covalent bonds, this means that graphite consists of _____ of carbon atoms which can _____ over each other. The atoms in diamond have _____ free electrons while the atoms in graphite have _____ free electron. This means that __________ is a conductor but __________ isn't.

Q3 This one is about **giant covalent structures**.

a) What sort of substances are **giant covalent structures**?

b) Do **giant covalent structures** have high or low melting and boiling points?

c) What feature of their **structure** gives them this **property**?

d) **Diamond** and **graphite** are **giant covalent structures** made from which **element**?

e) What is the difference in their **structure**?

f) Which of them **conducts electricity**?

g) Name a **giant covalent structure** made from **two different elements**.

Diamond is dead hard — so no messin' right...

Simple molecular compounds have loads of small molecules that are easy to pull away from each other. Giant covalent structures have one huge molecule containing billions of covalently bonded atoms — and they're really hard to pull apart. So that's why their properties are so different. Makes sense.

17.3

The Periodic Table

The Periodic Table is great — love it like you love your mother.

Q1 The Periodic Table is very useful. How much do you know about it ?

a) In the Periodic Table what is meant by a **Group**?
b) In the Periodic Table what is meant by a **Period**?
c) Roughly **how many** elements are there?
d) In what **order** are the elements listed?
e) What might be **similar** about members of the same group?
f) What might be **similar** about members of the same period?
g) Whose **idea** was it to put the elements in this order?
h) If an element is in Group I then **how many** electrons will it have in its outer electron shell?
i) If an ion has a 2+ charge, then **which group** is it most likely to be in?
j) If an ion has a 1- charge, then **which group** is it most likely to be in?

Q2 In this Periodic Table, some elements are shown as letters. They're **not** the correct symbols for the elements. Use the letters to answer the questions.

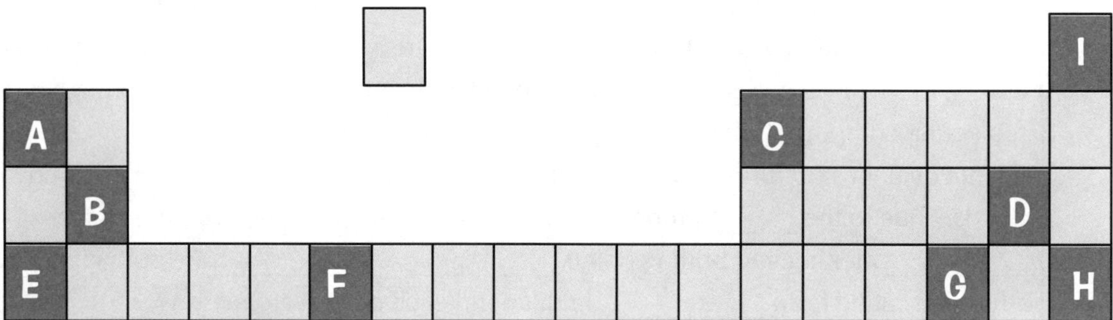

WHICH ELEMENT(S).........

a) are Noble gases?
b) are Halogens?
c) is in Group II?
d) is in the same period as D?
e) has three electrons in its outer shell?
f) has an atomic number of 3?
g) are non-metals?
h) is a transition element?
i) would form an ION with a charge of 1^+?
j) will not form an ion easily?
k) would form an ion by gaining 2 electrons per atom?
l) would form an ion with as many electrons as an atom of element (I)?
m) are the least reactive of those marked in the table?

Q3 **Complete** this table by filling in the **electronic configurations** of the elements:

Period	Group 1	Group 2	Group 3	Group 7	Group 0
2	Li 2,1	Be	B	F	Ne
3	Na	Mg	Al	Cl	Ar 2,8,8

Group 0: The Noble Gases

17.3

The Noble Gases think they're above all this reacting business. They're so smug about having a full outer shell, they just sit around all day like they're royalty...

Q1 Here's a few easy ones to start you off...

a) Why are the Noble gases known as group VIII
b) The Noble gases are "inert". **What** does this mean?
c) By referring to their atomic structure, **explain** why the Noble gases are "inert".
d) **Complete** the paragraph below using the word list.
Words can be used once, more than once, or not at all.

Periodic	inert	1%	diatomic	Noble	increase	shell	low	full
helium	individual		argon	neon	electrons	radon	radioactive	VIII

The ____________ gases are found in Group__________ on the ______________ Table. They are called Noble gases because they do not react with any other element, as they have a ______________ outer _____________ of _________. They are also called the _____________ gases. The Noble gases have very _____________ boiling points which _____________ down the group. The Noble gas with the largest atoms is ____________ and the one with the smallest atoms is ______________. Noble gases exist as __________ atoms rather than as __________ molecules. About ______________ of the air is made up of Noble gases.

Q2 The table below gives information about the Noble gases. Use it to **answer these questions:**

a) How do the **melting and boiling points** of the gases change as you go down the group?

b) **Complete** the table by estimating the melting point and boiling point of radon.

Noble Gas	Atomic Number	Density at STP g/cm^3	Melting Point °C	Boiling Point °C
Helium	2	0.00017	-272	-269
Neon	10	0.00084	-248	-246
Argon	18	0.0016	-189	-186
Krypton	36	0.0034	-157	-153
Xenon	54	0.006	-112	-107
Radon	86	0.01		

c) **Why** do the **densities** of the Noble gases increase down the group?

Q3 Why is neon used in **advertising signs**?

Q4 Give a **common use** for argon and state why it is used for that purpose.

Q5 Why is helium used in **meteorological balloons**, rather than argon?

Q6 The table below shows some details of the Noble gases. Have a look at it and answer the questions.

a) **Fill in the gaps** in the table.
b) **Write down** an element of Group 0 to match each of these descripions:
i) Gives out a light when a current is passed through it.
ii) Less dense than air.
iii) Used in lasers.

Noble Gas	Symbol	Atomic Number	Mass Number	No. of Protons	No. of Electrons	No. of Neutrons
	He		4	2		
Neon			20	10		
	Ar	18	40			
Krypton			84	36		
Xenon		54	131		54	
Radon		86	222			

17.3 Group I: The Alkali Metals

Q1 The table on the right shows four alkali metals and some of their physical properties.

Alkali Metal	Atomic Mass	Symbol	Boiling Point °C	Melting Point °C	Density g/cm³
Lithium	7		1342	181	0.535
Sodium	23		880	98	0.971
Potassium	39		760	63	0.862
Rubidium	85.5		688	39	1.53

a) Complete the table by filling in their **symbols**.

b) Caesium is the next alkali metal. Estimate its: **i) Boiling point** **ii) Melting point** **iii) Density**.

c) **Explain** why, as you go down Group I, the atoms get **bigger** in cross-section.

d) Which member of the group in the table is the **most dense**?

e) What must become **weaker** for the melting point to decrease down the group?

f) Over what **temperatures ranges** would you expect **i)** Rubidium, **ii)** Potassium, to be liquids?

Q2 **Complete** the table below, then answer the following questions:

Alkali Metal	No. of Protons	No. of Neutrons	No. of Electrons	Atomic Number	Mass Number
Lithium				3	7
Sodium	11				23
Potassium	19	20			
Rubidium				37	85
Caesium	55				133

a) Draw an atom of sodium showing its electron arrangement.

b) How many electrons has sodium in its outer shell?

c) Why does this make sodium so **reactive**?

d) What has to happen to an atom of sodium for it to achieve a **full** outer shell?

e) What is the **charge** of a sodium ion? **Explain** your answer.

f) When sodium bonds, it changes from an atom to an ion. What is meant by the term "**ion**"?

Q3 Put the metals in the box in order of reactivity, the most reactive first. Explain why the metals have this order of reactivity.

Caesium, Potassium, Lithium, Sodium, Rubidium.

Q4 Match up the alkali metal to its reaction in water.

A) Potassium
B) Sodium
C) Lithium

1) Ignites with yellow/orange flame, fizzes vigorously.
2) No flame, but fizzes.
3) Pops and ignites with a lilac flame, fizzes very vigorously.

Q5 When an alkali metal reacts with water, a gas is produced.

a) **Name** the gas that is produced. How could you test for this gas ?

b) **Complete** the equations to the right.

Sodium + Water →

Lithium + Water →

c) **i) Complete** and **balance** this equation: $K_{(s)} + H_2O_{(l)} \rightarrow KOH_{(aq)} +$

ii) What do the symbols (s), (l), (aq), and (g) stand for in chemical equations?

Group VII: The Halogens

17.3

Q1 Why are the halogens known as the Group VII elements?

Q2 Look at the information in the table.

Halogen	Melting Point °C	Boiling Point °C
Fluorine	-220	-188
Chlorine	-101	-35
Bromine	-7	58
Iodine		184

a) From the information given, **estimate** the melting point of iodine.

b) **Describe** the patterns (trends) in the melting and boiling points down the group.

Q3 All the halogens form diatomic molecules.

a) **Explain** what is meant by **diatomic**.

b) **Write** the formula for: **i)** the chlorine molecule **ii)** the iodine molecule.

Q4 The diagram on the right shows an atom of chlorine.

Atom of Chlorine

Cl

a) **Draw** a **molecule** of chlorine using this atom to help you.
b) What type of bonding do we call this?

Q5 The halogens also form another type of bond by gaining one electron.

a) What is this type of bonding called?
b) What would be the charge on a halogen ion?
c) **Name** a compound in which chlorine would gain an electron.
d) **Name** a compound in which chlorine would share an electron.

Q6 The reactivity of the halogens decreases down the group, but the reactivity of the alkali metals increases down the group. **Explain** this difference.

Q7 Halogens react with metals to form salts.

a) What is a salt?
b) Given that halogens are poisonous, where should reactions of metals and halogens be carried out?
c) **Write in** the salts formed from the following reactions:
d) Are the salts ionic or covalent compounds? **Explain** your answer.

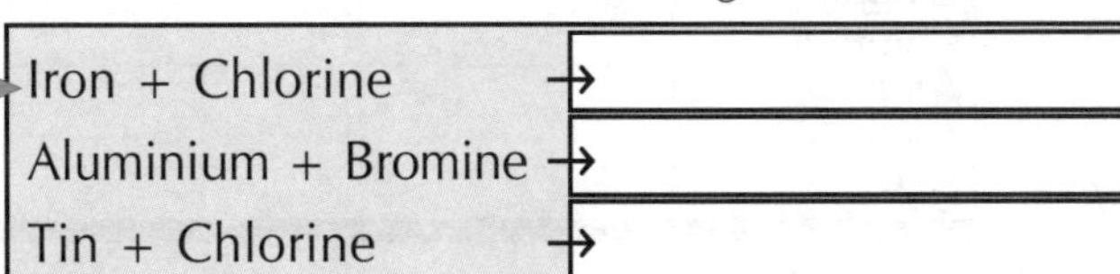

Q8 Chlorine is bubbled through sodium bromide as shown in the diagram.

a) **What** would you see happening in the test tube?
b) **Which** of chlorine or bromine is the most reactive?
c) **How** can you **explain** the results of the reaction?
d) **Write** an equation to explain the reaction.
e) **Complete** the equations below by writing the symbols and balancing them.

i) Fluorine + Sodium iodide →
ii) Chlorine + Sodium bromide →
iii) Chlorine + Potassium fluoride →
iv) Bromine + Potassium iodide →

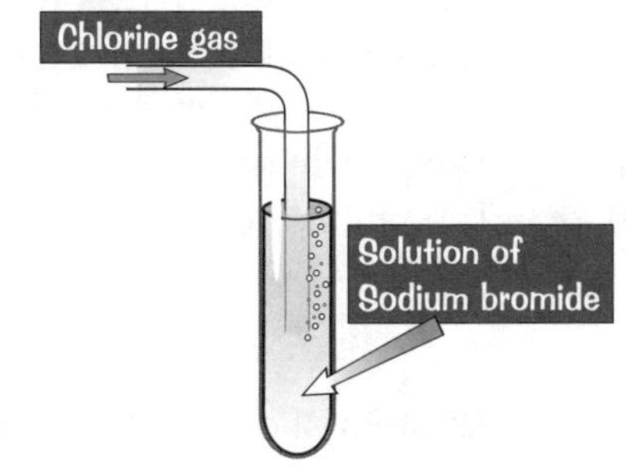

Just hand over the electrons and nobody gets hurt...

Wow, these guys want electrons bad — just one more and they'll have that nice full-outer-shell feeling...

17.4

Electron Arrangement

Q1 Answer these atom questions:

a) An atom can be compared to the solar system. **Explain** the similarity.
b) What keeps the electrons **attracted** to the nucleus?
c) Give **another** name for an electron orbit.

Q2 **Complete** the table to show the sizes of the electron shells.

Electron shell	Maximum number of electrons in the shell
1st	
2nd	
3rd	

Q3 **Complete** the table below showing the properties of the first 20 elements (you will need the Periodic Table at the front of the book).

Element	Symbol	Atomic Number	Mass Number	Number of Protons	Number of Electrons	Number of Neutrons	Electronic Configuration	Group Number
Hydrogen	H	1	1	1	1	0	1	—
Helium	He	2	4	2	2	2	2	0
Lithium	Li						2, 1	1
Beryllium								2
Boron				5				
Carbon								
Nitrogen		7						
Oxygen					8			
Fluorine							2, 7	
Neon								
Sodium		11						1
Magnesium								
Aluminium		13	27	13	13	14	2, 8, 3	3
Silicon								
Phosphorus								
Sulphur	S							
Chlorine								
Argon								
Potassium								
Calcium						20		2

Q4 Look at the table and answer these questions:

a) What is the link between **group number** and **number of outer electrons**?
b) What is the link between the **Noble gases** (group 0) and **full outer shells**?
c) Iodine is in group 7 — **how many** electrons does it have in its outer electron shell?
d) Xenon is in group 0 — **how many** electrons does it have in its outer electron shell?
e) The **number of electrons** in the outer shell governs which **property** of the element?

Q5 An atom of element X has two outer electrons that do not fill the outer shell.

a) **Name** its *group*.
b) Is it a **metal** or **non-metal**?
c) Name **another** element with similar chemical properties to X.

Industrial Salt

17.5

Q1 State the main **use** of solid rock salt, especially important in the **winter months**.

Q2 Where are large quantities of **salt** found?

Q3 **How** is most of the salt obtained from the ground?

Q4 What is the **common name** for concentrated sodium chloride solution?

Q5 Sodium hydroxide has many uses. It is obtained from rock salt industrially by electrolysis. What is **electrolysis**?

Q6 Sodium chloride is made into a solution before it is electrolysed.

a) **What** is this **solution** called?
b) **Why** does sodium chloride have to be made into a solution **before** electrolysis?

Q7 **Complete** the following sentences by **filling in** the missing words (words can be used once, more than once or not at all).

brine   electrolysis   hydrogen   lose Na^+ chlorine atoms
rock salt   sodium hydroxide Cl^- chlorine molecule Cl^- ions
gain   hydrogen molecule   industrial   Cl   chlorine
chloride H^+ hydrogen atoms   industrially

Sodium chloride has many __________ uses. Salt is mined as __________ __________. This is purified to give sodium chloride. Useful products are obtained from a solution of sodium chloride called __________ by __________. The ions produced are H^+, OH^-, __________ and __________. At the anode the __________ ions are deposited. They __________ electrons and become __________ atoms. Two __________ __________ join together to form a __________ __________. At the cathode the __________ ions are deposited. They __________ an electron and become a __________ atom. Two __________ __________ join together to form a __________ __________. All the products from the electrolysis of brine can be used, as __________ __________ solution is left in the reaction vessel.

Q8 Chlorine and hydrogen are formed by the electrolysis of brine. If a test tube of each were collected, how could you **test** which contained the chlorine and which the hydrogen (other than by looking at their colour)?

Top-tips: Make sure you learn about <u>electrolysis</u> — that's what you really need to know. You want to learn the three products and exactly how they're produced. And don't forget where the salt comes from.

17.5 Uses of Halogens and Salt Products

Q1 Chlorine is used in bleach. Bleach is made by dissolving chlorine in sodium hydroxide solution.

This is the reaction:

$$Cl_{2\,(g)} + NaOH_{(aq)} \rightarrow NaOCl_{(aq)} + NaCl_{(aq)} + H_2O_{(l)}$$

Balance the equation.

Q2 Give **two** other uses of chlorine.

Q3 Give **three** uses of sodium hydroxide.

Q4 **Fill the blanks** using the words below. Words can be used once, more than once or not at all:

sodium hydrogencarbonate hydrogen
chloride hydrocarbon sodium hydroxide
chlorine ammonia hydrogen fats
textiles margarine oven-cleaners

Brine is electrolysed to give the three products ______________, ______________ and ______________. ______________ is used in making PVC, disinfecting drinking water and in swimming pools. To manufacture PVC it is made into ______________, and this is added to a long chain ______________ molecule in such a way as to form PVC. Hydrogen is used to make ______________ such as ______________. ____________________ is used to make soaps and detergents, ______________, paper and ______________such as rayon wool and cotton.

Q5 During electrolysis, ions gain or lose electrons at the electrodes. Electrically neutral atoms or molecules are released.

Balance the following half equation, which shows what happens at the cathode during the electrolysis of sodium chloride.

$$\mathbf{Cl^- - e^- \rightarrow Cl_2}$$

Q6 What three things are required to **reduce** silver halides to silver?

Q7 What is the main **use** of silver halides?

Q8 Hydrogen halides are gases. If you **dissolved** one in water, would you get an acidic, alkaline or neutral solution?

Sodium hydroxide — what use are you eh?...

You've got to think of the chemical's properties — if you can see why it's good for a particular use, it's easier to remember. Check you know what's used in bleach, margarine, soap and insecticides.

Symbols, Formulae and Equations

17.6

Q1 **Write out** the first twenty elements of the Periodic Table with their symbols.

Q2 **Write out** the symbols for the following:

iron lead zinc tin copper

Q3 **Copy and complete** this table:

Name	Formula	Proportion of each element present in substance
Zinc oxide	ZnO	1 zinc 1 oxygen
Magnesium oxide		
	NaCl	
	HCl	
Sulphur dioxide		
		1 carbon 2 oxygen
		1 sodium 1 oxygen 1 hydrogen
Potassium hydroxide		
		1 calcium 1 carbon 3 oxygen
Copper Sulphate		
Sulphuric Acid		
	H_2SO_4	
		2 iron 3 oxygen
	$MgCl_2$	
	H_2	
		2 chlorine

Q4 **Complete** the following:

When **chlorine** reacts with a metal to make an ionic compound it forms a **chlor**_______.
When **oxygen** reacts with a metal to make an ionic compound it forms an **ox**_______.
When **sulphur** reacts with a metal to make an ionic compound it forms a **sulph**_______.

Q5 Answer the following questions about naming compounds.

a) What name would you give to a compound made from **SODIUM** and **BROMINE**?

b) What name would you give to a compound made from **SODIUM** and **FLUORINE**?

c) If a compound has "—ate" at the end of its name, what **element** will be present?

d) Some compounds have "—ite" at the end of their name, like sodium chlorite.
What **element** will be present if "—ite" is in the name of a compound?

e) Some toothpastes contain sodium monofluorophosphate.
What **elements** do you think are present in this compound?

Q6 **Complete** the following word equations:

a) Sodium + chlorine → __________ __________

b) Carbon + __________ → Carbon dioxide

c) Sulphur + oxygen → __________ __________

d) Zinc + oxygen → __________ __________

e) __________ + __________ → Iron sulphide

f) Potassium + chlorine → __________ __________

g) Lead + oxygen → __________ __________

h) __________ + __________ → Calcium oxide

17.6

Equations

You won't get anywhere with chemistry without getting used to equations. Especially symbol ones. Looks horrible but you'll be fine with a little practice...

Q1 **Complete** the following **word** equations:

a)	Iron	+	sulphur	→
b)	Iron	+	oxygen	→
c)	Magnesium	+	oxygen	→
d)	Sulphur	+	oxygen	→
e)	Hydrogen	+	oxygen	→
f)	Magnesium	+	sulphur	→
g)	Aluminium	+	chlorine	→
h)	Hydrogen	+	iodine	→
i)	Carbon	+	oxygen	→

Q2 Look at the following **equation**:

$$2HCl_{(aq)} + Mg_{(s)} \quad MgCl_{2(aq)} + H_{2(g)}$$

H Cl
H Cl
+
Mg
→
Cl Mg Cl
+
H H

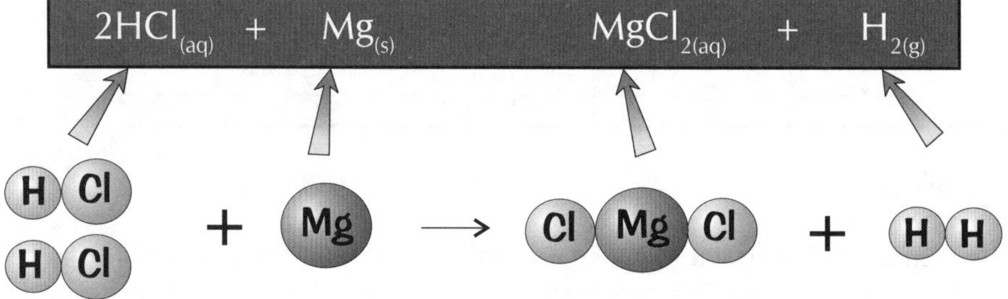

a) **What** do the terms (g), (aq) and (s) mean? What other similar symbol might be used?

b) **What** does the 2 before HCl mean?

c) **Why** is it $MgCl_2$ and not MgCl?

d) **Why** is it H_2 and not just H?

e) **Write out** the **symbol** equations below the picture equations, and **balance** them:

i)
K I
K I
+
Cl Cl
→
K Cl
K Cl
+
I I

ii)
Na
Na
+
Cl Cl
→
Na Cl
Na Cl

iii)
Li
+
O O
→
Li O Li

iv)
Li
Li
+
H O H
H O H
→
Li O H
+
H H

v)
Mg O O C O
+
H Cl
H Cl
→
Cl Mg Cl
+
H O H
+
O C O

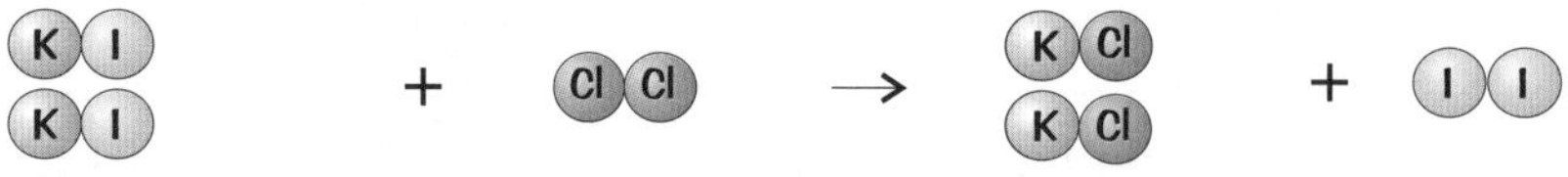

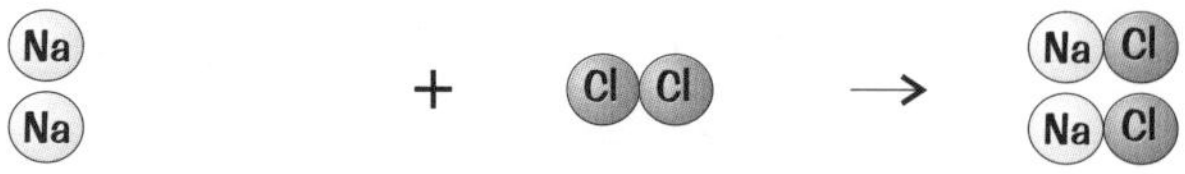

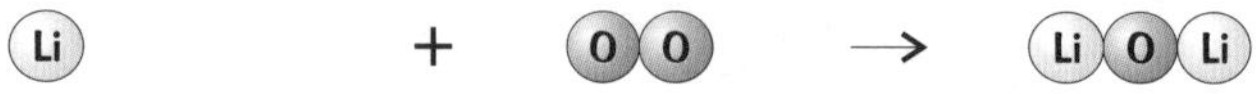

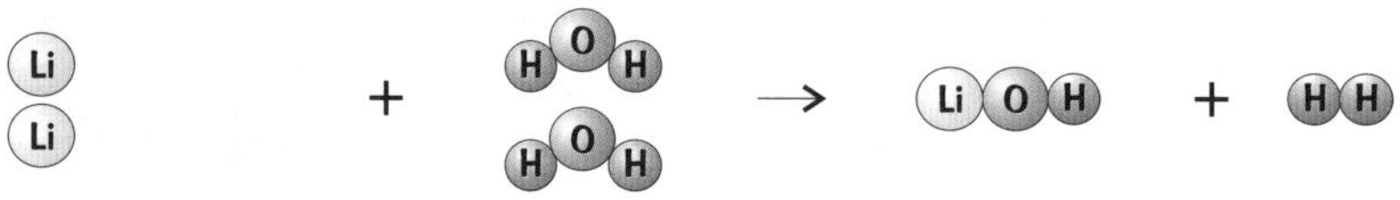

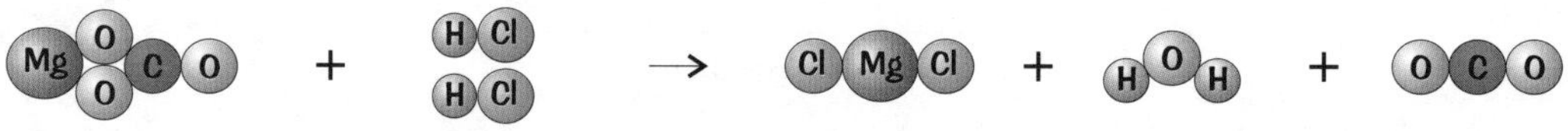

Equations

17.6

Q1 **Write** out the **symbol** equations for these word equations:

a) Carbon + oxygen → carbon dioxide

b) Zinc + sulphuric acid → zinc sulphate + hydrogen

c) Copper + chlorine → copper chloride

d) Hydrogen + copper oxide → copper + water

e) Magnesium + sulphuric acid → magnesium sulphate + hydrogen

Q2 **Balance** the following equations by putting the correct numbers before the formulae.

a) $N_2 + H_2 \rightarrow NH_3$

b) $CaCO_3 + H_2SO_4 \rightarrow CaSO_4 + H_2O + CO_2$

c) $H_2 + O_2 \rightarrow H_2O$

d) $Mg + O_2 \rightarrow MgO$

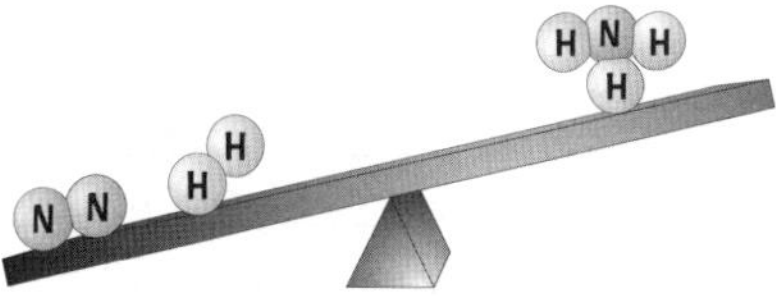

There's more...

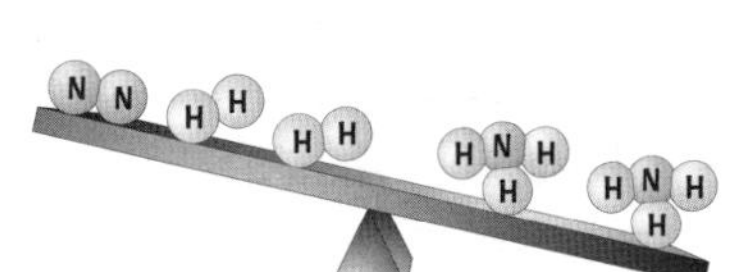

e) $Mg + H_2SO_4 \rightarrow MgSO_4 + H_2$

f) $H_2SO_4 + NaOH \rightarrow Na_2SO_4 + H_2O$

g) $Ca + H_2SO_4 \rightarrow CaSO_4 + H_2$

h) $H_2SO_4 + KOH \rightarrow K_2SO_4 + H_2O$

And more...

i) $Fe_2O_3 + CO \rightarrow Fe + CO_2$

j) $C_6H_{12}O_6 + O_2 \rightarrow CO_2 + H_20$

k) $CO_2 + H_2O \rightarrow C_6H_{12}O_6 + O_2$

l) $C_4H_{10} + O_2 \rightarrow CO_2 + H_2O$

m) $C_2H_4 + O_2 \rightarrow CO_2 + H_2O$

n) $C_3H_8 + O_2 \rightarrow CO_2 + H_2O$

o) $C_5H_{12} + O_2 \rightarrow CO_2 + H_2O$

p) $C_3H_6 + O_2 \rightarrow CO_2 + H_2O$

q) $C_2H_6 + O_2 \rightarrow CO_2 + H_2O$

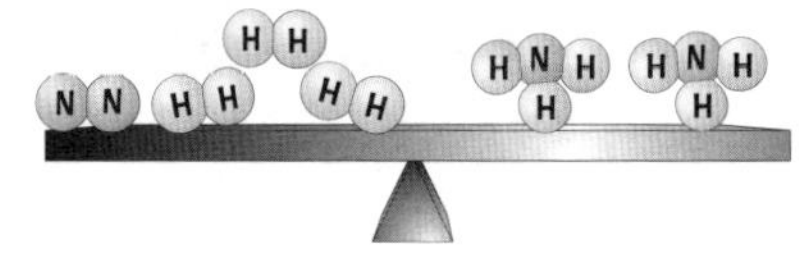

Right lad, you need six of one and half dozen of t'other...

Check each element, then check them all again. Keep checking till nothing needs changing, then it's got to be right. But don't change the numbers inside the formulae — that would completely change the reaction.

20.1 Speed, Distance and Time

This section is based on the thinkings of Sir Isaac Newton. His ideas now allow us to work out loads of things such as how far we have gone and how fast we got there — great.

Q1 Work out the speed of the items below in m/s:

This could be useful

a) An athlete who runs 100m (metres) in 10s (seconds).
b) A racing car zooming 240m in 12s.
c) A student, walking 600m in 240s.
d) A tortoise with a twisted ankle, shuffling 10m in 100s.

Q2 How long?

a) My flashy neighbour reckons his new racing bike can reach 18 m/s. He finished 10 laps of a 120m track in 70s. **Work out** his speed. **Could** he be telling porky pies?
b) A sprinter crosses the 100m race finish line. His speed throughout the race was 10 m/s, so **how long** did it take him?
c) The greyhound racetrack is 750m long. If Droopy's speed was 25 m/s, **what** was his time?

Q3 How far?

a) **How far** around the track would a racing car get, going at 90 m/s for 30s?
b) Concorde can travel at 650 m/s. **How far** can it go in 25s, travelling at this speed?
c) Find **how far** a cheetah could get if its speed is 30 m/s (70 mph) and it runs for 500s.
d) **How far** would a roadrunner go travelling at a speed of 25 m/s (56 mph) for 700s?

Q4 **Complete the sentences**:

Use these words: fast, direction, how, direction.

Speed is ___________ ___________ you're going with no regard to ___________ .
Velocity, however, must also have the ___________ specified.

Q5 A car travels 600m in 30s.

a) Find its average **speed**.
b) The car's average speed is usually different from its speed at any particular instant in time. **Explain** the reason for this.
c) **How far** would the car travel at the same speed in 1500s?

Q6 **Find** the speed (in m/s) of:

a) A train travelling 1200km in 8 hours.
b) A walker who travels 12km in 2½ hours.

Q7 How far does:

a) A cyclist travel in 3 hours at an average speed of 12 km/h?
b) A ship travel in 5 hours at an average speed of 25 km/h?

Q8 **Find** the velocity of a car travelling 2000m due North in 100s.

Velocity and Acceleration

20.1

Q1 **How long** does it take:

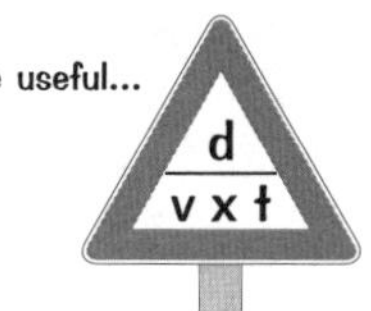

a) A car to cover 560km at an average speed of 70 km/h (in hours)?
b) Light to travel from the Sun to the Earth (150,000,000km) at a speed of 300,000 km/s? (Answer in minutes and seconds).

Q2 Find the **velocity** of a walker travelling a distance of 1000m East in 500s.

Q3 Find the **velocity** of a bird flying 450m South-East in 5s.

Q4 A walker starts in Barchester at 10am. She walks 5km North-East to Histon, getting there at 11am. She takes a half-hour break, then walks back to Barchester in 50 minutes.

a) What is her **velocity** (in m/s) when walking to Histon?
b) What is her **velocity** when walking back to Barchester?
c) What is her **average speed** for the whole trip?

Q5 Here's a really useful equation in a fantastic grey box:

$$a = \frac{\Delta V}{\Delta t}$$

a) From the equation, state what **a**, **ΔV** and **Δt** stand for.
b) State the usual **units** of **a**, **ΔV** and **Δt**.
c) **Explain** how acceleration is different from speed and velocity.

Q6 **Complete these sentences** using words from the list below. Use each word once only.

acceleration, second, 3 m/s, second, acceleration, 4 m/s, velocity, velocity

a) A motorbike has a steady ____________ of 3 m/s^2. This means that every ____________ its ____________ changes by ____________.

b) A car has a steady ____________ of 4 m/s^2. This means that every ____________ its ____________ changes by ____________.

Q7 PC Bacon is cruising along in his car at 15 m/s.

a) He keeps on going for an hour. **How far** does he go, in kilometres?
b) A car shoots past at 80 mph. How fast is the car going in **kilometres per hour**, and in **metres per second**? (One mile is about 1.6 kilometres).

c) PC Bacon gives chase, and accelerates steadily at 1 m/s^2 up to 40 m/s. **How long** does this take?
d) After travelling along for 3 minutes at 40 m/s, he catches up with the speeding car. **How far** has he travelled since reaching 40 m/s?
e) The speeding car is now travelling at 28 m/s. PC Bacon flags it down, and it pulls over into a layby. The car takes 15s to halt. **What** is its deceleration?

Was I speeding, officer?... Speed and velocity — they're not the same. They both say how fast a thing is going, but velocity also gives the direction, e.g. 30 m/s North. Remember Speed = Distance ÷ Time — writing them in a formula triangle makes everything a lot easier.

20.1 Describing Motion Graphically

Q1 This question is about a car whose motion is described by a velocity/time graph.

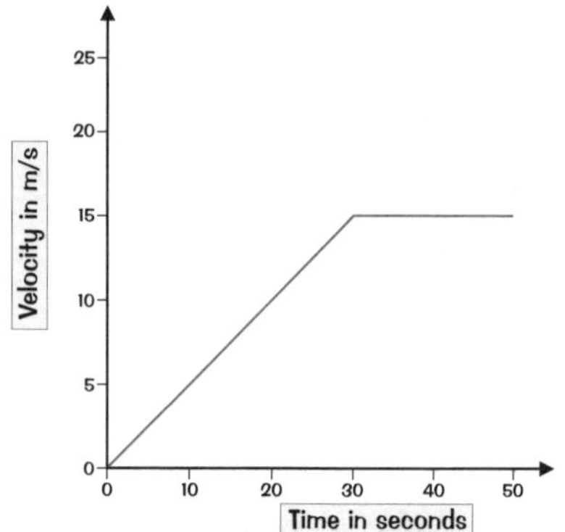

a) **How far** does the car travel in the first 30 seconds?

b) **Describe** the motion of the car in the next 20 seconds.

c) **Copy** the graph with the time axis extended to 100 seconds. Then **complete** the graph using the following information:
   (1) Between the times of 50 and 60 seconds, the car undergoes a steady acceleration to 20 m/s.
   (2) For the next 20 seconds the car's speed is steady at 20 m/s.
   (3) During the next 20 seconds, the car slows to a stop at a steady rate.

d) **Calculate** the acceleration occurring in **c) (1)**.

e) **Calculate** the deceleration occurring in **c) (3)**.

f) **Work out** the distance travelled during the last 40 seconds of this short trip.

Q2 This question is about Barry riding his new bike.

a) **How far** does Barry travel during the first 20 seconds of his journey?

b) Between the times of 20 and 40 seconds. **What is** Barry's **deceleration**?

c) How far does Barry travel during the period of deceleration described in **(b)**?

d) **What happens** over the next 20 seconds of the journey?

e) **How far** has Barry travelled in total over the whole 60 seconds?

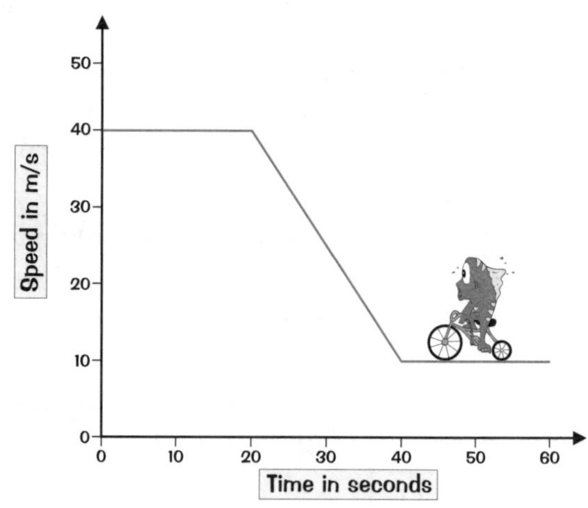

Q3 **Draw** a distance/time graph using these measurements taken during a bike journey.

Distance (m)	Time (s)
0	0
20	5
40	10
60	15
80	20
100	25
100	30
50	35
0	40

a) **Describe** the motion of the bike for the whole journey (write on the graph).

b) **Calculate** the speed of the bike between the times of 20 and 25 seconds.

c) **For how long** is the bike stationary?

d) **Calculate** the speed of the bike between the times of 30 and 40 seconds.

e) What is the **total distance** covered by the cyclist?

Mass, Weight and Gravity

20.2

Acceleration — very important if you're a wannabe boy-racer.
But it'll only happen if you've got unbalanced forces.

Q1 Fill in the **gaps** using the words below. Use each word **once** only.

bodies, large, attraction, weak, strong, field, centre, newtons, weight

Gravity is the force of ____________ between __________. Between objects on Earth, it is a ____________ force, but if the mass is very very __________ as with a planet or a star, the gravity can be very ____________. The region where a gravitational force can be felt is often referred to as a gravitational ______________.
The Earth's gravitational field attracts every object on Earth. This gives an object a _____________. Weight is measured in ______________, and always acts towards the __________ of the Earth.

Q2 "Mass"and "weight" are used in everyday language almost as if they were the same thing.

Draw a table with **two** columns, one headed "**mass**" and the other "**weight**".
Decide which information belongs to which column, and write them in:

- amount of matter
- measured in Newtons
- measured by a balance
- not a force
- measured by a spring balance
- is a force
- caused by the pull of gravity
- same anywhere in the universe
- measured in kilograms
- is lower on the moon than on Earth

Q3 Be very careful how you use the words weight and mass.

a) "A bag of flour weighs one kilogram".
Explain why this statement is not accurate.

b) Rewrite the above statement so that it is accurate.

c) **Copy and complete** the table opposite for a range of masses on Earth (g = 10 N/kg).

Mass (g)	Mass (kg)	Weight (N)
5		
10		
100		
200		
500		
1000		
5000		

Q4 The strength of gravity on Earth is **g = 10 N/kg**.
Find the **weight** of rocks with the following masses:

a) 5kg **b)** 10kg **c)** 2.5kg

Find the **mass** of rocks with the following weights on Earth:

d) 30N **e)** 150N **f)** 450N

If Freda had known about the Moon's low gravity, she never would have entered the high jump contest.

Q5 The strength of gravity on the Moon is g = 1.6 N/kg. Find the **weight** of green cheese on the moon with the following masses:

a) 5kg **b)** 10kg **c)** 2.5kg

Find the **mass** of rocks with the following weights on the Moon:

d) 16N **e)** 80N **f)** 960N

20.2 Force, Mass and Acceleration

Q1 Use the list on the right to identify forces **a)** to **f)**.

a) Acts straight downwards.	TENSION
b) Slows things down.	GRAVITY or WEIGHT
c) In a rope or cable.	LIFT
d) Due to an aeroplane wing.	THRUST or PUSH or PULL
e) Speeds something up.	REACTION FORCE
f) Acts straight upwards on a horizontal plane.	DRAG or AIR RESISTANCE or FRICTION

Q2 This question concerns a stationary object — a mug of tea. Mmmmmm, nice.

a) **Copy** the diagram and **draw in** the two vertical forces. **Label them**.
b) **Explain** how you'd know that these two forces were equal.
c) **What** would happen if there was only one **vertical** force?

Q3 A fish is hanging on the end of a fishing line.

Copy the diagram and **draw in** the 2 vertical forces. **Label them**.

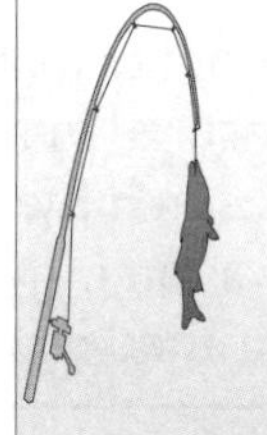

Q4 A car is moving forward with a **steady** horizontal velocity.

a) **Copy** the diagram and **draw in** the **two** vertical forces. **Label them**.
b) **Draw** in the **two** horizontal forces. Is one force bigger than the other?

Q5 **Complete** the following sentences with the words below:

unbalanced faster greater greater thrust upwards
downwards weight reaction drag drag force smaller

Acceleration means "getting ___________". You only get acceleration with an overall resultant (___________) force. The ___________ the unbalanced ___________ the ___________ the acceleration. The ___________ the unbalanced force, the smaller the acceleration. A car which is accelerating forward has a larger ___________ than ___________ force, but the vertical forces (___________ and ___________) are the same. A skydiver accelerating ___________ has a weight force downwards, and a smaller ___________ ___________.

Force, Mass and Acceleration

20.2

Q1 Chose the correct word from each pair to complete these statements about braking force:

The greater the speed of a vehicle:

a) The **greater** / **smaller** the force needed to stop it in a certain time.

b) The **greater** / **smaller** the distance needed to stop it with a certain braking force.

Q2 This diagram shows how the force of friction can be measured.

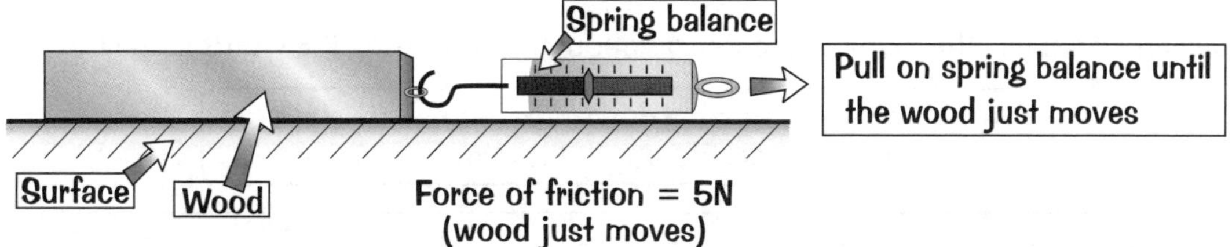

a) What's the **maximum** force you can apply before the wood starts to move?
b) Give **two** ways you can **increase** the force of friction.
c) Give **two** ways of **decreasing** the friction.

Q3 Why do:

a) Skiers wax their skis?
b) Machines have to be lubricated by oil?
c) Climbers wear rubber-soled shoes?
d) Ballroom dancers wear leather-soled shoes and dance on a highly polished floor?

Q4 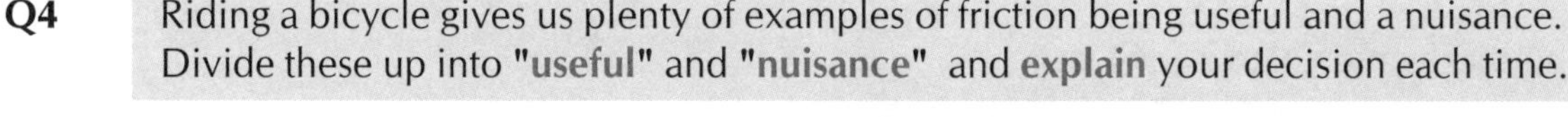
Riding a bicycle gives us plenty of examples of friction being useful and a nuisance. Divide these up into "**useful**" and "**nuisance**" and **explain** your decision each time.

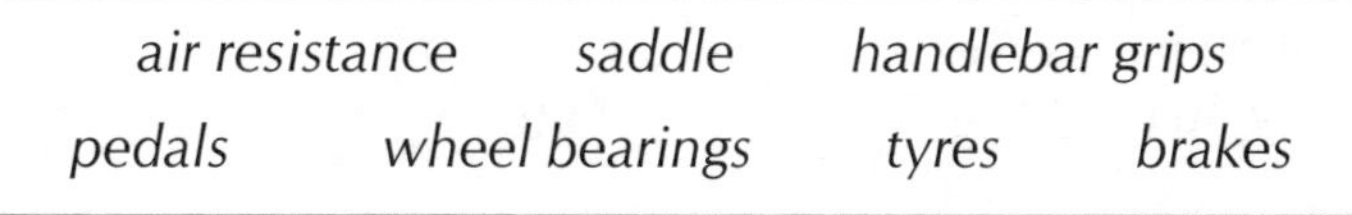
air resistance *saddle* *handlebar grips*
pedals *wheel bearings* *tyres* *brakes*

Q5 Friction causes wear and heating. Answer the following questions about these **two** effects of friction.

a) **Give three examples** where friction acts between surfaces that are **sliding** over each other.
b) Friction produces **heat** energy. Give two examples where this is **useful**.
c) What can be used to keep **friction** in **machinery** as **low** as possible?
d) **Explain** what will happen to an engine running without oil?
e) **Explain** why brakes might need to be replaced more often for a racing car than for a car that is only used around town (30 mph speed limit).

Luke — Feel the forces...

Friction is always there to slow things down — you can't afford to ignore it, so learn all the stuff on these pages. Remember the three ways that friction occurs — solids gripping each other, solids sliding past each other and drag from fluids. Friction causes wear and heating, machinery needs oil to lubricate it and stop it from wearing down — or even worse, welding itself together from the extreme heat. Eeek. Don't forget that friction can be helpful as well as a nuisance, try walking on ice if you don't believe me.

20.2 Force, Mass and Acceleration

Q1 It's important to know about stopping distances if you drive a car — and if you're doing science GSCE...

a) **What two stages** occur when a driver decides to stop their car?

b) **Name three factors** which increase the overall stopping distance of a vehicle?

c) **What** can happen if a driver brakes **too hard**?

Q2 **Newton's** Second Law of Motion states that a **non-zero resultant force** causes **acceleration.**

Copy and complete the following sentences about this law, using the words in the box below.

force unequal slowing down speeding up stopping accelerate decelerate direction starting

If there is an unbalanced __________, then an object will __________ or __________ in that __________. This change in motion can take five different forms: __________, __________, __________ __________, __________ __________ and changing direction. On a force diagram, the arrows will be __________.

Q3 There's a nice, easy relationship between force, mass and acceleration — you need to remember it.

a) **Complete** the equation, "F = "

b) **Rearrange** the equation as "a = ".

c) **What size** of acceleration does a force of one Newton give a mass of one kg?

Q4 **Find** the acceleration of these objects:

a) Resultant Force 100N, mass 10kg.

b) Resultant Force 500N, mass 25kg.

c) Resultant Force 75N, mass 2.5kg.

Q5 When Sarah is sitting in her go-kart, the total mass is **50kg**. Starting from rest at the top of a hill, she experiences a force of **100N** down the hill, and a constant resistance of **10N** in the opposite direction. She sets off with a tiny push, and travels for ten seconds before the hill levels off.

What is her **velocity** when she reaches the bottom?

Q6 A circus cannon is fired, giving Coco the Clown an acceleration of 5 m/s^2. He has a mass of 90kg.

a) What force propelled Coco?

b) What force is exerted on the cannon?

c) If the cannon has a mass of 450kg, how fast will it accelerate, and in what direction?

Newton – an ancient relative of Mr. Kipling...

Diagrams, diagrams, diagrams. They're very important. I reckon they're well useful — they help you to visualise the effect of each force. Remember that things <u>weigh</u> what they do because of the <u>force</u> of <u>gravity</u> acting on them. Learn <u>Newton's laws</u> of motion and things get a whole lot easier. Trust me.

Force, Mass and Acceleration

20.2

Q1 Complete the following sentences using these words:

adding subtracting resultant forces direction overall motion same accelerate decelerate steady

> In most real situations, there are at least two _______ acting on an object along any given _______. The _______ effect of these forces will decide the _______ of the object — whether it will _______, _______ or stay at a _______ speed. The overall effect is found by _______ or _______ the forces which point along the _______ direction. The overall force you get is called the _______.

Q2 A car of mass 2,000kg has a faulty engine which provides a driving force of 5,500N at all times. When it reaches 70 mph the drag force acting on the car is 5,400N.

a) **Draw a diagram** for both cases (rest and at 70 mph) showing all the forces acting on the car.
b) **Find** the car's acceleration when first setting off from rest. (Ignore the drag).
c) **Find** the car's acceleration at 70 mph.

Q3 What is another name given to each of the following?

a) The downward force acting on falling bodies.
b) Air resistance.
c) The maximum velocity reached by a falling object.
d) A useful piece of equipment to increase air resistance.
e) A shape which will decrease air resistance.

Q4 **Plot the graph** of velocity (in m/s) [vertical axis] against time (in s) [horizontal axis] showing the motion of a human skydiver after jumping out of an aeroplane. Then answer the questions **below**:

Velocity (m/s)	Time (s)
0	0
4.5	2
16.5	4
23.0	6
29.0	8
36.0	10
43.5	12
50.0	14
56.0	16
60.0	18
60.0	20

a) **Find** the terminal velocity of the skydiver *(and remember to to give the units).*
b) **Estimate** the velocity of the skydiver after:
i) 5s **ii)** 12.5s.
c) At **what time** does the skydiver reach **terminal velocity**?
d) The skydiver opens her parachute 20s after jumping out of the aeroplane. **Describe** the extra force acting on her and its effect upon her speed.
e) **Will** the skydiver reach a new terminal velocity? **Explain** your answer.

Q5 **Draw** the diagrams below showing the resultant forces. If the body is accelerating, write down the direction (up, down, left or right) in which it is accelerating.

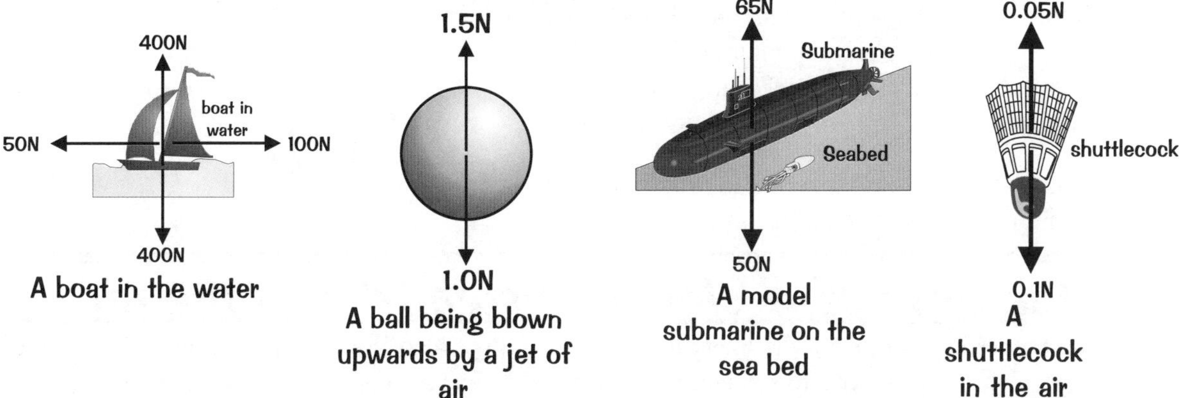

A boat in the water

A ball being blown upwards by a jet of air

A model submarine on the sea bed

A shuttlecock in the air

20.3 Work and Energy

The energy used or work done can be calculated using the size of the force exerted and the distance over which it acts. Don't exert too much force on this page.

Q1 The table shows how the force exerted by a sprinter changes with the type of training shoe worn. It also shows the distance moved by the sprinter in a time of 2 seconds.

Copy the table and complete the final column showing the work done.

Brand of trainer	Force (N)	Distance (m)	Work Done
Two Stripes	4.2	1.6	
Big Cross	5.6	0.8	
Off Balance	4.8	1.2	
Obverse	5.9	1.4	
High Vest	4.5	0.9	

a) What **units** should be used for the work done column?

b) What **force** is the work mainly done against?

The sprinter decides to test the Two Stripes shoe further by doing a 200m run. For 15 seconds of this time, she runs at a constant velocity of 9m/s.

c) If the sprinter has a mass of **50kg**, what is her **kinetic energy** during those 15 seconds?

Q2 My old car breaks down. Luckily the road is flat. There is a garage 1500 metres away. The car manual says it needs a minimum force of 700N to push the car along a flat road.

a) What is the **minimum energy** I will need to give the car to get it to the garage?

The car goes over a broken bottle, still 600m from the garage. A tyre bursts and the force of friction increases the required pushing force to 900N.

b) Calculate the **total energy consumption** in this case.

Someone mentions that there is another garage only 1300m away from where my car broke down, but the last 100m are uphill, and the pushing force here would have had to be 1150N.

c) Would I have saved any energy by pushing the car to this garage, assuming that in both cases I had avoided any broken bottles?

Q3 Scott and Sheila are waterskiing over a 400m course. When it's Scott's turn, a forcemeter on the tow rope registers a force of 475N. When Sheila has a go, the forcemeter registers 425N.

a) Calculate the **energy** needed to pull each skier over the course.

b) Why would the **total energy** consumed by the boat be **more** than this in each case?

Scott now starts to show off by giving piggyback rides to passing sharks. He does this 4 times, each for 30m. For the remainder of the 400m course, he is by himself. During each piggyback, the forcemeter measures 720N.

c) Calculate the **energy** needed to pull Scott and his fishy friends over the course in this case.

Like the tortoise — slow and steady wins the race...

The slower something is moving the lower its kinetic energy. Also the lighter something is, the lower its kinetic energy too. Make sure to remember work done = force x distance. Learn that and you're sorted.

Orbits

20.4

Objects are attracted to each other by a gravitational force. Between you and me this force is tiny but between planets and satellites the force is strong enough to keep them in orbit.

Q1 This question consists of a number of statements about our solar system.

For each statement, say whether it is **true or false**, and give a **reason** for your decision.

a) All the planets are visible because of light they produce themselves.

b) The planets in the solar system orbit around a massive object.

c) All planets have spherical orbits.

Q2 Like all members of the Solar System, comets orbit around the Sun.

a) Draw a diagram showing the **shape of the orbit** followed by a comet around the Sun.

b) Give the **name of the orbit** formed by the path of a comet.

c) **Explain how** this shape differs from the paths followed by the planets.

Q3 NASA has spent a lot of money putting the Hubble telescope into space.

a) What are the advantages of having a telescope in space?

b) Why is this helpful to astronomers?

Q4 The planet Jupiter has four large moons. Information about them is given in the table.

a) Which moon is the largest?

b) Which moon takes the longest time to orbit Jupiter?

c) Europa and Io are of similar sizes. Why does Europa take more time to complete one orbit?

d) As described above, four moons orbit Jupiter. Why doesn't Jupiter orbit its moons instead?

Name of Moon	Diameter (km)	Time to Orbit Jupiter (Earth Days)
Europa	3126	3.5
Callisto	4820	16.7
Io	3632	1.8
Ganymede	5276	7.2

20.4 Orbits

Q1 Artificial satellites have been used for different purposes since the first successful launch in the 1950's. Today, satellites play an important role in our lives. The following statements can describe the motion of satellites.

- **A** in a high orbit
- **B** in a low orbit
- **C** move across the sky
- **D** above the atmosphere
- **E** in a polar orbit
- **F** in an equatorial orbit
- **G** orbits in a few hours
- **H** orbits in 24 hours

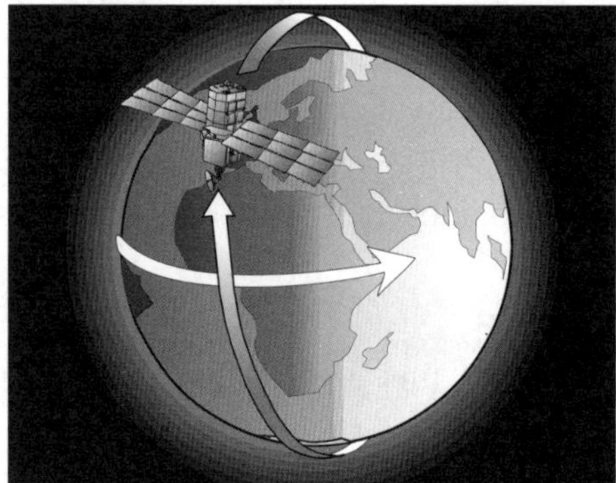

Which of the statements above will apply to:

- **a)** Communications satellites?
- **b)** Most weather satellites?
- **c)** Spy satellites?
- **d)** Satellites broadcasting TV pictures?

Q2 If the space shuttle is in orbit, more than one Earth-based station is needed to communicate with it.

Why would **one station** be no good?

Q3 Work out which of these statements are **true** and which are **false**. If it's wrong, rewrite it correctly.

- **a)** The Earth, the Sun, the Moon and all other bodies attract each other with a force called gravity.
- **b)** As the distance between two bodies increases, the force due to gravity between them increases more than in proportion to the increase in distance.
- **c)** The nearer an orbiting body is the longer it takes to make a complete orbit.
- **d)** To stay in orbit at a fixed distance, smaller bodies must constantly adjust their speed.
- **e)** Comets orbit the Sun in perfect circles.
- **f)** A satellite in a geostationary orbit around the Earth will always stay in the same position above the Earth.
- **g)** Monitoring satellites are put in geostationary orbits.

Q4 Scientists believe that we may be able to detect living organisms on other planets by the **chemical changes** they produce in the atmosphere of their planet.

How have the living organisms on Earth affected its atmosphere?

Top-tips: It's pretty tricky to get your head around orbits. To stay in orbit at a fixed distance, smaller bodies, including planets and satellites, must move at a matching speed around larger bodies. If you're stuck look in the revision guide (available from good schools and booksellers everywhere...)

The Universe

20.5

The Milky Way in which we live is a very small part of the universe.

Q1 The exploits of Mouldy and Scally on the well known Z-files may one day represent science fact rather than science fiction.

a) Without sending a space craft there, **how** could astronomers **detect possible life** on another planet?

b) **What** does SETI stand for? Explain fully what they do.

c) **How** would SETI astronomers know that a radio signal was from a specially made transmitter?

d) **How** do scientists use robots to explore other planets?

Q2 Black holes are a very strange phenomenon. Fill in the blanks below using each of these words.

black hole	matter	gas	electromagnetic
compact	neutron star	light	stars
gravitational	supernova	dense	X-rays

At the end of its life, a large star may explode into a ________. Clouds of dust and ________ are thrown into space, and what is left behind is called a ________ ________. If enough ________ is left behind, this may be so ________, and its ________ field so strong, that nothing can escape from it, not even ________ or other forms of ________ radiation. When this occurs it is known as a ________ ________. Black holes cannot be seen but their effects can be observed. For example, ________ can be detected that are emitted when gases, from nearby ________, spiral into a black hole.

Q3 Our Solar System is part of the Milky Way.

a) **What** is the Milky Way?

b) At night time, a milky white band can be seen stretching right across the sky. **What characteristic** of the Milky Way gives rise to this appearance?

"Ob bu datak" — take me to your teacher...

The universe is massive. It's so big we don't really know how big it is. There are strange things out there like black holes, there may even be life forms that we could find. This stuff is dead easy to remember — you must have seen loads of films and TV shows about it. I'm not saying you can spend all your revision time watching ET though — you've still got to learn it...

20.5 The Universe

Q1 Below are some facts about our Milky Way. For each one, decide whether it is **true** or **false**.

a) Neighbouring stars in the Milky Way are usually much further apart than the planets in the Solar System.
b) The Milky Way is about 10,000 light years across.
c) The Milky Way is at the centre of the Universe.
d) There are many known solar systems in the Milky Way.
e) Our Solar System is at the centre of the Milky Way.
f) The Milky Way has spiral arms.
g) The stars we see at night are part of the Milky Way.
h) The Milky Way takes a long time to rotate.
i) The Milky Way is the biggest of its kind.
j) The Milky Way is separated from its neighbours by lots of empty space.
k) There are still gas clouds in the Milky Way.
l) No more stars will form in the Milky Way.
m) Galaxies are often millions of times further apart than the stars within a galaxy.

Q2 The energy given out by the Sun and other stars is generated by **nuclear fusion** reactions taking place in the stars.

a) Describe what happens in a nuclear fusion reaction.
b) Name the two main elements that undergo fusion reactions.

One result of nuclear fusion is that nuclei of the heaviest elements are present in the sun. Atoms of these elements are also present in the inner planets of the solar system.

c) What does this suggest about the formation of the solar system?

Q3 Theories of the origin of the universe have to take in to account that **light** from other galaxies is shifted to the **red** end of the spectrum.

a) What is the name of this effect?
b) Is the light from further away galaxies more or less shifted than that from closer galaxies?

The current explanation for this effect is that galaxies are moving away from each other with a speed proportional to their distance apart.

c) What does this explanation suggest about the formation of the universe?
d) What is the name for this theory?

The Life Cycle of Stars

20.5

Q1 A bunch of universe-loving astronomers have been studying groups of stars. They have used their observations to come up with an idea for how they think some of the stars evolved.

This "**Life Cycle**" is illustrated in the diagram below.

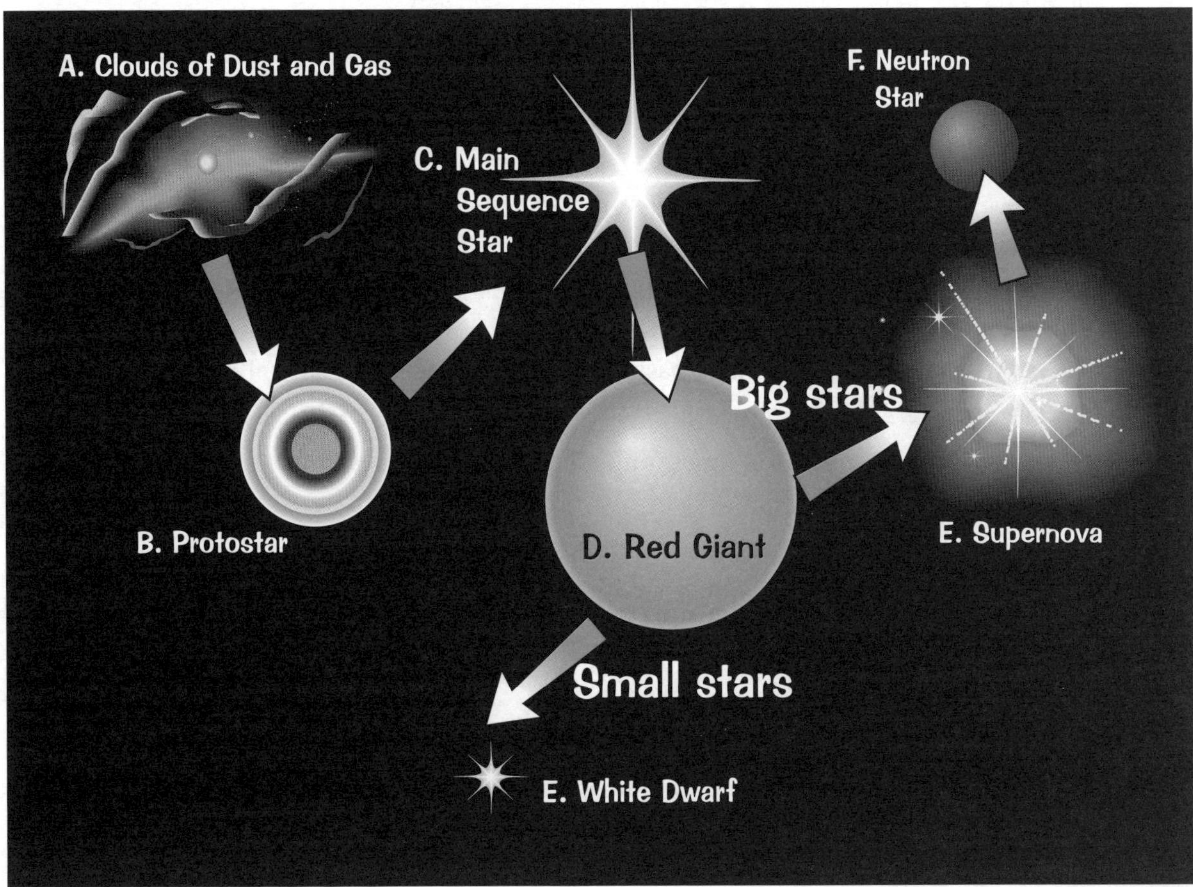

a) Stars are formed when clouds of dust and gas are drawn together. **What force causes** this to happen?

b) At a certain stage in the life cycle, the star may **expand**. **What causes** the force which leads to **expansion**?

c) **What** is the **relationship** between these two forces in our sun at the moment?

d) **How** does the matter making up neutron stars and black holes **differ** from the matter we are used to on Earth?

e) When studying life cycles astronomers need to study a **group of stars** rather than just one or two. **Explain why**.

I'm going to be a star. A star I tell you...

I'll bet you never realized how dull the universe really was until you got to this section. You've still got to know all those details though so learn, learn, learn until you can do all the questions. All of them.

21.1

Waves: Basic Principles

May there be light in your pre-exam lives, and if music be the food of love then turn off your stereos. They'll only distract you. OK, enough of that. Do some questions.

Q1 Copy the following sentences and **fill in the gaps**.

- **a)** There are two different types of wave motion: ________ and ________.
- **b)** The number of waves per second passing a fixed point is called the ________, and is measured in ________.
- **c)** The time taken for two adjacent crests to pass a fixed point is called the ________, and is measured in ________.
- **d)** The maximum distance of particles from their resting position is called the ________.
- **e)** The highest point of a transverse wave is called a ________.
- **f)** The lowest point of a transverse wave is called a ________.
- **g)** The distance travelled each second by a wave is called its ________ and is measured in ________.
- **h)** Waves will change their speed and wavelength when they go into different materials. This is called ________.
- **i)** Waves will spread out when they pass through a small gap. This is called ________.

Q2 What does a wave transfer?

Q3 You can send a wave along a piece of string by shaking one end up and down (see diagram).

- **a)** **What** do we call the up and down movement of the string?
- **b)** **How** would you **increase** the **frequency** of this wave?
- **c)** How would you **increase** its **amplitude**?
- **d)** This wave is a transverse wave. **Explain** why a longitudinal wave of a similar frequency **can't** be made to travel along the string.

Q4 You are floating in the sea, measuring waves (as you do). You time 5 seconds between one crest passing and the next.

- **a)** What is the **frequency** of this wave?
- **b)** By watching the waves move along a breakwater you estimate that the distance between 10 crests is about 30m. Work out the average **wavelength** of the waves.
- **c)** **How far** have the waves travelled each time a crest passes you?
- **d)** **How long** does it take for one wave to pass you?
- **e)** How far does this wave travel in **one** second?
- **f)** What is the **speed** of the wave?
- **g)** **Which way** do you move as the wave passes through you?

Q5 There are six equations below, some of which are incorrect / incomplete. Write down the correct versions, first in words, then using the usual symbols.

Frequency = Speed x

Frequency = $\frac{\text{Wavelength}}{\text{Speed}}$

Wavelength = $\frac{\text{Speed}}{\text{Frequency}}$

Speed = $\frac{\text{Frequency}}{\text{Wavelength}}$

Speed = Frequency x

Frequency = $\frac{\text{Speed}}{\text{Wavelength}}$

Reflection and Refraction

Q1 Like sound, light can be reflected off surfaces. Complete the gaps in the sentences below. You've got no words to help you, so you'll really need to know your stuff.

a) Some objects give out their own light. All other objects we see because they ________ light.

b) Some objects reflect light without sending it off in many different directions. This is called a ________ reflection and objects which do this look ________.

c) Most objects send the reflected light in many different directions, giving a ________ reflection. These objects look ________.

d) The law of reflection states that "the angle of ________ is ________ to the angle of ________."

Q2 What is the name for a beam of light used to represent a light path?

Q3 What is the name for the line drawn at right angles to a mirror surface?

Q4 The diagrams 1, 2 and 3 shows rays arriving at a surface.

Make a copy of each diagram. Complete the labels and draw the reflected rays.

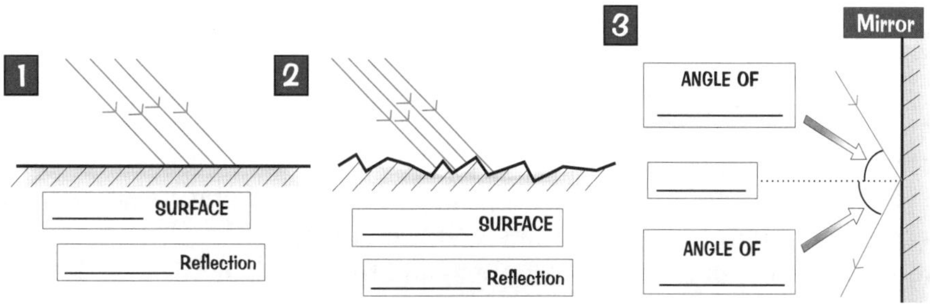

1
________ SURFACE
________ Reflection

2
________ SURFACE
________ Reflection

3
Mirror
ANGLE OF ________
____
ANGLE OF ________

Q5 Have a look at this plan view of two people sitting on a park bench.

They can see some statues reflected in the window.

Use the law of reflection to decide **which of the statues**, A, B, C and D, each person can see.

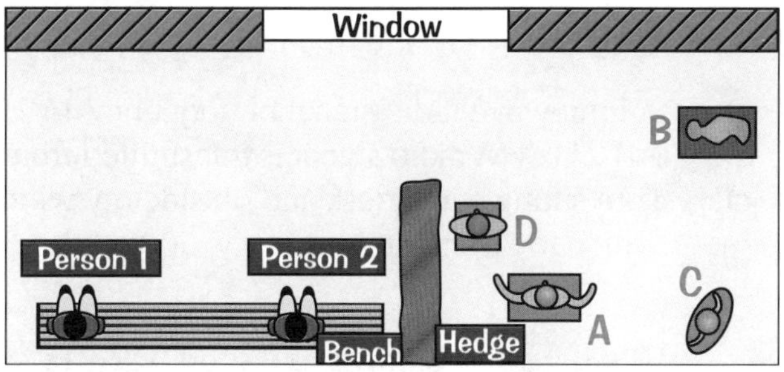

Window
B
D
Person 1
Person 2
C
A
Bench
Hedge

Q6 **Fill in the gaps** or **choose the correct words** for the following sentences about refraction.

a) Light travels at different __________ in different media.

b) Light will **speed up / slow down** when it travels from air into glass.

c) When the light goes back into air it will **speed up / slow down**.

d) The change of speed occurs at the ______________ of the two media.

Q7 What is meant by the "**normal**" to a surface?

Q8 Does the **frequency** of light change as it enters a different medium?

21.1 Diffraction

Q1 Study the rays in the two diagrams on the right.

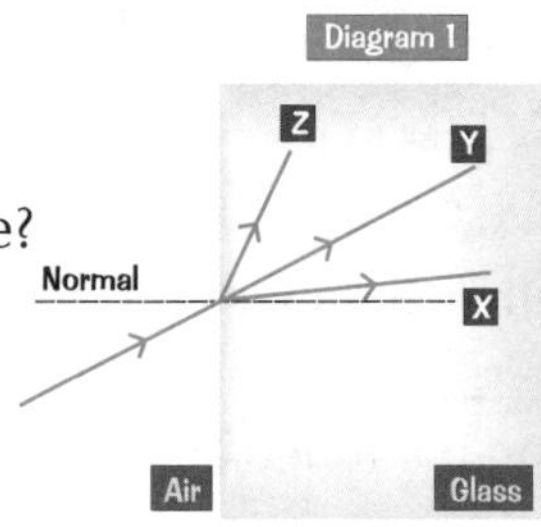

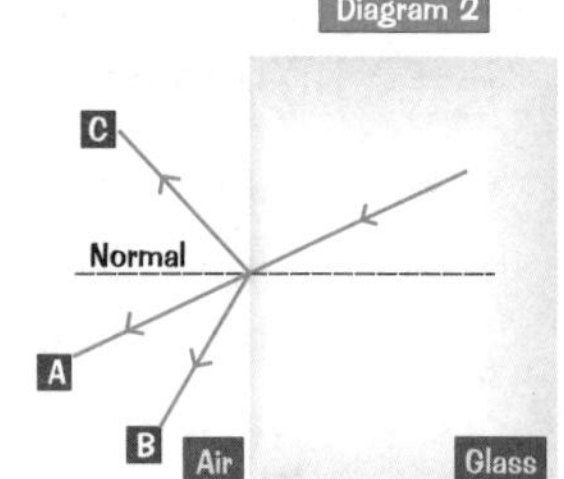

a) In Diagram 1, a ray **enters** a glass block. **Which ray** (X, Y or Z) shows how it would continue?

b) In Diagram 2, a ray **leaves** the block. **Which ray** (A, B or C) shows its path correctly?

Q2 **Choose the right words** to make these sentences correct.

When a ray of light enters a glass block it is bent [**towards** / **away from**] the normal.
When a ray of light leaves the glass block it is bent [**towards** / **away from**] the normal.

Q3 **Fill in the gaps** in the following sentences.

a) Waves will __________ when they go through a ____________ or past an ___________.

b) This effect is called _____________.

c) The _____________ the gap the more diffraction there is.

d) If the gap is about the same size as the ______________ of the wave, a ______________ shaped wave will be produced.

Q4 A sound wave and visible light wave pass through a doorway 75cm wide.

a) What **frequency of sound** has a wavelength of 75cm? Can a human **hear** this sound?

b) If the visible light wave has a frequency of 5×10^{14} Hz, what is its wavelength?

c) You can **hear** around corners but not **see** around them. Use the results of your calculations from **a)** and **b)** to explain this.

(In your calculations, take the speed of sound to be 330 m/s and the speed of light to be 3×10^8 m/s)

Q5 Would there be much **diffraction** in the following situations? What would be the effect?

a) A long-wave radio signal of frequency 1MHz passes between two blocks of flats 250m apart.

b) A 1GHz FM radio signal is transmitted from the far side of a short tunnel that is 6m wide.

c) I am sitting at my desk and outside my window (50cm wide) someone's serenading me with a toy trumpet (frequency 5000Hz).

Q6 The diagrams below show short wave TV waves and long wave radio waves approaching a hill.

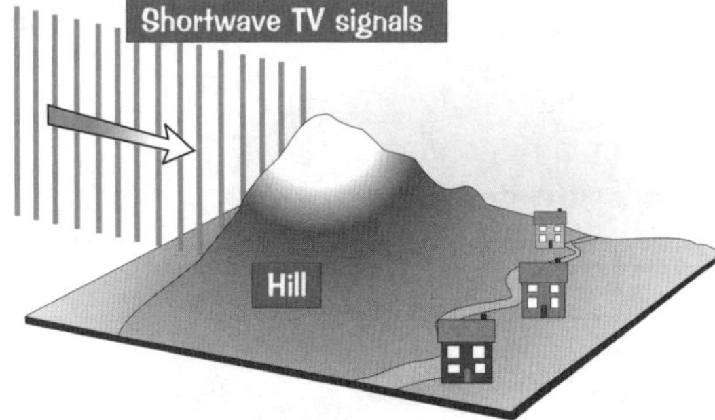

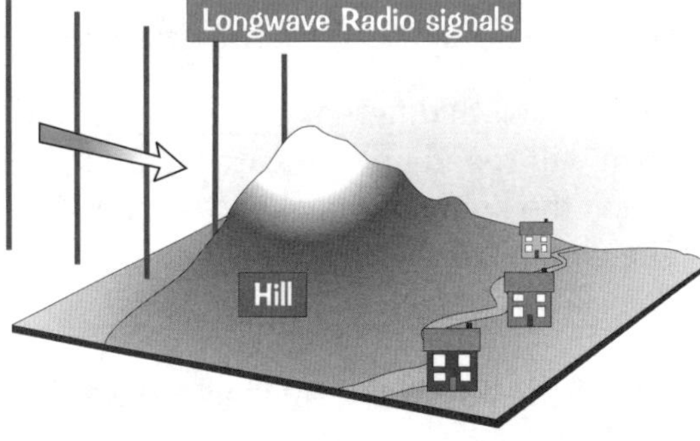

a) Copy and complete the pictures above, showing how the hill changes the direction of the EM wave.

b) Suggest a reason why people in these houses can **listen** to the cricket on long wave Radio 4 but not **watch** it on the television.

The Electromagnetic Spectrum

21.2

Q1 Copy and complete the following paragraphs about electromagnetic waves.

a) Electromagnetic (EM) waves form a continuous ____________. For a given __________ all EM waves travel with roughly the same ______________. In a ____________ this ____________ is about 3 x 10^8 m/s. There are _____________ main types of EM wave. The correct order for these types of EM wave is (beginning with longest wavelength):
_______ ______, _______________, _______ ________, _______ ________, ________ ________, ____________ and ________ _________.

b) _____________ waves have the lowest frequency and the __________ wavelength. _________ _________ have the highest frequency and the _____________ wavelength. Our eyes are sensitive to EM waves from the ________________ spectrum only.

Q2 Decide whether each of the statements **a)** to **j)** below are **true or false**. **If false**, write down what the **highlighted words** should be replaced with.

a) **Microwaves** are used to communicate with satellites.
b) **Microwaves** are the same thing as heat radiation.
c) **Gamma rays** both cause and cure cancer.
d) Only **visible light** will show diffraction.
e) **Radio waves** can have wavelengths of many metres.
f) **X-rays** are used to take pictures of bones because they are relatively safe.
g) **Infrared** radiation causes skin cancer.
h) **Microwaves** are absorbed by water.
i) **Long wave radiowaves** are able to diffract long distances round the Earth.
j) **Visible light** has a wavelength of about a ten thousandth of a millimetre.

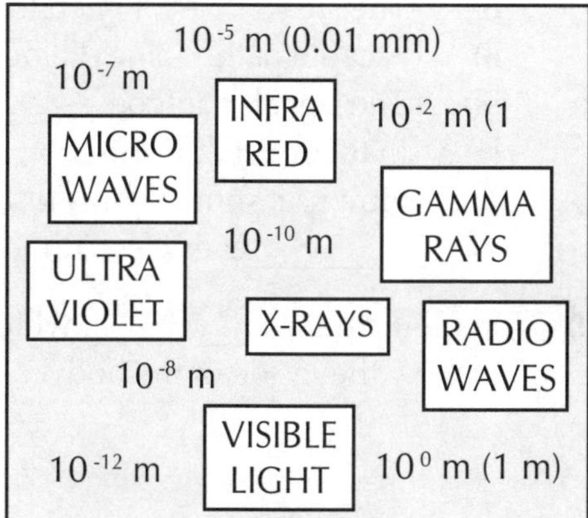

Q3 The diagram shows parts of the electromagnetic spectrum and wavelengths for the different radiations — but they're all mixed up.

a) **Draw** your own diagram of a spectrum, but with the types of radiation and wavelengths in the correct order, from the shortest to the longest wavelength.
b) What is the **speed** of an electromagnetic wave in a vacuum?
c) Calculate the **frequency** for each type of wave.
d) How many times longer is a typical visible light wave than an X-ray wave?
e) How many times longer is a microwave than a typical visible light wave?

10^{-5} m (0.01 mm)
10^{-7} m
INFRA RED
10^{-2} m (1
MICRO WAVES
GAMMA RAYS
10^{-10} m
ULTRA VIOLET
X-RAYS
RADIO WAVES
10^{-8} m
VISIBLE LIGHT
10^{-12} m
10^{0} m (1 m)

A cold and calculating mind...

Once you've got the hang of them, 'doing' questions like calculations, and 'fill in the blank'-type things are much easier to get marks on than 'thinking' questions (the innocent-looking-but-evil 'explain why' and 'in what way' questions). Often though, a question will have several parts, with only the last one needing much thinking. Even if that bit stumps you, you should be able to clean up on the rest.

21.2 The Electromagnetic Spectrum

Nearly at the end of the book now, so you must feel proud of yourself — unless you started from the back, in which case you've still got loads to go. Ah well...

Q1 An electromagnetic wave is drawn on an A4 piece of paper so that one wavelength fills the page. You're told that it's drawn **actual** size.

What two types of EM wave could the drawing represent?

Q2 A commonly used microwave wavelength is 3cm. What is its frequency?

Q3 A **special property** of light is shown in the diagrams below. Complete these sentences about it.

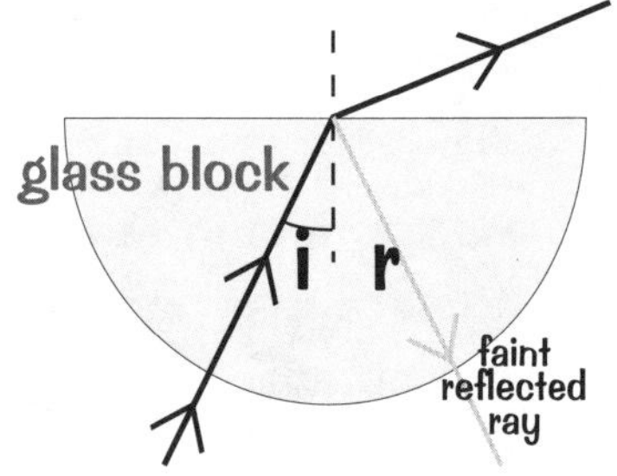

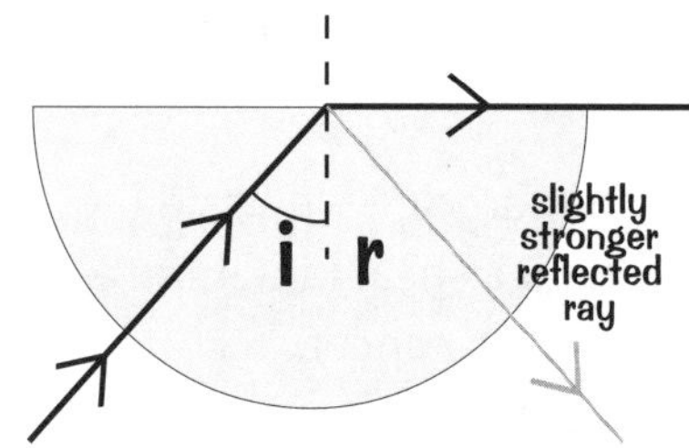

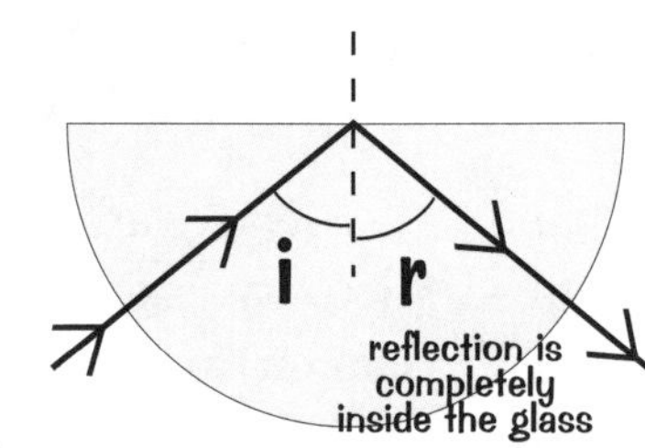

a) When light attempts to exit a **dense** medium (e.g. glass), at an angle to the normal greater than the ________ ________, **all** of the light is reflected inside the medium.

b) This phenomenon is called ________ ________ ________.
It has important practical uses, for example in **optical fibres**, ________ and ________.

c) Optical communications have several advantages over **electrical signals** in wires. Fill in the blanks to say what they are.

- i) The signal doesn't need to be ________ as often.
- ii) A cable of the same diameter can carry a lot more ________.
- iii) The signals can't be ________ into, or suffer ________ from electrical sources.
- iv) In theory, **no information whatsoever would be lost** at each ________.
  However some light is lost due to **surface imperfections**, so the signal still needs ________ every few km.

d) In **medicine**, an ________, which consists of a narrow bunch of optical fibres, is used to view the inside of the body.

Q4 Draw a **simple** labelled diagram to illustrate each of the three practical uses given in **Q3b**.

Top tips: **Practical applications are important, and much loved by examiners. Make sure you understand why the stuff on this page is relevant to the real world. Don't forget the diagrams.**

The Electromagnetic Spectrum

21.2

Q1 This table is all mixed up. **Redraw** it with the information in the **correct** places.

Type of Radiation	Effects on Living Tissue	Uses
Gamma	• probably none	• communication • broadcasting • radar
X-Ray	• heating of water in tissues can cause "burning"	• imaging internal structures in the body • studying the atomic structure of materials
UV	• kills living cells in high doses • lower doses can cause cells to become cancerous • causes tanning	• fluorescent tubes • tanning • security marking
Visible	• kills living cells in high doses • lower doses can cause cells to become cancerous • kills cancerous cells	• kill bacteria in food • sterilise medical equipment • treat tumours
IR	• kills living cells in high doses • lower doses can cause cells to become cancerous	• radiant heaters • grills • remote controls • thermal imaging
Microwave	• causes burning of tissues	• satellite communication • cooking
Radio	• activates sensitive cells in the retina	• seeing • optical fibre communication

Q2 Radiation absorption by biological tissues can have harmful consequences.

a) When radiation is absorbed, the energy it carries can be converted into **two** forms. Name them.

b) In general, is **short wavelength, high frequency** radiation more or less harmful than **long wavelength, low frequency** radiation?

c) Jessica Rarebit is sunning herself. Write down **two** ways in which she can protect against electromagnetic waves in the sunlight which are likely to cause **sunburn** or **skin cancer**.

d) Professor Lex Ray is conducting highly dodgy experiments with radioactive sources which are emitting gamma rays. What steps can he take to protect himself?

21.2 Digital and Analogue Signals

Q1 Information such as speech or music can be converted into electrical signals.

a) What are the **two** ways of transmitting this information?

b) Write down how they are **different**.

c) **List three** examples of devices which use each type of signal.

Q2 Decide whether the following statements are **true or false**. If false, write out the correct version.

a) The **amplitude** and **frequency** of **digital** signals vary continuously.

b) **Digital** pulses can take one of only **two** forms: ON or OFF.

c) Clocks, phones and dimmer switches can **all** be **analogue** devices.

d) Clocks, phones and on/off switches can **all** be **digital** devices.

e) **Digital** pulses can take one of only **two** forms: 1 or 0.

f) The problem with **digital** signals is that they lose quality over relatively short distances.

g) **Digital** signals are capable of transmitting far more information than analogue ones (within a given time).

Q3 Signals often need to be **amplified** along their route or at their destination.

a) **Why** is this necessary?

b) **What else** usually happens to a signal between its source and its destination? *(Hint: it picks up something unwanted).*

c) In what ways do analogue and digital signals differ in their response to amplification? **Why** is this?

Q4 Rearrange these pictures into **two sets of seven** (including arrows) to show:

a) **Digital** signals being amplified.

b) **Analogue** signals being amplified.

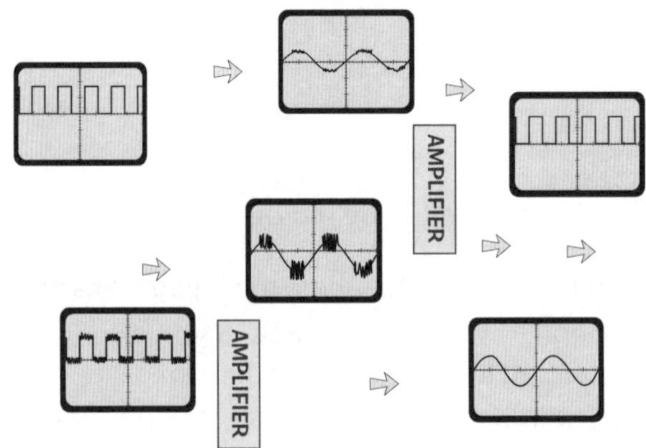

Pulsating stuff this...

This all follows on neatly from optical fibres and what-not, so you can bet you'll get a question on it. Make sure you know the <u>differences</u> between analogue and digital signals, and <u>why</u> digital signals are better. And "because we can watch the footy and loads of cool movies" is not an exam answer.

Radioactive Substances

21.3

Radioactivity has provided the plot for far too many really pointless movies. But it does have its uses, and examiners like asking about them (the uses that is, not the movies).

Q1 The diagram below shows alpha, beta and gamma radiation being fired at a line of obstacles.

a) Copy the diagram. For each particle, draw a line to show the path it travels before it's absorbed.

b) Give a reason why alpha particles only penetrate a short distance into a material.

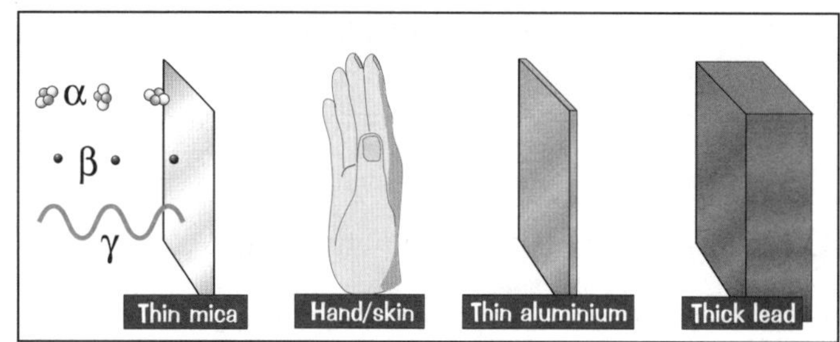

Q2 When radiation travels through matter it can cause ionisation.

a) Explain what is meant by the term "ionisation".

The diagram below shows a simplified drawing of an experiment to demonstrate that radiation can ionise matter.

The space between the plates is filled with argon gas at low pressure. A current is measured.

b) Name the two different particles formed when radiation from the source ionises an argon atom.

c) Describe how this leads to a current in the circuit.

d) The argon gas is removed from between the plates, leaving a vacuum behind. Explain why there is now no current flow.

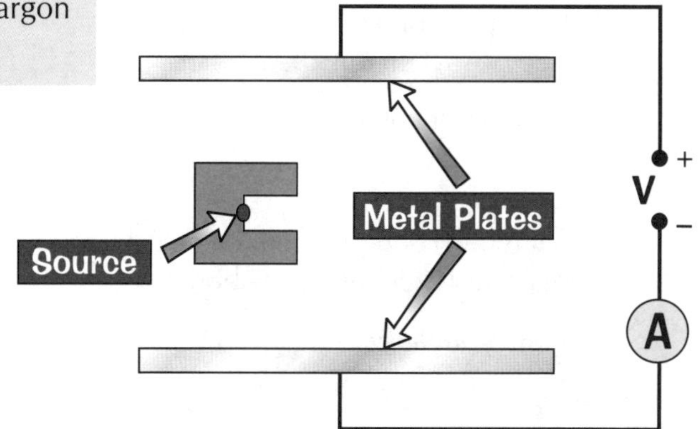

Q3 Radioactive iodine-131 is commonly used in medicine as a tracer.

a) Explain what you understand by the word "tracer".
b) Where will iodine-131 be concentrated if injected? Why is this?
c) What type of radiation is emitted by iodine-131?
d) Why would an alpha-emitting isotope be unsuitable for use in medicine as a tracer? Give two reasons.

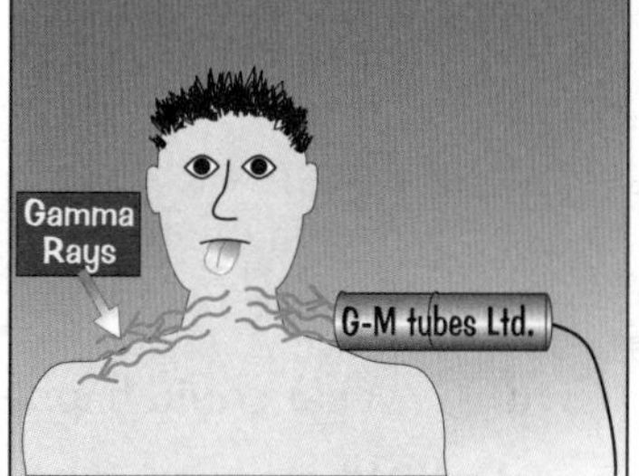

Q4 This question concerns the treatment of cancer using radiotherapy.

a) High doses of gamma rays can be used to treat cancers. What effect do gamma rays have on living cells?
b) Explain why a patient on a course of radiotherapy feels very ill.
c) For the treatment to be a success, what two factors does the radiotherapist need to consider before starting the treatment?

21.3 Effects of Radiation

Q1 Radioactive particles can be harmful to living cells.

a) Which **types of radiation** can do this damage?
b) What **process** usually has to happen for damage to occur?
c) Which part of the cell controls **cell function**?
d) What do we call a cell that has been **slightly altered**, but not killed?
e) Why are these cells so **dangerous**?
f) Name the **condition** commonly caused by these cells?

Q2 Different types of radiation cause varying degrees of damage to cells.

a) Which of these is likely to cause the most damage to cells — an **alpha particle**, a **beta particle** or a **gamma ray**?
b) Why's this type of radiation more dangerous? Give **two reasons**.

Q3 List **at least three factors** which determine how much harm is done to a person when exposed to radiation.

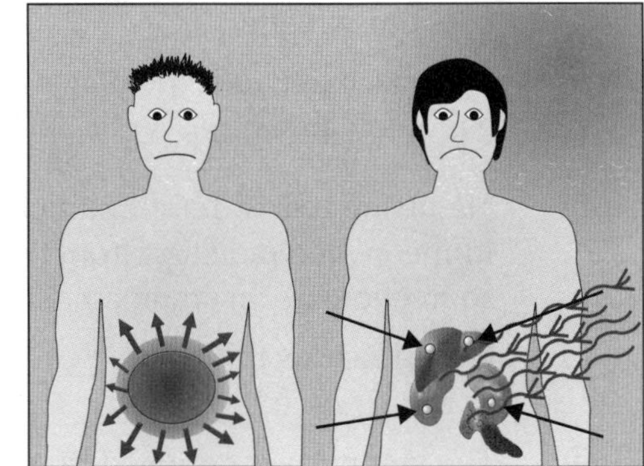

Q4 What type(s) of radiation are most dangerous when **outside** the body?

Explain your answer.

Q5 What type(s) of radiation are most dangerous when **inside** the body?

Explain your answer.

Q6 In the Health Services, radiation is used in the treatment of many cancers.

a) What **type of radiation** is generally used?
b) What does the radiation do?
c) Why does the radiation need to be **very well-targeted**?

The medical physicists who are responsible for calculating the doses need to ensure that the dose of radiation isn't too low or too high.

d) What could happen if the dose is **too low**?
e) What about if the dose is **too high**?

It was a long time before anyone discovered what had happened to the children in the shed that day.

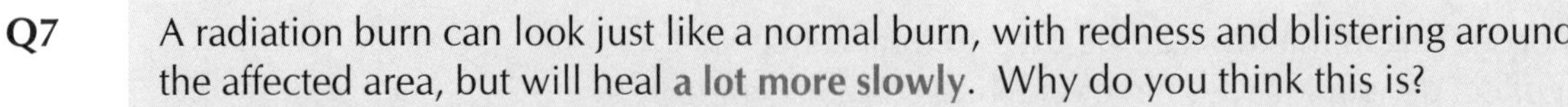

Q7 A radiation burn can look just like a normal burn, with redness and blistering around the affected area, but will heal **a lot more slowly**. Why do you think this is?

Q8 **Young** children and developing embryos are particularly susceptible to the effects of radiation. Why is this?

Atomic Structure

21.4

Q1 The diagram shows the particles that constitute an atom.

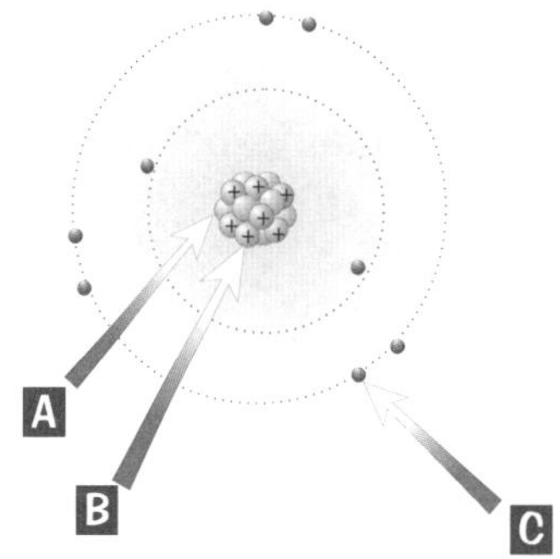

a) **Name the particles** labelled A, B and C.

b) What stops the electrons from flying away from the nucleus?

c) How many **neutrons** are there in the nucleus if there are 16 nucleons in this atom?

Q2 The following paragraph describes the structure of an atom. **Copy and complete.**

All atoms consist of a ____________ and a number of ____________.
The __________ is made up of ____________ and neutrons.
____________ have a positive charge and
__________ are electrically neutral. Most the __________ of the atom
is concentrated here but it takes up a relatively small ____________.
The __________ orbit the __________. They carry a negative charge
(and are really really ____________). The ratio of the mass of an
electron to the mass of a proton or neutron is about __________.
The masses of the __________ and the proton are almost ____________.

Q3 **Complete the table** below which summarises the relative mass and electrical charges of the sub-atomic particles.

Particle	Relative Mass	Electric Charge
Proton		
Neutron		
Electron		

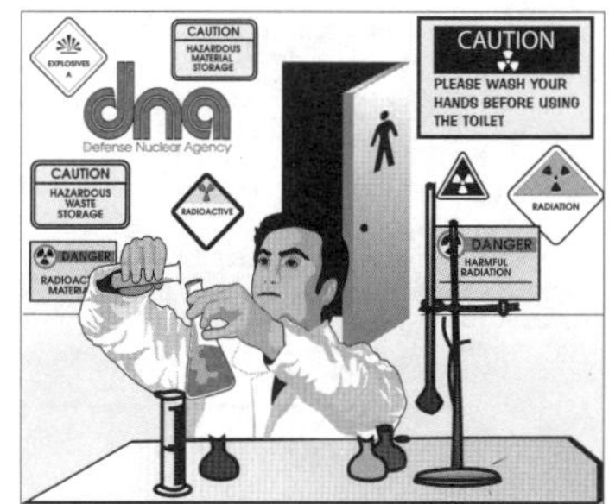

Q4 The diagram below shows the apparatus used by Lord Rutherford to probe the structure of the atom.

a) **Name the particles** that are directed at the gold foil.

b) Why does this apparatus need to operate in a **vacuum**?

c) Which of the detectors measures the **highest** count rate?

d) Some particles are detected at Y. **Explain** this observation using your knowledge of atomic structure.

e) Just a very small fraction of the incident particles are scattered more than 90° by the foil (some of these are detected by detector Z). What does this tell you about the **nuclei** of the gold atoms?

f) Gold was chosen as the target for this experiment. Give a **reason** for this choice.

g) Explain why a **gaseous** target would be unsuitable.

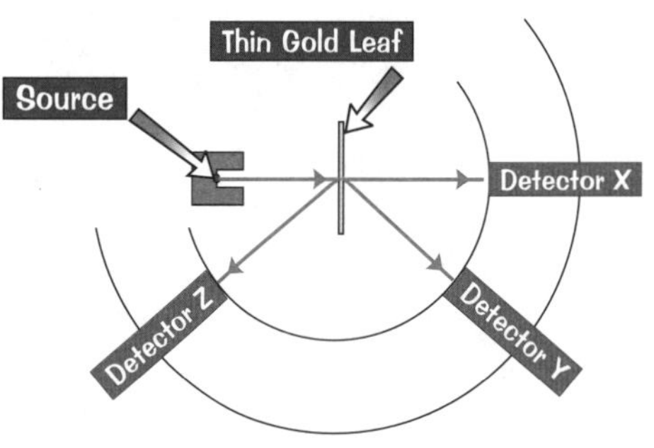

21.4 Atomic Structure

Q1 A stable atom of bismuth has a **mass number** of 209.

a) Explain what is meant by "**mass number**".

The **atomic number** of bismuth is 83.

b) **Calculate** the number of neutrons in the nucleus of a **stable** bismuth atom.
c) **Describe** how the structure of an **unstable** atom of bismuth will be different to a **stable** atom of bismuth.

Q2 Copy the table opposite and **fill in the missing data.**

	Number of electrons	Number of protons	Number of neutrons	Mass Number	Symbol
oxygen-16		8			${}^{16}_{8}O$
aluminium-27	13				
radium-226		88			
strontium-90	38				
hydrogen-3		1			

Q3 **Copy and complete** the following paragraph about isotopes using the given words. You may use a word more than once.

atomic mass alpha decay neutrons electrons stable beta three element energy protons

Isotopes of the same ________ have equal numbers of ________ and ________ but different numbers of ________. Hence they have the same ________ number but a different ________ number. Every ________ has at least ________ different isotopes but usually only one or two ________ ones. If a radioactive isotope decays, radiation is emitted. If an ________ or a ________ particle is emitted then a different ________ is formed.

Q4 Information about six atoms A, B, C, D, E and F is given below.

Atom A: 8 neutrons, mass number 16
Atom B: 3 electrons, mass number 7
Atom C: 8 protons, mass number 17
Atom D: 6 neutrons, mass number 11
Atom E: 3 neutrons, mass number 6
Atom F: 6 protons, mass number 12

For **three** of the atoms you don't need the mass number to identify the element. Which are they?

Q5 How do the **mass number** and **atomic number** of a nucleus change if it emits:

a) an alpha particle? **b)** a beta particle? **c)** gamma radiation?

Radioactive Decay

21.4

Q1 A sample of a radioactive substance was found to be emitting 8000 beta particles a second at the beginning of an experiment. Fifteen minutes later, it was emitting 4000 beta particles a second.

a) What is the **half-life** of the radioactive substance?
b) **How many minutes** after the start would you expect to measure a count rate of 1000 particles per second?
c) **What count rate** would you expect to measure after **two hours**?

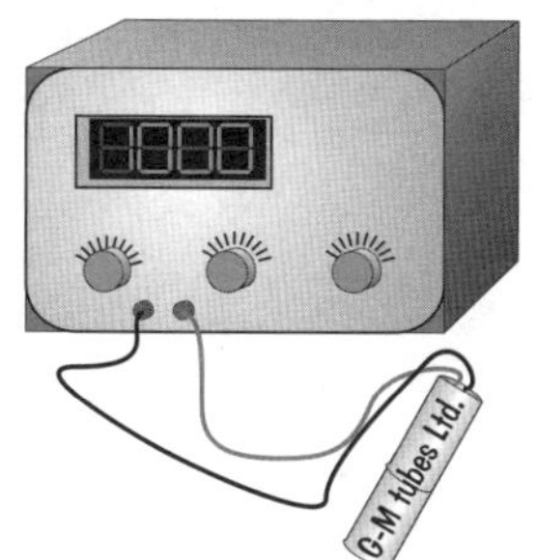

Background radiation from radioactive materials in the ground or in the air is about 2 counts per second.

d) How long would it take the count rate from the substance to fall **below this background count**?

Q2 The count rate from a radioactive material was measured using a G-M tube and counter. The results are given below:

Count rate in counts per second	95	73	55	42	32	23	18
Time in seconds	0	10	20	30	40	50	60

a) **Plot a graph** of count rate in counts / second (vertical axis) against time in seconds (horizontal axis).
b) **Find the half-life** of the material by finding how long it took the count rate to fall from 90 to 45.
c) Another material has a very low activity which makes it difficult to measure its activity above the background radiation. **Describe** how you might overcome this problem.

Q3 The half-life of carbon-14 is 5,600 years. Carbon-14 makes up about 1 part in 10,000,000 of the carbon in air. For each item in **a)** to **c)**, calculate **how long ago** it was living material.

a) An axe handle containing 1 part in 20,000,000 carbon-14.
b) A spear handle containing 1 part in 80,000,000 carbon-14.
c) A fossil containing 1 part in 320,000,000 carbon-14.

Q4 **Fill in the gaps** in the paragraph below.

Carbon-14 makes up about one ten-______ of the carbon in the air (Carbon-______ is the main isotope of carbon). This level stays fairly ______ in the atmosphere. The same proportion of C-14 is also found in ______ things. However, when they ______, the C-14 is trapped and it gradually ______. By simply measuring the ______ of carbon-14 found in an artifact, you can easily calculate how ______ ago the item was ______ material using the ______ of 5,600 years.

Q5 Lead-210 (atomic number 82) decays with the emission of a beta particle. Bismuth-210 is formed, which decays with the emission of a beta-particle to form polonium-210.

a) **Draw** the above decay series, showing the mass and atomic numbers for all the atoms.
b) The graph opposite shows how the activity of bismuth–210 varies with time. **Estimate** the half-life of bismuth-210.
c) Polonium-210 decays with the emission of an α-particle. An isotope of lead is formed. What is the **mass number** of this isotope of lead?

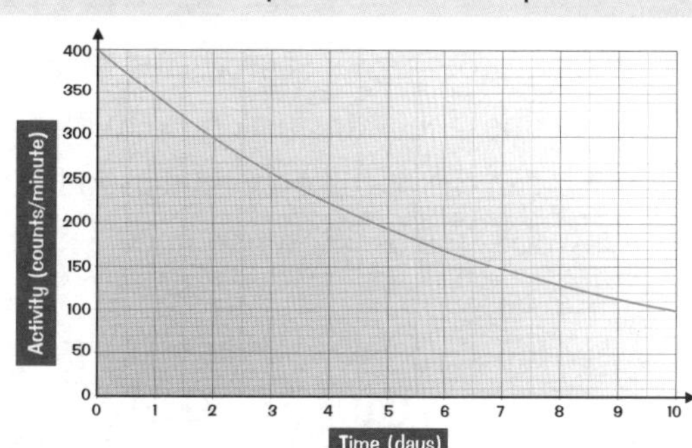

21.5 Sound Waves

Q1 What has to happen for a sound wave to be created?

Q2 What **vibrates** in the objects below to start a sound?

Drum

Violin

Loudspeaker

Voice

Q3 Are sound waves **longitudinal** or **transverse**?

Q4 Answer these questions using the six frequencies which are listed below.

2Hz, 20Hz, 200Hz, 2000Hz, 2kHz, 20kHz

a) Which two frequencies are **identical**?
b) Which is closest to the lowest frequency **humans** can hear?
c) For which one could you easily count the vibrations without instruments?
d) Which is closest to the **highest** frequency humans can hear?

Q5 Sarah is experimenting with an oscilloscope and a signal generator connected to a loudspeaker.

She draws an oscilloscope trace for a range of frequencies and amplitudes (see opposite) but gets the labels mixed up.

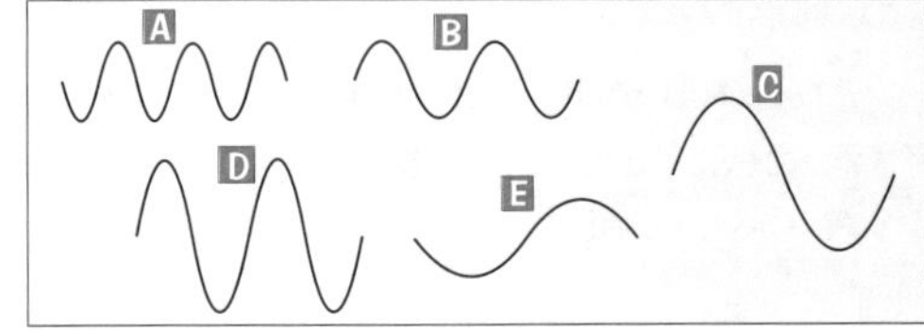

a) Study the traces above and complete the missing data in the table opposite.

b) What is the difference in the sound of the traces B and D?

Oscilloscope Trace	Frequency (Hz)	Amplitude (V)
	100	2
	100	4
	200	2
	200	4
	300	2

Q6 A signal generator can be used with a loudspeaker and amplifier to make sounds of a large frequency range (see below). An oscilloscope displays the sounds as traces.

a) What **kind of signal** is produced by a signal generator?
b) What does the **loudspeaker** do to this signal?
c) What can the oscilloscope be used for in this set up?
d) Why does the oscilloscope need a microphone attached to it?

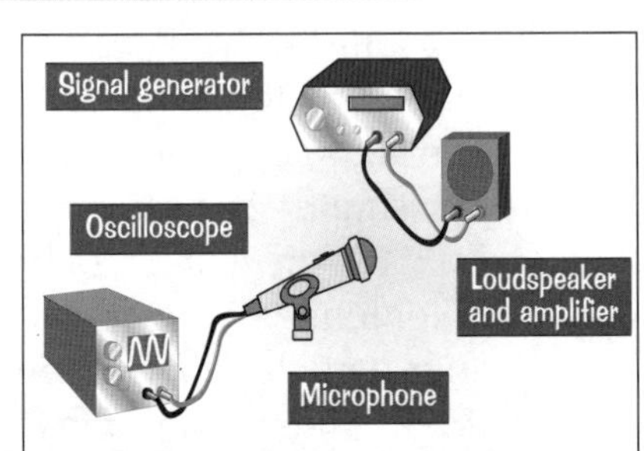

Ultrasound

Q1 Copy and complete the following:

"Sounds above 20 000Hz have too high a ____________ to be heard by the human ear. Such sounds can be converted from ______________ oscillations using a loudspeaker. Sounds above this frequency are called ______________."

Q2 Calculate the wavelengths of the following ultrasound frequencies (in air).

— Take the speed of sound in air to be 330m/s.

a) 25kHz **b)** 30kHz **c)** 50kHz **d)** 100kHz

Q3 You should be able to describe several applications that humans have found for ultrasound.

Below is a table summarising six uses of ultrasound. The information is all mixed up.

Application	Category of use	Ultrasound used to	Basic principles
Removal of kidney stones	Industrial	Image the foetus	Use of energy in ultrasound to physically alter material
Quality control	Medical	Shatter stones allowing them to be passed out in urine	Use of energy in ultrasound to physically alter material
Removal of tartar	Military / Scientific	Break up tartar deposits on teeth	Use of energy in ultrasound to physically alter material
Sonar	Medical	Check for cracks in metal castings	Detection of reflected ultrasound to build image
Pre-natal screening	Industrial	Cleaning delicate mechanisms without dismantling them	Detection of reflected ultrasound to build image
Cleaning	Medical	Measure distances to objects or map the sea bed	Detection of reflected ultrasound to build image

Redraw the table with the information in the **correct places**.

Q4 Why is ultrasound...

a) better than X-rays for looking at a foetus?
b) better for cleaning delicate mechanisms than traditional methods?
c) better for treating kidney stones than open surgery?
d) the chosen method for checking for flaws in metal castings?
e) used to remove tartar?

Ultrasound — Mancunian for very good...

Most of your extended electromagnetic wave questions are going to be about one of five things: Radio, light, ultrasound, X-rays, or gamma rays. That's because they have important practical applications. I know I'm banging on about this, but you've just got to learn them.

21.6

Seismic Waves

Q1 The diagram shows the model we have developed for the Earth using information from seismic waves.

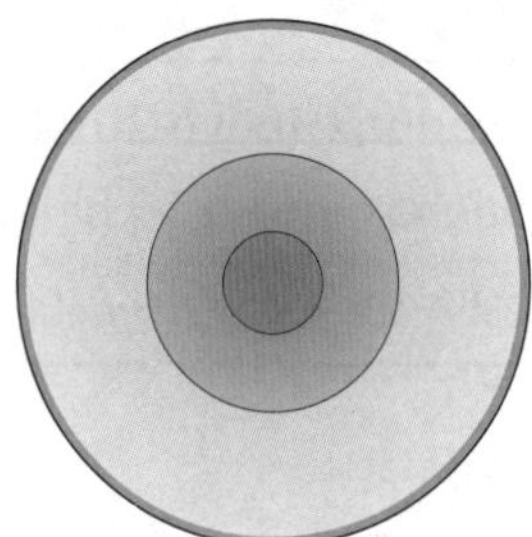

a) **Copy** the diagram and label the different layers that make up the Earth.

b) The measurement of seismic waves can be used to learn about the interior of the Earth. **Why** is this a more convenient method than drilling into the earth to take measurements?

Q2 Study the diagram of the Earth on the right. It shows an earthquake sending four S–Waves into the Earth.

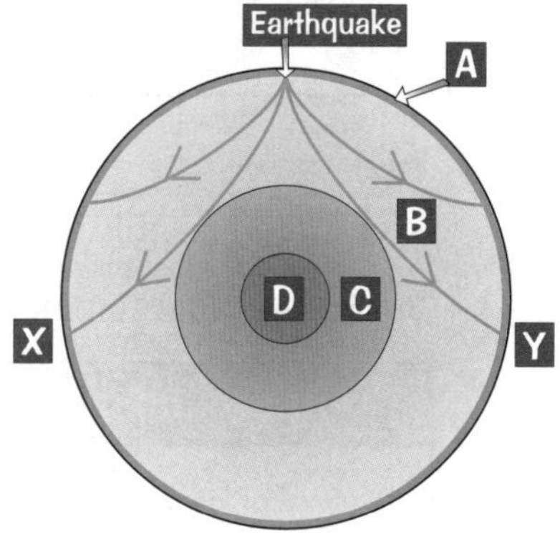

a) Describe what an "**S–Wave**" is.

b) What is the name for the region on the earth's surface beyond X and Y?

c) Why are there no S-waves detected beyond X and Y?

d) Describe the **state** of the rocks in layer B.

Q3 The paths of the **S–Waves** travelling through layer B are bent.

a) What property of the rock in layer B is steadily changing to account for this observation?

b) Now compare this effect with the refraction of light waves. Give **two reasons** why we can say that the S–Waves in layer B are **refracted**.

Q4 Give **three** ways in which P–Waves are different from S–Waves.

Q5 The diagram below shows the paths for some **P–Waves** travelling through the Earth.

a) Point D is at the boundary of which two layers?

b) The direction of the waves at D and E changes suddenly. Why does this happen?

c) Detectors are placed on the Earth's surface between points P and R. Describe where you would **not** expect to detect any P–Waves.

d) What property do P-waves have that allows them to reach the parts that other waves can't?

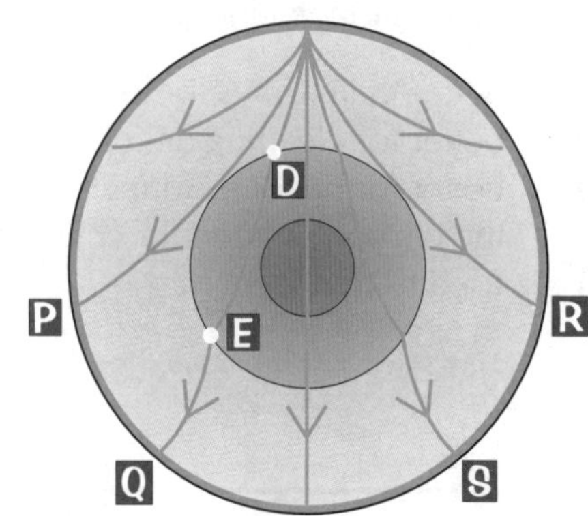

Q6 After an earthquake, would you expect to feel the P–Wave first, or the S–Wave? **Explain** your answer.

Module Three — Environment

12.1 — Population and Where Species Live

Page 1 — Population and Habitat

Q1 Predators are animals which kill and eat other animals. Prey are the animals eaten by predators. Examples could include foxes (predators) eat rabbits (prey), etc.

Q2 Possible table:

Factor	Examples
Competition for water	Weeds and wheat
Competition for light	Trees and grass
Competition for nutrients	Sycamore and oak trees
Competition for food	Blackbirds and thrushes
Competition for space	Weeds and carrots
Predation	Mice eaten by owls
Grazing	Grass eaten by cows
Amount of food available	Mice for owls to eat
Disease	Myxomatosis in rabbits

Q3 The Sidewinder's movements help to keep it cool by keeping some of its body off the hot sand. Different parts of the body are in contact at different times as it moves. It also allows the sidewinder to get a grip in the sand.

Q4 Burrows are likely to be cool during the day, allowing the animals to come out at night when it is cooler on the surface. Prey will be hidden from predators (and predators will be hidden from their prey). As it is cooler underground, the animals may be able to conserve moisture. However, it is unlikely that there will be any food in the burrow, and the animals will need to forage at night. It may be difficult to find food in the dark, and predators may be hunting then, too.

Q5 a) The plants are able to continue their species without trying to grow when there is insufficient water.
b) The plants can reach down to where there may still be water/minerals, etc.
c) The roots can absorb surface water, e.g. if there is light rain or early morning dew.
d) Plants can continue to live even when there is no ground water.
e) Leaves are a potential source of water loss through transpiration, and so water can be conserved this way.
f) Water can be lost by evaporation through stomata. This is reduced if the stomata are only open at night when it is cooler.
g) The thorns put off grazing animals that might try to eat the plants or get at their stored water.

Q6 Lemmings are small, so will lose heat quickly. They have fur and live in burrows to reduce their heat loss (their rounded bodies will keep their surface area to volume ratio down). Their ears are small and hidden by fur which again reduces heat loss. Their fur is light brown for camouflage in the tundra. They can hide from predators in their burrows.

Q7 Linked, food, increase, predators, food, decrease.

Page 2 — Population and Habitat

Q1 a) There are extremes of temperature in the Arctic; it can be quite warm in summer, but the temperature is below freezing for most of the year. There can be strong winds, which would make it seem much colder. There is relatively little rainfall, with most falling in the summer, so it is quite dry.
b) Plants grow close to the ground to withstand the strong winds. Their small leaves will reduce water loss.
c) The cold will be a major problem in the Arctic, and adaptations such as fur and lots of fat can be expected. Animals may also live in burrows to escape the cold and strong winds. Grazing animals might find it difficult to find food if the plants are low growing with small leaves.

Q2 a) Aids heat loss.
b) The desert is very dry. Being able to hold lots of water prevents dehydration.
c) The desert is hot and dry, not sweating and not producing much urine means that the camel doesn't get dehydrated.
d) This helps camouflage the camel.
e) Large feet spread the weight of the camel and stop it sinking into the soft sand.
f) Having no layer of body fat helps the camel to lose body heat, which helps it as the desert is hot.
g) Tolerating big changes in its body temperature means the camel doesn't need to sweat. This prevents dehydration.

Q3 Any three of these points:
1) It is strong, agile and fast, which helps it catch prey.
2) It has strong jaws and sharp teeth for killing prey.
3) Good stereo vision with both eyes facing forwards, which helps it to find prey.
4) It has a camouflaged body for stalking prey.
5) It has the right sort of teeth for chewing meat.

Q4 Any three of these:
Temperature, amount of light, availability of water, availability of oxygen and availability of carbon dioxide.

Page 3 — Population and Habitat

Q1 Plants — space, water, nutrients from soil.
Animals — space, water and food

Q2 a) Fast and agile, so can escape from predators.
b) Brown colour so camouflaged.
c) Good all-round vision helps it spot predators.
d) Good hearing helps it hear predators
e) Other rabbits can see the bright white tail when the rabbit is running.

Q3 Minimum, reduces, thick, insulation, sheds, prevent, white, camouflage, powerful, runner, prey.

Module Three — Environment

12.2 — Energy and Biomass

Page 4 — Food Chains and Pyramids

Q1 Grass is eaten by cows which are eaten by people.

Q2

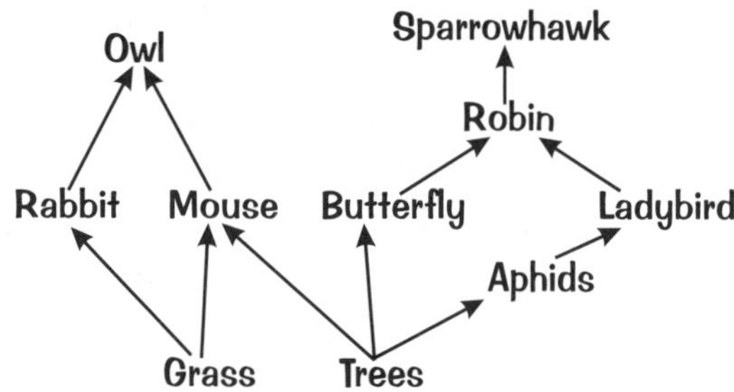

Q3 a) A pyramid of numbers shows the numbers of organisms at each trophic level in a food chain.

b) Row F is the most likely to represent the numbers of organisms.

c) The size of the organism increases going from left to right along this food chain.

d) Pyramid A.

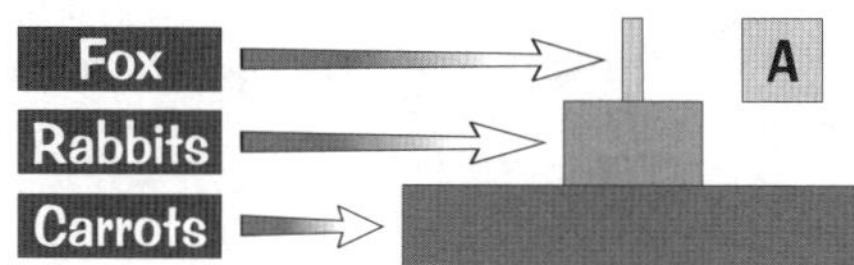

e) The larger the organism, the narrower its bar.

Q4 a)

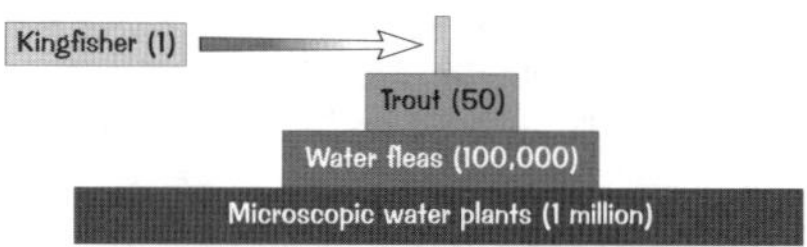

b)

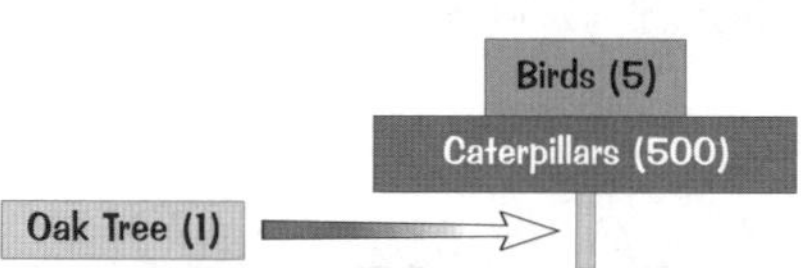

c) It is not always possible to draw the bars to scale because the numbers at each level can be very different. For example, it the kingfisher bar was 1mm wide, the microscopic water plants bar would be 1km wide!

d) A pyramid of numbers can have a non-pyramid shape if there is a single, large producer.

e) & f)

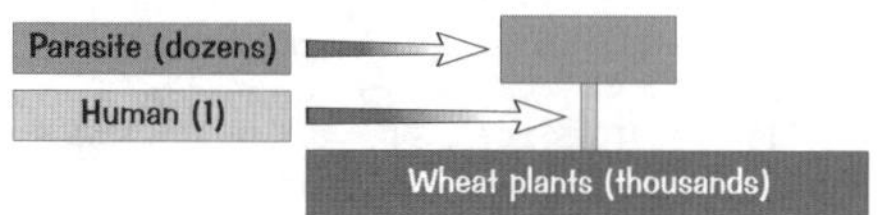

Similar to answer for **d)**, the parasites survive off a single large producer — a human.

g) Any suitable non-pyramidal example with relevant labelling and explanation.

Page 5 — Food Chains and Pyramids

Q1 Biomass is the mass of living organisms at a particular trophic level. Pyramids of biomass show the mass of living organisms at each trophic level in a food chain.

Q2 a) Pyramid:
(10cm for the phytoplankton works well).

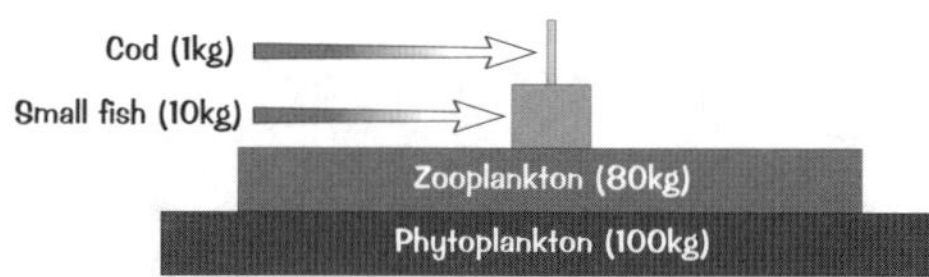

b) If the biomass of the lowest trophic level is very large compared to the top level, a scale drawing will need a bar that is too small to draw accurately. A vertical line can be used then.

c) The most mass is lost zooplankton → small fish (70kg).

d) The greatest proportion is lost small fish → cod (90%).

e) Biomass is lost through waste materials and nutrients used for respiration.

f) 1kg of dry cod would eat 10kg of dry small fish. Since both fish have the same proportion of water in their bodies, 1kg of wet cod would eat 10kg of wet small fish.
so 7.5kg of wet cod would eat 75kg of wet small fish.
So 1 cod would eat 75 ÷ 1.5 = 50 small fish

Q3 a) Pyramid A — A large producer could support many herbivores, which then support fewer carnivores, so the first bar is small.

b) Pyramid B — Pyramids of biomass have the proper pyramid shape.

c) Pyramid D — Parasites are smaller than their hosts, so there will more of them, giving a wider final bar.

d) Pyramids B or D — The bottom bar would be the largest because many algae would be needed.

Q4 Less, biomass, narrower, numbers.

Page 6 — Food Chains and Pyramids

Q1 5 herons, 8000kg

Q2 a) Producers – green plants.

b) Photosynthesis.

c) It reduces.

Q3 He should grow vegetables, wheat and other crops that can be eaten by humans. This is because material and energy is lost at each stage in a food chain. This means that the efficiency of food production can be improved by reducing the number of stages in food chains.

Q4 a) Energy and materials are always lost in organisms waste materials. Organisms use energy for respiration.

b) Respiration, heat, very, constant, higher.

c) The goldfish is cold blooded, so it doesn't have to use energy regulating its body temperature. The mouse does, so it needs more energy, which it gets through food, to live.

d) 10%

Module Three — Environment

Q5 a) They don't use energy moving or lose much energy through heat loss to their surroundings. This means they require less energy to live, so don't require as much food. This makes farming them cheaper.

b) Hormones are used to regulate the ripening of fruit on the plant and during transport to consumers. This decreases the amount of fruit that goes bad before it gets to consumers, so the amount of wastage is reduced.

c) The advantage is that the cost of food production is reduced, so food is cheaper for shoppers. The disadvantage of battery farming is that the chickens have to be given lots of antibiotics to keep them healthy. This is as the warm, crowded in which they are kept helps the spread of disease. The disadvantage of adding hormones to fruit is that the hormones may not be very good for humans.

12.3 — Waste Materials

Page 7 — Waste Materials and The Cycles

Q1 a) For growth and other purposes.
b) In animal waste materials or through the decomposition of dead plant and animal material.
c) So plants have the materials they need to grow and live.

Q2 a) Decomposers.
b) The bacteria and fungi obtain nutrients for respiration, and for growth and repair.
c) Carbon dioxide will be returned to the atmosphere.
d) Minerals and nitrogen compounds.
e) Bacteria and fungi are important because they remove dead animals and plants, they release valuable minerals and nutrients from them. These minerals and nutrients are vital for the healthy growth of plants (without plants, the carbon cycle would cease).

Q3 a) Warm
b) Moist
c) plenty of

Q4 a) To decompose the sewage.
b) Decomposing microorganisms there need plenty of oxygen.
c) The decomposed material in compost is full of the nutrients that plants need to grow.

Q5 Processes which return materials to the environment.

Page 8 — The Carbon Cycle

Q1 a) Photosynthesis
b) Respiration.
c) Clockwise from top: carbon dioxide, photosynthesis, carbon, respiration.
d) Fats, proteins and carbohydrates.

Q2 a) It becomes part of the fats and proteins in the animals' body.
b) Respiration.

Q3 When plants and animals die, some animals and microorganisms feed on their bodies. Carbon is released into the atmosphere as carbon dioxide when these organisms respire.

Q4 Carbon dioxide, green, respiration, fats, carbohydrates, proteins, eating, decomposed, microorganisms, respire.

Page 9 — The Nitrogen Cycle

Q1 a) They absorb nitrates in the soil.
b) Making proteins.
c) Making proteins.
d) Eating plants.

Q2 a) Putrefying bacteria.
b) Ammonium compounds.
c) Nitrifying bacteria convert ammonium compounds to nitrates.

Q3 Some is used when plants respire, some is used when animals respire, some is used when the decomposing bacteria respire and some is present in the nitrates returned to the soil.

Q4 a) False - they get it as nitrates from the soil.
b) False - they return carbon dioxide.
c) True
d) True
e) False - they need it to make proteins.
f) False - putrifying bacteria do this.
g) True.
h) False - get from eating plants.

Page 10 — Waste Materials and The Cycles

Q1 Clockwise from top: nitrates in soil, animals eat plants, animal protein, death and decay, nitrifying bacteria.

Q2 First column: Plants absorb nitrates and when they die they are decomposed to leave ammonium compounds, among other things. Also animals eat plants and produce waste. The waste contains ammonium compounds and when animals decompose they leave ammonium compounds as well.
Second column: Nitrifying bacteria convert ammonium compounds to nitrates in the soil.

Q3 a) Sewage works and compost heaps.
b) Warm.
c) Fats, carbohydrates, proteins would all do.
d) Photosynthesis
e) The microorganisms that do the decomposing release carbon dioxide into the atmosphere when they respire.
f) Nitrifying bacteria.
g) Proteins.

12.4 — Humans' Effect on The Environment

Page 11 — Our Effect on The Environment

Q1 Building, quarrying, farming, dumping waste.

Q2 Air: sulphur dioxide, carbon dioxide, nitrogen oxides.
Land: pesticides, herbicides.
Water: sewage, fertiliser, pesticides, herbicides.

Module Three — Environment

Q3 i) Cutting down trees will increase the amount of carbon dioxide in the atmosphere as it reduces the amount removed and "locked up" as wood.
ii) Trees which have been cut down will either decompose or be burnt. Both processes release CO_2.
iii) The cows will produce methane — another greenhouse gas.

Q4 a) The rate of use of raw materials in increasing along with the size of the population.
b) They are in danger of running out as we use them quicker and quicker.
c) Larger as from the graph we can see there are roughly 6 times as many people alive now as there were 200 years ago, so the effects of our actions are going to be larger.
d) More waste is being produced now, so it is important that it is handled properly, as more pollution will be caused if it is not.

Q5 a) Carbon dioxide
b) Two reasons, 1: it has increased the release of carbon dioxide (due to the burning and rotting of the felled trees) 2: It has reduced the rate at which carbon dioxide is removed from the atmosphere and "locked-up" as wood.
c) Burning them will produce sulphur dioxide and nitrogen oxides and these gases are the cause of acid rain.
d) There are limited supplies of fossil fuels and as the population grows we need more and more energy. So unless we have other energy sources we will run out of fossil fuels and have no way to make energy.

Page 12 — The Greenhouse Effect

Q1 a) Natural sources of carbon dioxide: Respiration, forest fires, volcanoes, rain reacting with limestone, spring waters.
b) The release of carbon from fossil fuels has increased dramatically with time, especially since 1950. This is probably due to increased use of oil for vehicles, and coal and natural gas for energy.
c) The amount of carbon dioxide in the atmosphere has risen steadily since 1850. This is probably due to the release of carbon dioxide from burning fossil fuels.
d) Approximate increase in carbon from fuels 1875–1975:
$5.7 \div 0.2 = 28.5$, i.e. 25 to 30 times increase.
e) Approximate increase in carbon dioxide 1875–1975: $0.033 \div 0.029 = 1.1$, i.e. not a lot. (The scale of the graph is misleading, as it does not start at zero.)
f) Carbon dioxide can be absorbed by plants for photosynthesis. It can dissolve in water. It can be incorporated into shells of sea creatures. It can eventually form rocks such as limestone.
g) Carbon dioxide is a greenhouse gas. If there is more of it in the atmosphere, it should absorb more heat energy. The temperature of the Earth's atmosphere should rise as a result.

Q2 a) By farting. Or possibly, 'they emit methane as a by-product of digestion
b) Some of the crops rot in the water. This produces methane.
c) More farming will be needed to provide food for the growing population, so the amount of methane produced by these two sources will increase.

Page 13 — The Greenhouse Effect

Q1 a) Although there are fluctuations, there is a clear trend of increasing temperature with time.
b) Both carbon dioxide levels and temperature follow the same trend upwards. However, there have been years in which the temperature has fallen even though the amount of carbon dioxide has risen, e.g. 1880 to 1885, and 1965 to 1970. Therefore, there must be other factors involved.
c) As the temperature has risen, so has the sea level. This is probably due to ice melting at the poles and in glaciated regions.
d) If carbon dioxide levels continue to rise, it would be expected that sea levels and temperature would rise as well. The rise in temperature will change the climate. The rise in sea level will cause flooding in low-lying areas of the world.

Q2 a) It might not be the only factor, but the graphs seem to show that the increase in carbon dioxide is causing an increase in temperature. Therefore it would seem wrong to say it wasn't causing global warming.
b) It would cost a lot of money for industry to reduce its emissions.
c) Planting trees would reduce the amount in the atmosphere, but only once the trees had grown.

Q3 a) Carbon dioxide and methane absorb most of the energy radiated by the earth. Some of this energy is re-radiated back to Earth, keeping it warmer than it would be without the insulating layer.
b) The Earth would be much colder.

Page 14 — Acid Rain

Q1 a) sulphur + oxygen → sulphur dioxide
b) The gases dissolve in the water vapour in rain clouds.
This makes the rain acidic.
c) Car exhausts, planes, trains... any form of fossil fuelled transport.

Q2 a) It won't be able to photosynthesise, so it won't be able to make food.
b) Trees will be able to absorb the dissolved aluminium and this will poison them.
c) It means they won't be able to absorb nutrients from the soil as well.

Q3 a) Water plants will be poisoned by the aluminium and will lose leaves due to the acid.
b) The crustaceans, and animals that depend upon them for food, directly or indirectly, will die.
c) The fish will be unable to obtain enough oxygen and so will die.

Page 15 — Pollution

Q1 a) "Development that meets the needs of today's population without harming the ability of future generations to meet their own needs." Mmm, sounds good.
b) Without it the human race may have problems in the future caused by it's actions in the present.

Module Four — Inheritance and Selection

Q2 a) By replacing the nutrients which crops remove from the soil.
b) It will be washed into the river.
c) Eutrophication.

Q3 a) Correct sequence: Excess fertilisers leach from the soil and are washed into the lake.
Water plants in the lake start to grow rapidly.
There is increased competition between the plants, and some die as a result.
The number of microbes that feed on dead organisms increases.
The microbes take more oxygen from the water for their respiration.
Fish and other aquatic animals die of lack of oxygen.
b) The plants grow more quickly because they have received additional nitrates and phosphates.
c) The plants are likely to be competing for light and space. Nitrates, phosphates and water are likely to be in excess.
d) The oxygen content of the water goes down because additional decomposer microbes use the oxygen to respire.
e) In a eutrophic lake, the nitrates are not limiting because they are being added to the community from outside. Eutrophication kills animals and eventually plants. Therefore, the microbes are not recycling the nutrient but causing increasing death followed by yet more decay.

Q4 a) Food
b) Sewage contains the same nitrates/phosphates as chemical fertilisers so you get the same results.

13.1 — Individual Differences

Page 16 — Variation

Q1 a) i) a and c
ii) They are the only two that have all the same features not affected by the environment. (roll tongue, brown hair and brown eyes)
b) i) Ability to tan; hair colour **ii)** Sex, tongue rolling, eye colour.

Q2 Discontinuous, range, inherited, environmental.

Q3 Asexual, exact, two, parent, gametes.

Q4

Organism	Number of chromosomes in a body cell	Number of pair of chromosomes	Number of chromosomes in each gamete
Fruit Fly	8	4	4
Kangaroo	12	6	6
Rye Plant	20	10	10
Chicken	36	18	18
Mouse	40	20	20
Humans	46	23	23
Crayfish	200	100	100

Page 17 — Variation

Q1 Asexually, produce, copies, without, offspring, parent, clones, exactly, genes, parent, reproduction, less, sexual, mixing, two.

Q2 a) Chromosomes are found in the nucleus of body cells.
b) Twenty-three.
c) Hair colour, blood group, inherited diseases, eye colour.
d) The other characteristics are caused by environmental factors.

Q3 a)

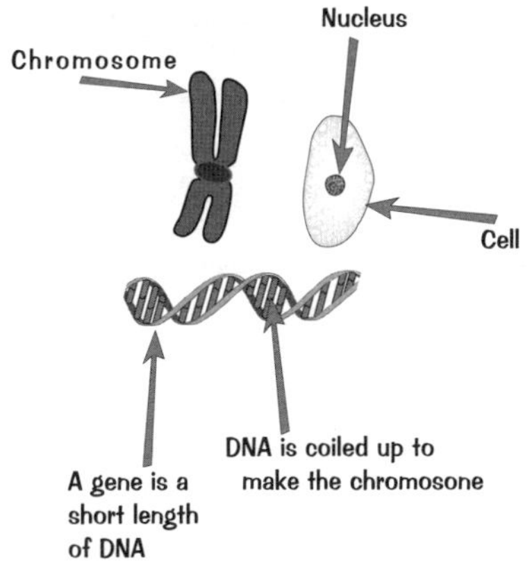

b) Genes give chemical instructions to cells to determine how they grow. Different instructions produce different cells with different characteristics. A gene instruction for black hair will be not be the same as a gene instruction for blond hair and will produce different cells.
c) divide, new, identical, divide, multiply, replicating, growth, replace.

Page 18 — Mitosis and Meiosis

Q1

Asexual Reproduction	Sexual Reproduction
Offspring are clones of parent	Offspring are not genetically identical to parents
Only one parent is needed	Two parents are needed
No joining of sex cells needed	Male and female gametes join

Q2 A 1 Initially the DNA is very mixed up and evenly distributed within the nucleus.
2 Chromosomes are formed by the organisation of DNA strands into a chromosome structure. The double arms of the chromosome structure are duplicates of each other.
3 The chromosomes line up along the centre of the cell and cell fibres pull them apart.
4 Membranes begin to form, surrounding the two sets of chromosome sections produced in stage three. These become the nuclei of the two daughter cells.
5 Two separate cells are produced, identical to the parent cell in stage one. The threads begin to unwind and become mixed up and evenly distributed within the nucleus.

B 1 The chromosomes pair up. There are 46 human chromosomes so there are 23 pairs. In each pair one chromosome is from your mother the other is from your father.
2 The pairs of chromosomes now split up, separating those from your father from those from your mother. The two nuclei produced from this splitting are different, containing a mixture of chromosomes from both your mother and father. Each nucleus now only has 23 chromosomes.
3 The chromosomes themselves now split forming duplicates of themselves within two nuclei.
4 There are now two sets of duplicate cell pairs produced when the chromosomes split in stage three. The cells are called gametes.

Module Four — Inheritance and Selection

13.2 — Breeding Plants and Animals

Page 19 — Selective Breeding

Q1 People, varieties, characteristics, breed, selective, milk, colour, alleles, variety.

Q2 a) Pointed ears, long tail, long hair, sticking up ears, pointed snout, etc.
b) Have greater variety of alleles - haven't been selected for aesthetic purposes which sacrifice health.
c) The breed would eventually disappear.

Q3 a) The process where people breed animals with the best characteristics is called *artificial* selection.
b) Selective breeding *decreases* the number of alleles in a population
c) Farmers often selectively breed to *increase* yields of food produced.
d) Selective breeding involves *sexual* reproduction.
e) Breeding characteristics like floppy ears into dogs is *disadvantageous* to the dog.

Page 20 — Cloning

Q1 a) Asexual
b) i) Have same genes / or similar. **ii)** Clones
c) i) Grow quickly / Need less space / Can grow all year round / New plants are disease free / All plants have the same requirement / Easier to harvest.
ii) Reduce gene pool / Vulnerable to diseases.
d) Cuttings

Q2 a) Asexual
b) Identical
c) Different
d) i) New plants are produced quickly, identical to parent plant.
ii) Less variety, reduction in gene pool.

Q3 a) Plants that are produced by cuttings grow into new plants by *mitotic* cell division.
b) Tissue cultures are a useful way of producing large numbers of *identical* plants from a small number of cells.
c) Genetically identical plants are produced by *asexual* reproduction.
d) Growing plants from tissue cultures *decreases* the gene pool.
e) Cloning techniques are also used in producing identical animals by splitting embryo cells *before* they specialise.

Page 21 — Cloning

Q1 genetically, asexual, mitosis, cuttings, tissue, identical, cells, splitting, embryo, host, naturally.

Q2 a) Mitosis.
b) Because they are genetically identical.
c) i) Fast, identical to parent. **ii)** Reduces variety / gene pool.
d) i) Cloning. **ii)** Can quickly produce offspring with exactly the same wool.

Q3 a) Enzymes.
b) Human, protein.
c) Insulin.

13.3 — Evolution

Page 22 — Evolution

Q1 changed, Darwin, degenerate, adaptations, environment, organisms, food, existence, fittest, characteristics, nature, survival, natural, evolution.

Q2 All giraffes had short necks, mutation resulted in some giraffes having longer necks than others, the giraffe population had individuals whose necks varied in length, natural selection resulted in longer necked offspring surviving, only long necked giraffes survived the competition for food.

Q3 a) Fish.
b) Number of reptiles in diagram declining 60 million years ago.
c) Mammals
d) They show changes and development of organisms over millions of years.
e) Fossilisation is rare / did not occur.

Page 23 — Natural Selection

Q1 variation, species, disease, die, environment, offspring, natural, alleles, favourable, survive.

Q2 a) i) Mutation. **ii)** Predation / amount of food / disease.
b) Black moths were camouflaged from their predators and not eaten as much.
c) In polluted / industrial areas, black moths survive. In cleaner areas (Scotland and Southwest) light moths survive.
d) It can breed with a light moth and produce fertile young.
e) Natural selection.

Q3 a) The frequency of alleles which determine useful characteristics *increases* in a population.
b) Factors like disease cause a population to *decrease*.
c) Organisms that are the best survivors are those that are *best suited to their environment*.
d) Survivors pass their genes on to their *offspring*.
e) Natural selection is the process by which *evolution* takes place.
f) In order for changes to occur in the characteristics of a population *mutation* must take place.

Q4 a) The young may develop abnormally or even die young.
b) The mutant cells may start to multiply in an uncontrolled way and invade other parts of the body. This is known as cancer.
c) A good example of a neutral mutation is the appearance of blue budgies within a population of yellow ones.
d) Bacteria have also been known to mutate overcoming the effects of antibiotics.

Page 24 — Evolution and Fossils

Q1 a) False, Lamarck believed that animals evolve features according to how much they use them. Darwin believed in "Survival of the fittest".
b) True.
c) True.
d) False, Animals that adapt well to their environment are more likely to survive.
e) True.

Module Four — Inheritance and Selection

Q2 a) A– Fossils formed in this way usually develop from hard parts of animals such as **bones** , **teeth** and **shells**. When animals die their bodies settle on the ocean floor.

B– When they die, hard parts of animals don't **decay** easily. **Sediment** collects around the dead animals and they become buried.

C– Over a long period of time the hard parts **decay** and are replaced by **minerals**. A rock like substance is formed in the same shape as the original hard part known as a fossil.

D– The sediment surrounding the **animal** remains also turns to rock, but the fossil stays distinct inside the rock.

b) Within the amber there is no oxygen or moisture for the decay microbes.
Glaciers are too cold for decay microbes to work.
Waterlogged bogs are often too acidic for decay microbes to work.

c) fast, swamp, oxygen.

Page 25 — Mutations

Q1 Chromosome, naturally, mitosis, nucleus, divide, mutations, ionising, mutagens, carcinogens, harmful, sex, replication, neutral, beneficial, antibiotics, genetic.

Q2 a) Sunlight contains harmful ultraviolet light, which causes mutations and can lead to skin cancer.

b) A radiographer must stand behind a protective screen to prevent exposure to harmful X-rays emitted from the X-ray machine.

c) Carbon tetrachloride is a strong chemical that was found to be carcinogenic.

d) Workers used to form an accurate point to their brushes by sucking the ends to a point in their mouths.

13.4 — Inheritance

Page 26 — Cystic Fibrosis

Q1 Genetic, recessive, membranes, allele, both, carriers

Q2 Carrier - Cc; normal - CC; sufferer - cc

Q3 a) **i)** Both parents, two children (Cc)
ii) 1/4 children (cc)
iii) 2/4 children (CC and cc)
iv) Parents and 2/4 children (Cc)

b) Carry recessive alleles, but are not sufferers.

c) See diagram:

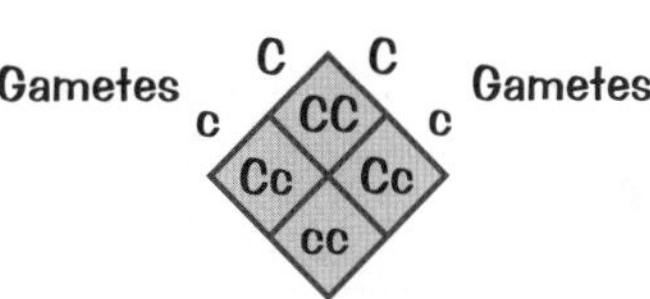

Page 27 — Cystic Fibrosis

Q1 a) Cystic fibrosis is an *inherited* disease.

b) Cystic fibrosis is caused by a *recessive* allele

c) Children can inherit the cystic fibrosis disease when *both* of their parents have the recessive allele.

Q2 a) Father = Cc, Mother = CC.

b) No

c) i) No

ii) each one has a 50% chance of carrying the disease.

d) 50%

e) 50%

f) i) No **ii)** He could have the same genotype whether one or both parents were carriers.

Q3 a) See diagram:

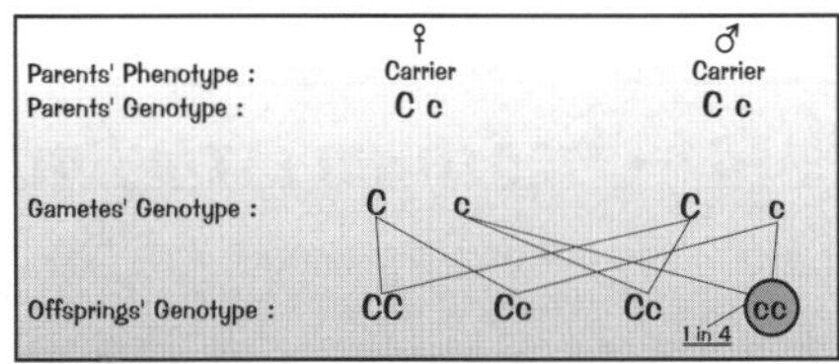

b) No

c) They have a recessive allele but do not suffer from the disease.

Q4 Genotype for a carrier = Cc; Produced in the lungs of sufferers = mucus; The normal, homozygous, dominant condition = CC; Has the cystic fibrosis allele but no ill-effects = carrier, Cc;
One in four chance of a child having this genotype from two carrier parents = CC, cc.

Page 28 — Genetic Diseases

Q1 Red, recessive, carrier, malaria, protected, alleles, oxygen.

Q2 a) Since the carriers of the sickle cell allele are more immune to malaria, more people with this allele will survive in malaria infected areas. Hence the high distribution of the allele in these areas.

b) i) They are protected against malaria.

ii) Their offspring may develop the disease.

Q3 a) See diagram :

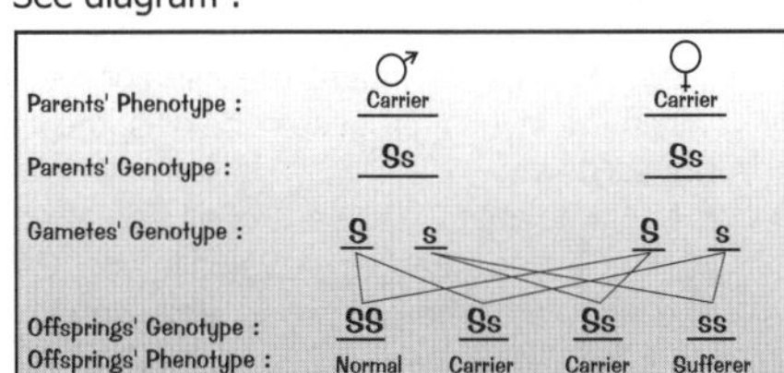

b) i) 1 in 4 (25%).

ii) They are deprived of oxygen (because red cells stick in their capillaries).

c) i) Lack of iron / haemoglobin in blood.

ii) They are protected against malaria.

Page 29 — Genetic Diseases

Q1 Dominant, one, allele, nervous

Q2 a) 1 in 2 (50%)

b) i) They don't have carriers - disease usually appears in childhood.

ii) Symptoms don't appear until after age 40 when sufferer has already had children.

Q3 Interbreeding in small community / with relatives.

Module Seven — Patterns of Chemical Change

Q4 a) See diagram:
b) 1 in 2 (50%)

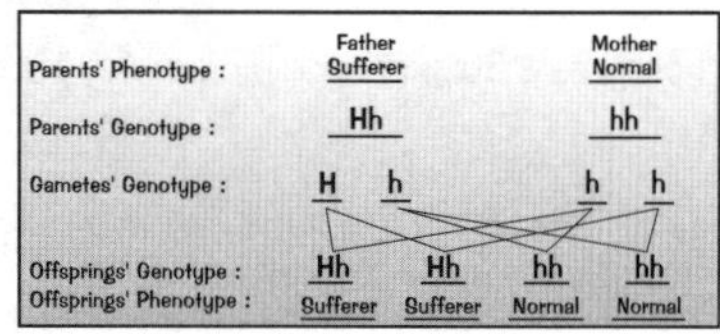

13.5 — Controlling Fertility

Page 30 — Menstrual Cycle Hormones

Q1 a) Progesterone and Oestrogen.
b) It would increase it.
c) Egg development and release would be stopped.
d) Yes. Levels of the hormones would fall back to normal after a period of time.

Q2 a) Pituitary gland and ovaries
b)

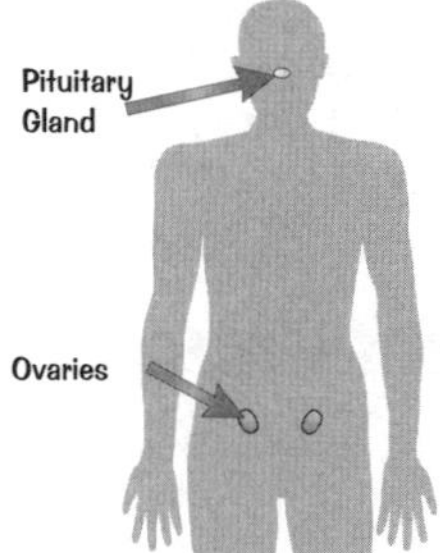

Q3 a) FSH (follicle stimulating hormone) can be used to increase the fertility of women.
b) FSH stimulates the ovaries to produce oestrogen which then stimulates the release of an egg.

Q4 Oestrogen – Stops production of FSH, causes the lining of the uterus to thicken and the release of an egg on day 14.
Progesterone – Maintains the lining of the uterus. When the level of progesterone falls, the lining breaks down.
LH – Stimulates the release of an egg after 14 days.
FSH – Causes an egg to develop in one of the ovaries and stimulates them to produce oestrogen.

Page 31 — Menstrual Cycle Hormones

Q1 a) A = progesterone
B = oestrogen
b)

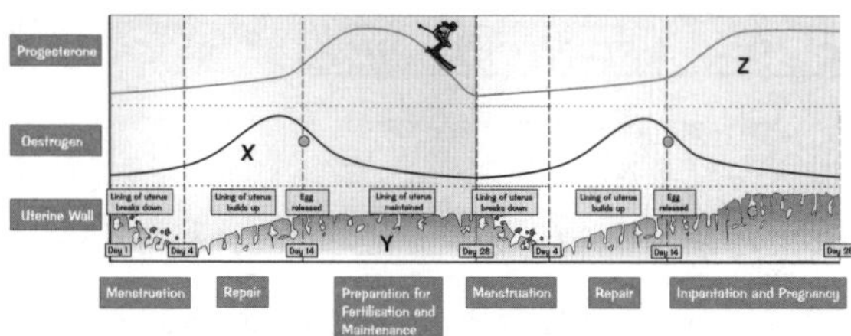

c) LH
d) FSH

Q2 a) Oestrogen.
b) Progesterone.

Q3 The pituitary gland and ovaries are the target organs, the hormones released during the cycle act upon them.

Q4 a) Progesterone.
b) Progesterone is needed to maintain the lining of the uterus, to ensure that the baby is kept healthy.

Q5 a) FSH.
b) Oestrogen.
c) High levels of FSH can result in difficult and dangerous multiple births. The high levels of FSH stimulate production of oestrogen, if oestrogen levels get too high then natural production of FSH is hampered and will eventually stop.

16.1 — Reaction Rates

Page 32 — Rates of Reaction

Q1 Match, egg, digestion, concrete, rust.

Q2 **a)** (B) or (C) **b)** (B) or (C) **c)** (A)

Q3 Catalysts are used up in reactions - false; catalysts are specific to certain reactions - true; enzymes are biological catalysts - true; reactions slow if catalysts are used - false; enzymes increase the activation energy - false; reactions will speed up if they are heated - true; reactions slow down if they are diluted - true; increasing concentration increases the rate of reaction - true; pressure increases the rate of gaseous reaction - true; reactions are fast at the start - true.

Q4 Heating the acid, using more conc. acid, using powdered metal not ribbon, using a catalyst, shaking the flask also works because it keeps the magnesium in contact with the acid.

Q5 Reacting magnesium with sulphuric acid, using a gas syringe to measure the amount of hydrogen given off etc.

Q6 Marble chips reacting with hydrochloric acid. The mass of the reaction vessel contents can be measured and seen to change as CO_2 escapes.

Page 33 — Rates of Reaction

Q1 a&b)

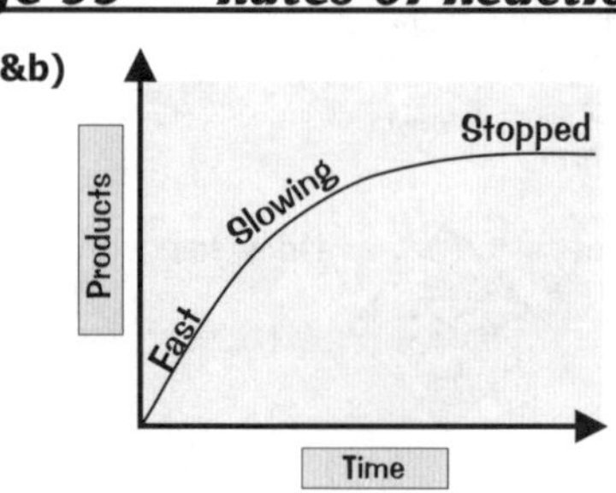

c) Reaction: start, middle, end
Speed: fast, slowing, stopped

Q2

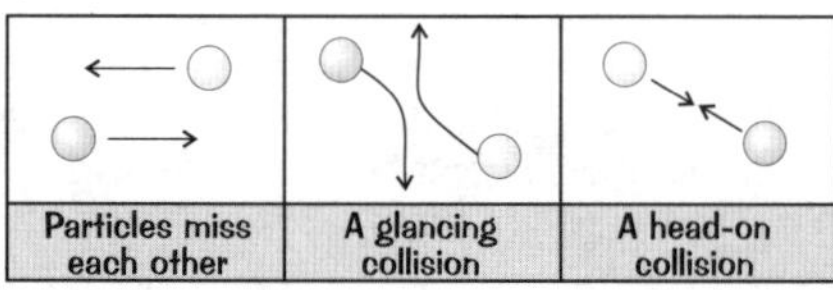

Module Seven — Patterns of Chemical Change

Page 34 — Collision Theory

Q1 Collide; energy; collision theory; concentration; catalyst;

Q2 a) Faster; more often; energy; faster.
b) Particles; faster;
c) Surface area; faster.
d) Moderate; successful; collision; faster.

a
Fast | Slow
Hot | Cold

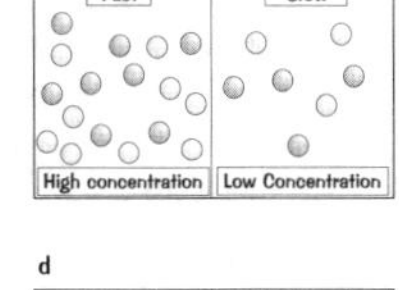

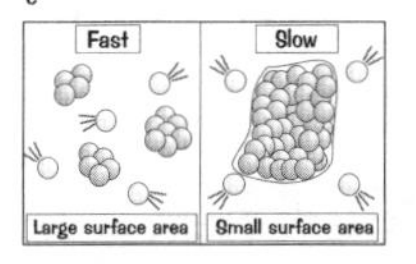

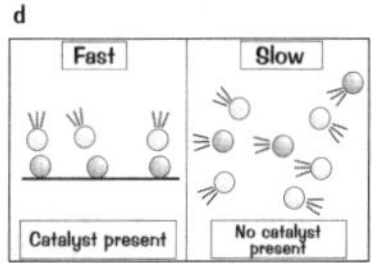

Q3 Reacting particles must collide with enough energy in order to react. (There is an activation energy barrier.)

Page 35 — Experiments on Rates of Reaction

Q1 a)

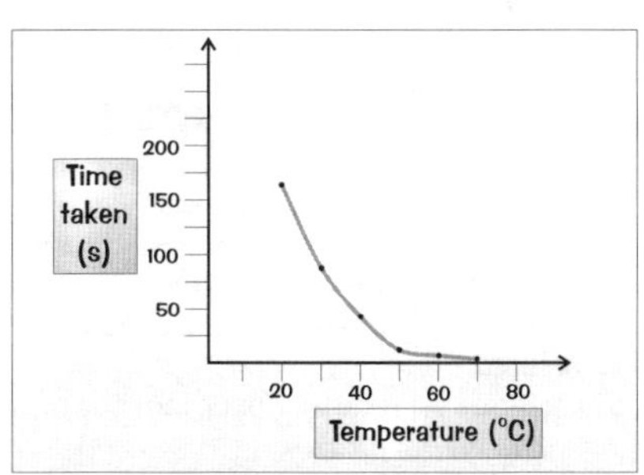

b) The higher the temperature, the less time is taken.

c)

Temperature (°C)	20	30	40	50	60	70
Time taken (s)	163	87	43	23	11	5
Rate (1/t)	0.0061	0.0115	0.0233	0.0435	0.0910	0.2000

d)

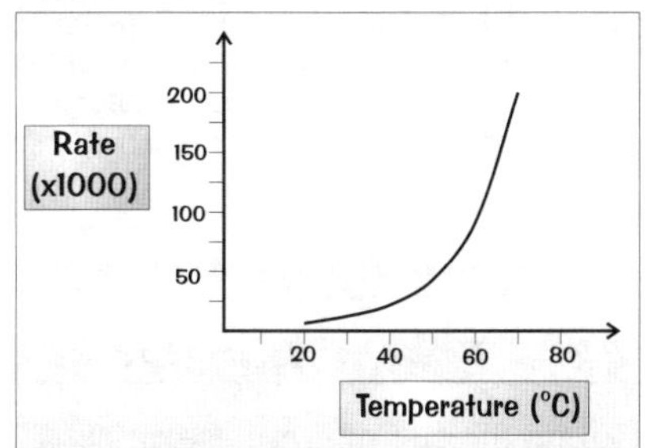

e) The higher the temperature, the faster the rate of reaction.

f) Higher temperatures give particles more energy, which makes them move faster. As the particles are moving faster, there are more collisions, and as they have more energy, more of these collisions are successful. Both mean a faster reaction rate.

Q2 a)

Volume of sodium thiosulphate (cm³)	50	40	30	20	10
Volume of water (cm³)	0	10	20	30	40
Time taken (s)	80	101	137	162	191
Rate (1/t)	0.0125	0.0099	0.0073	0.0061	0.0052

b)

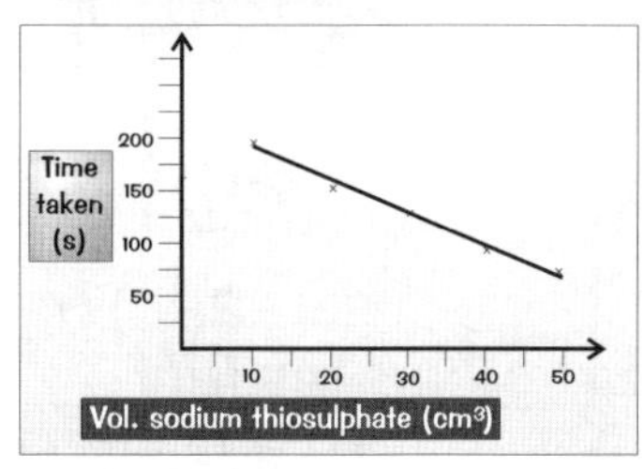

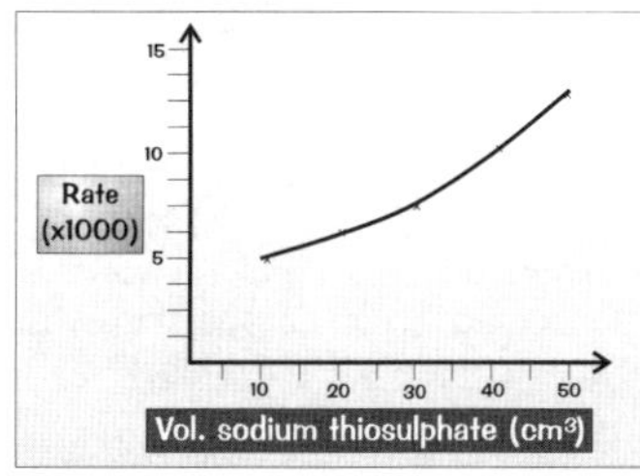

c) The greater the concentration the faster the reaction or the higher the rate.

d) With more particles in the solution there is a greater chance of a collision. More collisions means a faster reaction.

Page 36 — Catalysts

Q1 a) Copper doesn't react.
b) Zinc reacts slowly.
c) Zinc and copper react much better together.
d) Copper acts as a catalyst.
e) Copper is not used up, confirming its action as a catalyst.

Q2

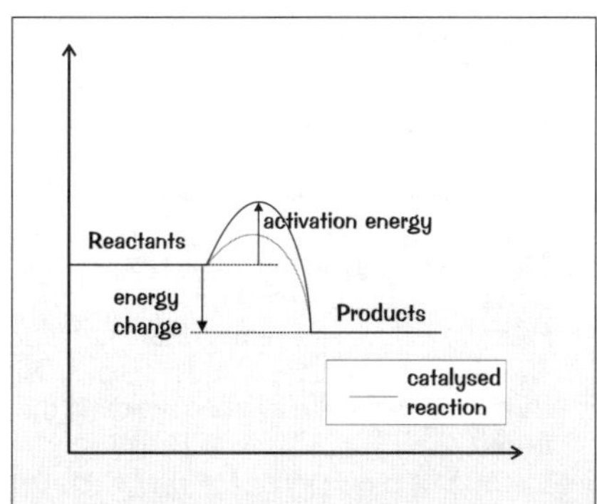

Q3 Catalysts speed up the reaction therefore it takes less time to make more product. Catalysts also lower the operating temperature and this saves money.

Q4 a) **i)** Tubes 2 & 3... Trypsin does not work on the protein on film B - enzymes are substrate specific.
ii) Tubes 2 & 4 - boiling stops the enzyme working.
iii) Tubes 2 & 5 - some substances can block or inhibit the action of enzymes.

b) Tube 1 is included as a control to show that film does not disintegrate of its own accord.

Module Seven — Patterns of Chemical Change

Page 37 — Hazards

Q1

Oxidising
Example: Liquid Oxygen

Harmful
Example: Methanol

Highly Flammable
Example: Petrol

Corrosive
Example: Sulphuric Acid

Toxic
Example: Cyanide

Irritant
Example: Bleach

Radioactive
Example: Uranium

Explosive
Example: Hydrogen

Q2 To give information about dangerous substances in an easily recognizable form, and so that the warnings can be understood all around the world; e.g. if a British tanker crashed in Europe, they would still be able be able to understand the label.

Q3 Using extreme care/ at least eye protection/wipe up spills/ industrial fully protective clothing might be used.

Q4 a) To inform the public and the emergency services that the tanker is carrying a cargo which is corrosive.
b) They might need to know more details about the substance in large amounts in order to decide how to deal with it.
c) Because the emergency services might need the advice of a specialist i.e. someone who is familiar with the substance and can tell them how to handle it.
d) Clear area, fully protect clothing and flush drains completely.

16.2 — Enzymes

Page 38 — Enzymes

Q1 a) Food spoilage is caused by reactions of bacteria and fungi.
b) The temperature in the fridge is about 5 °C and this slows the bacteria's reactions.
c) Freezing reduces the temperature further and effectively stops the spoilage reactions. Microbes can't grow when the available water in the food is frozen.

Q2 i) Biological detergents may contain protein-digesting and fat-digesting enzymes
ii) Isomerase is used to convert glucose syrup into fructose syrup, which is much sweeter and therefore can be used in small quantities in slimming foods
iii) Proteases are used to 'pre-digest' the protein in some baby foods.

Q3 a) CO_2 turns limewater milky.
b) Enzymes can be used to bring about reactions under normal conditions of temperature and pressure when otherwise they would require expensive equipment and high energy expenditure. They can also be carefully selected to catalyse a precise reaction.
c) A huge variety of enzymes exist, unlike non-biological catalysts (hence they can be carefully selected to do a very precise job). Also, metal catalysts are finite resources, and hence may be scarce and expensive (e.g. platinum).
d) Enzymes are extremely sensitive to ambient conditions (e.g. temperature, pressure). Non-biological catalysts are less fussy. Enzymes can only be used when manufacturing in a batch process (i.e. they become used up) non-biological catalysts allow continuou s production.

Page 39 — Enzymes

Q1 a) $C_6H_{12}O_6 \rightarrow 2\,C_2H_5OH + 2CO_2$ + energy
b)

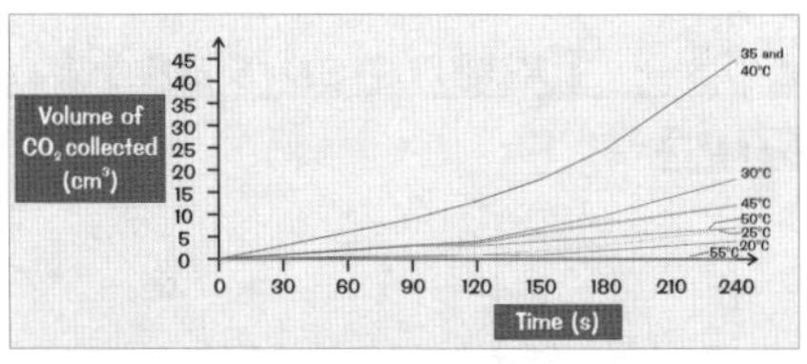

Temperature (°C)	20	25	30	35	40	45	50	55
Rate (cm³/min)	2	4	8	20	20	4	2	0

c) Optimum temperature is between 35 and 40 °C
d) Above the optimum temperature the enzyme is denatured.
e) Fermentation products - beer, lager, wine, bread.

Q2 a) Pasteurised milk is used to make yoghurt and cheese.
b) Fresh milk contains other bacteria, which may spoil the foodstuff.
c) Cheese — lactic acid producing bacteria makes the milk go acidic then further bacteria activity gives a sour (mature) taste and texture. Yoghurt is made at 45 °C - enzymes produced by bacteria make lactic acid (sour taste). Lactic acid is produced in these fermentation processes rather than alcohol.

16.3 — Energy Transfer in Reactions

Page 40 — Energy Transfer in Reactions

Q1 Energy (heat), exothermic, energy (heat), endothermic, Exothermic, hot, given out, Endothermic, cold, taken in, ΔH, endothermic, negative, energy, exothermic, endothermic, energy, break, energy, made.

Q2 a) Burning fuel = exothermic
b) Neutralisation = exothermic
c) Thermal decomposition of calcium carbonate = endothermic
d) Rapid oxidation of iron = exothermic
e) Rapid dissolving of NH_4NO_3 = endothermic

Module Seven — Patterns of Chemical Change

Q3 a) Breaking one N≡N bond needs 945kJ/mol
b) Breaking the H-H bond needs 435kJ/mol
c) Making the N-H bond releases 389kJ/mol
d)

```
                      2×/  H  \
                        |  |  |
N≡N  +3×(H-H) ⇌         |  N  |
                        \H   H/
```

e) Breaking reactant bonds needs
N ≡ N + (3 x H-H) = 945 + (3 x 435) = 2250kJ/mol
f) Making product releases
6 x N-H = 6x389 = 2334kJ/mol
g) Overall energy change is 2250 - 2334 = -84kJ/mol
More energy is released. It is exothermic, overall energy change is -84kJ/mol

Page 41 — Energy Transfer in Reactions

Q1 a)

```
  H H
H-C-C-H   +   3 x (O=O)  ⇌  2 x (O=C=O)   +   3 x ( H-O-H )
  H OH
```

b) Breaking bonds
C-H x 5 = 413 x 5 = 2065; C-O x 1 = 360; O-H x 1 = 463; Total =2888kJ/mol
O=O x 3 = 497 x 3 = 1491
Total = 2888 + 1491 = 4379kJ/mol.

c) Released on making
4 x C=O = 740 x 4 = 2960;
6 x O-H = 6 x 463 = 2778;
Total energy released = 5738kJ/mol.
d) Overall energy change:
Energy in - Energy out =4379 - 5738 = -1359kJ/mol
e) A negative value means exothermic reaction.

Q2 a) 4 x C-H (413) = 1652kJ/mol
2 x 0=0 (497) = 994kJ/mol Total =2646kJ/mol
b) 2 x C=0 (740) = 1480kJ/mol
4 x O-H (463) = 1852kJ/mol Total =3332kJ/mol
c) Overall energy change
= energy in - energy out
= 2646 - 3332
= -686kJ/mol (exothermic)
d)

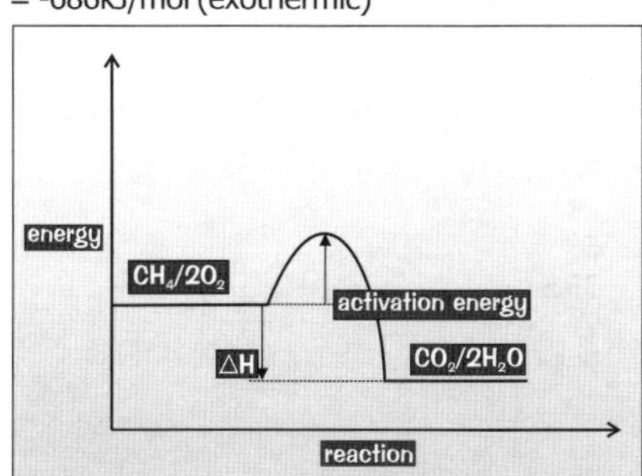

e) exothermic

Q3 a&b)

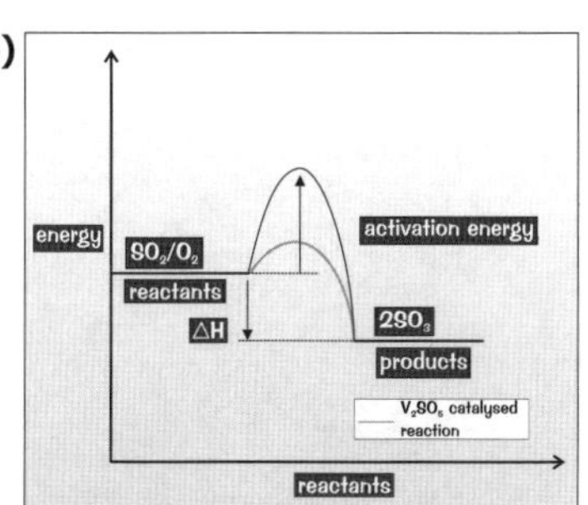

16.4 — Fertiliser

Page 42 — Ammonia and Fertilisers

Q1 It produces ammonia, which is needed to make fertilisers, explosives and plastics.

Q2 a) Air **b)** Methane, crude oil, water.

Q3 a) To give a large surface area for the reactants to be in contact.
b) Speeds it up.
c) Turns ammonia gas into a liquid to be decanted off.
d) These conditions favour the reaction, making ammonia.
e) Molecules collide with less energy — less effective collisions and this would slow the rate of reaction.
f) **i)** $N_2 + 3H_2 \rightleftharpoons 2NH_3$
ii) equilibrium or reversible reaction
g) Despite the catalyst and favourable conditions the equilibrium still leaves much of the raw materials unreacted. This is compensated by recycling these gases for another pass around the chamber.

Q4 Expensive: need thicker piping and chambers which is less cost effective.

Q5 Ammonia; Haber Process; fertilisers; nitrogen; hydrogen; 450; pressure; 200; unreacted; recycled; molecules; hydrogen; molecule; nitrogen.

Q6 a)

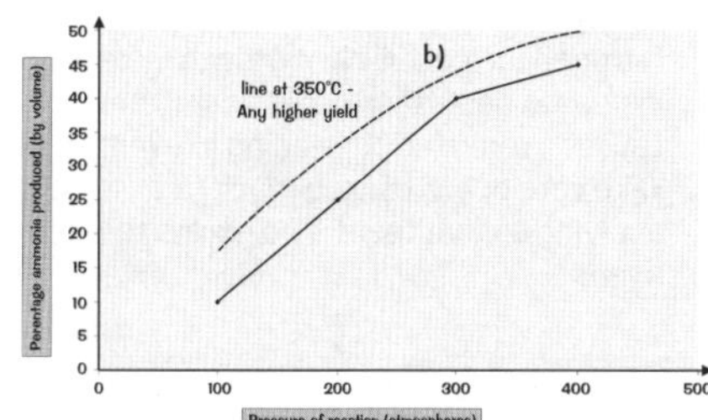

c) The reaction goes at a slower rate which is not economically viable.

Page 43 — Ammonia and Fertilisers

Q1 a) Gives out heat.
b) Increases the yield by moving the reaction equilibrium to the right hand side.
c) Since the forward reaction is exothermic, increasing the temperature will stimulate the reverse reaction to try to remove this excess heat. So the yield is lowered, but the rate is increased (poor yield produced fast).
d) At higher temperature the rate of reaction is greater. The lower yield is more than compensated by the much greater reaction rate.
e) Higher pressure brings the reactants closer together so the molecules collide much more frequently and react more often. The yield is increased because the forward reaction, which tries to reduce the pressure, is favoured. Thus increased pressure increases the yield.
f) Without the catalyst the rate is far too slow. Also enables reaction to take place at a lower temperature.

Module Seven — Patterns of Chemical Change

Q2 a) $4NH_{3\,(g)} + 5O_{2\,(g)} \rightarrow 4NO_{(g)} + 6H_2O_{(l)}$: nitrogen monoxide and water
b) Hot platinum catalyst
c) $4NO_{(g)} + 3O_{2\,(g)} + 2H_2O_{(g)} \rightarrow 4HNO_{3\,(g)}$
d) Nitric acid.
e) Neutralisation.
f) Ammonia + Nitric acid → Ammonium nitrate ($NH_{3(aq)} + HNO_{3(aq)} \rightarrow NH_4NO_{3(aq)}$ or $NH_4OH_{(aq)} + HNO_{3(aq)} \rightarrow NH_4NO_{3(aq)} + H_2O_{(1)}$)
g) Nitrogen.
h) For making proteins and chlorophyll.

Page 44 — Ammonia and Fertilisers

Q1 a) Natural fertilisers would have to be used (e.g. manure, potash)
b) Fewer crops could be grown (lower yields).

Q2 They are compounds such as ammonium nitrate. This hasn't been produced by living things like organic fertilisers.

Q3 Oxidised; fertilisers; nitrogen monoxide; cooled; water; oxygen; nitric acid; nitric acid; neutralised; ammonia; ammonium nitrate.

Q4 Soluble — but easily leached.

Q5 a) Bacteria
b) Oxygen — the fish suffocate and die
c) Eutrophication
d) Nitrogen increases, plant growth increases, and the increased population density competing for oxygen causes overcrowding, leading to eventual death.
e) Take care not to use too much fertiliser when applying so that there is no excess to leach into rivers.

16.4 — Reversible Reactions

Page 45 — Simple Reversible Reactions

Q1 a) $NH_3 + HCl \rightarrow NH_4Cl$ $NH_4Cl \rightarrow NH_3 + HCl$
b) Reversible reaction - the reaction goes both ways, reactants make products but products also break down to reactants.
c) $NH_3 + HCl \rightleftharpoons NH_4Cl$

Q2 a) Heat the blue crystals
b) Add water
c) $CuSO_4 + 5H_2O \rightleftharpoons CuSO_4.5H_20$

Q3 a) Balanced; equilibrium; equilibrium; static; down; up; activity; change; dynamic; dynamic; closed; open.
b) Dynamic.
c) Closed
d) Open system. There would cease to be an equilibrium.

Q4 a) Equilibrium being established
b) Point B represents equilibrium
c) This is a dynamic equilibrium

Page 46 — Simple Reversible Reactions

Q1 a) Increasing temperature will favour the products (reaction goes to right).
b) Increasing pressure will move equilibrium to left (to decrease volume, as fewer moles of gas on left).
c) Doubling the concentration of N_2O_4 will favour the products (send the reaction to the right).

Q2 a) Increasing pressure will favour products.
b) Increasing temperature will favour reactants.
c) Adding nitrogen will make more product.
d) Removing ammonia will also favour products.

Q3 a) $N_{2(g)} + 3H_{2(g)} \rightleftharpoons 2NH_{3(g)}$
b) Iron catalyst
c) Catalyst speeds up reaction.
d) Fine pellets have a large surface area - more contact area for reactants.
e) Optimum conditions from graph are high pressure and low temperature.
f) High pressure sends the reaction to the right and favours more product (4 moles of gas on left : only 2 on right).
g) Extreme high pressure is expensive and dangerous. 200 atms represents a working compromise. Lower temperatures give a higher percentage yield but take much longer to do so. 450 °C gives an acceptable yield very quickly (balance between % yield and RATE of reaction).

Q4 a) **i)** Increasing temperature would favour backward reaction (less product).
ii) Increasing pressure would favour products (3 moles of gas on left: 2 on right).
b) Optimum conditions would be low temperature and high pressure
c) High temperatures speeds up reaction. Less product more quickly is better economically than a large yield of product obtained over a very long time.
d) Extreme pressures (1000 atm) are expensive to achieve and dangerous - need really thick reaction vessels.

16.5 — Calculations

Page 47 — Relative Formula Mass

Q1 a) 40
b) 23
c) 56
d) 35.5
e) 27
f) 201

Q2 a) 2
b) 32
c) 71
d) 160
e) 28
f) 38

Q3 a) 80
b) 36.5
c) 58.5
d) 28
e) 103
f) 134

Module Eight — Structures and Bonding

Q4 a) 44
b) 18
c) 28
d) 233
e) 461
f) 102

Q5 a) 158
b) 154
c) 192
d) 74
e) 294
f) 331

Page 48 — Percentage Element in a Compound

Q1 a) 27.27% **k)** 82.35%
b) 42.86% **l)** 57.5%
c) 52.35% **m)** 36%
d) 54.76% **n)** 52.94%
e) 80% **o)** 51.61%
f) 50% **p)** 40%
g) 50% **q)** 38.61%
h) 40% **r)** 20.81%
i) 60% **s)** 35%
j) 11.11% **t)** 21.21%

Q2 a) M_r of CH_4 = 16 % carbon = $\frac{12}{16}$ x 100 = 75%

b) M_r of C_6H_6 = 78 % carbon = $\frac{72}{78}$ x 100 = 92.31%

c) M_r of C_2H_5OH = 46 % carbon = $\frac{24}{46}$ x 100 = 52.17%

C_6H_6 has the greatest proportion of carbon.

Q3 a) Al_2O_3

Q4 c) Magnetite (Fe_3O_4)

Q5 a) 39.32%
b) 28.57%
c) 100%
d) 69.64%

Q6 0.33%

Page 49 — Empirical Formulae

Q1 a) CH_3
b) Na_3AlF_6
c) NH_3
d) $N_2H_4O_3$

Q2 a) $AlCl_3$
b) sulphur trioxide — ratio of sulphur to oxygen in the compound is 1:3.
c) $Ca(OH)_2$ — calcium hydroxide
d) x = 5

Page 50 — Reacting Amounts Calculations

Q1 a) 8.8g **b)** 880g **c)** 5.6g

Q2 8.8g

Q3 112 tonnes.

Q4 230g of sodium.

Q5 14.336g

Q6 a) 1,889g (1.889kg)
b) 3,778g (3.778kg)
c) 8,500g (8.5kg)
d) 1,889kg (1.889 tonnes)

Q7 24g

Page 51 — Calculating Volumes

Q1 a) 48 litres
b) 2.4 litres
c) 2.4 litres
d) 476 cm^3
e) 6 litres
f) 60 litres
g) 2400 cm^3
h) 102 000 cm^3

Q2 a) 4 g **b)** 0.5 g **c)** 24 g **d)** 4 g
e) 28 g **f)** 21.25 g **g)** 16.5 g **h)** 21.4 g

17.1 — Bonding

Page 52 — Atoms and Molecules

Q1 a) A **b)** B, D or F **c)** C **d)** E **e)** B or D **f)** F **g)** D

Q2 Dalton

Q3

Name	Molecular formula	Structural formula	Molecular model
Water	H_2O	H–O–H	
Ammonia	NH_3	H–N(–H)–H	
Ethane	C_2H_6	H_3C–CH_3	
Carbon dioxide	CO_2	O=C=O	

Q4 A = silicon
B = oxygen
C = covalent bond

Module Eight — Structures and Bonding

Page 53 — Atoms

Q1 a) Smallest particle of an element with the properties of that element. The basic building block of all matter.
b) 3 main particles.
c) Protons, neutrons and electrons.
d) Small structure consisting of protons and neutrons at the centre of the atom making up almost all the mass.
e) A group of electrons with the same energy.

Q2 a) Nucleus **b)** Electron **c)** Shell

Q3

Particle	Mass	Charge	Where it is found
Proton	1	+1	In the nucleus
Electron	Negligible	-1	Orbiting the nucleus
Neutron	1	0	In the nucleus

Q4 a) In the nucleus. **b)** Empty space.

Q5 The electrons.

Q6 7

Q7 a) The number of protons.
b) The total number of protons and neutrons.
c) A = Mass number; Z = Atomic number; A–Z = number of n^0(neutrons).
d) 3 **e)** 3 **f)** 4
g) Atomic number (Z) indicate the number of protons/ electrons (which defines an element).

Q8 a) $p^+ = 6$, $e^- = 6$, $n^0 = 6$.
b) $p^+ = 19$, $e^- = 19$, $n^0 = 20$.
c) $p^+ = 1$, $e^- = 1$, $n^0 = 0$.

Q9 a) Isotopes are different atomic forms of the same element, which have the same number of protons but a different number of neutrons.
b) Carbon 14 (^{14}C).
c) No.

Page 54 — Electron Arrangement

Q1

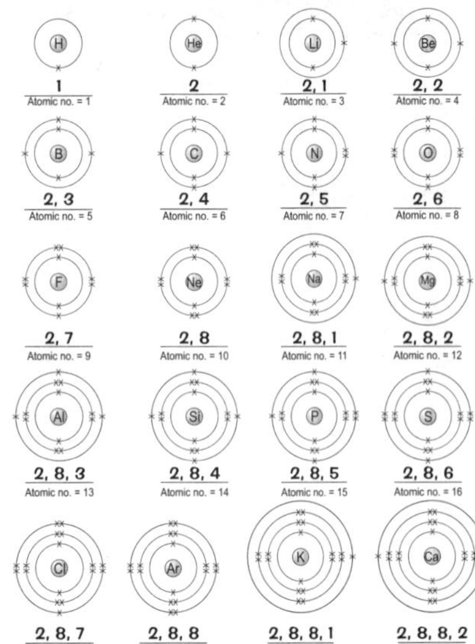

Page 55 — Covalent Bonding

Q1 A molecule is a group of atoms bonded together and capable of free existence.

Q2 Bonding.

Q3 One or more pairs of electrons.

Q4

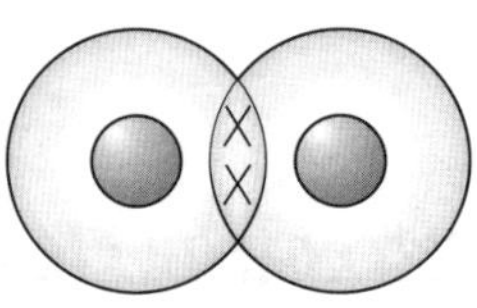

Q5 So they have a more stable, full outer shell of electrons.

Q6

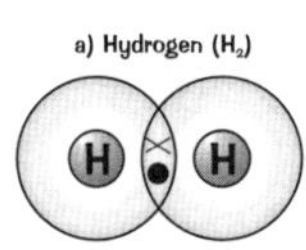

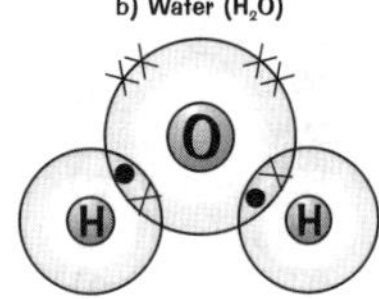

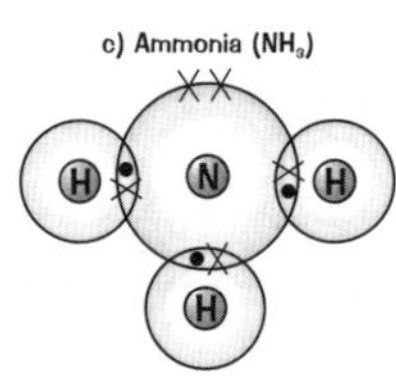

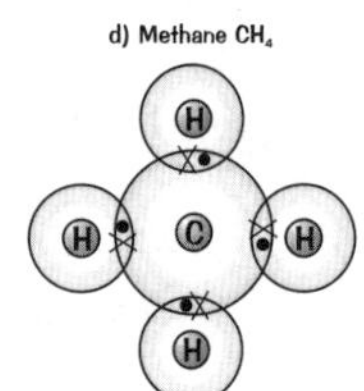

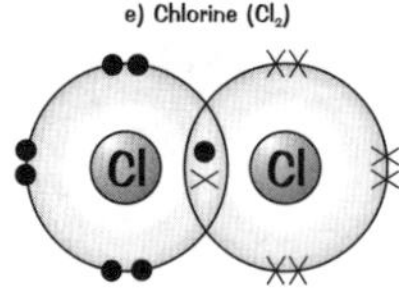

Q7 Sharing 2 pairs of electrons.

Q8

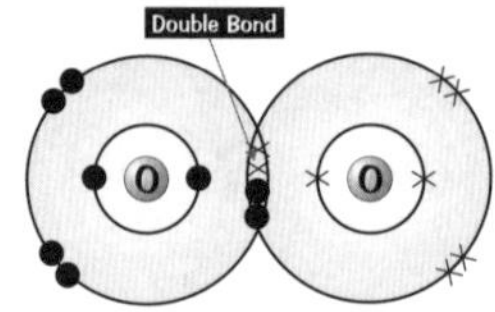

Module Eight — Structures and Bonding

Page 56 — Ions

Q1 a) An atom or molecule that is charged because it has gained or lost electrons.
b) Na^+, O^{2-} or any other sensible example.
c) NH_4^+, CO_3^{2-} or any other sensible example.
d) Neutral; protons; –ve; positively charged; negatively charged.

Q2

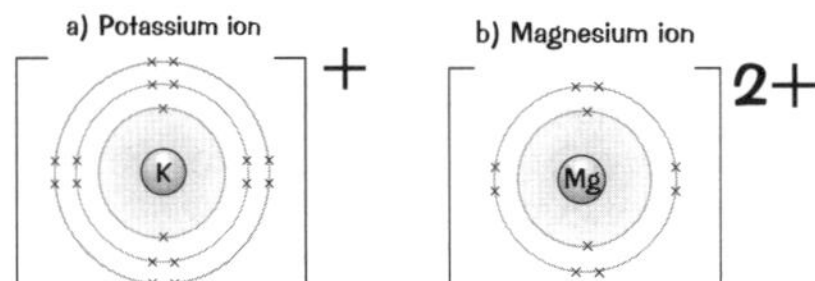

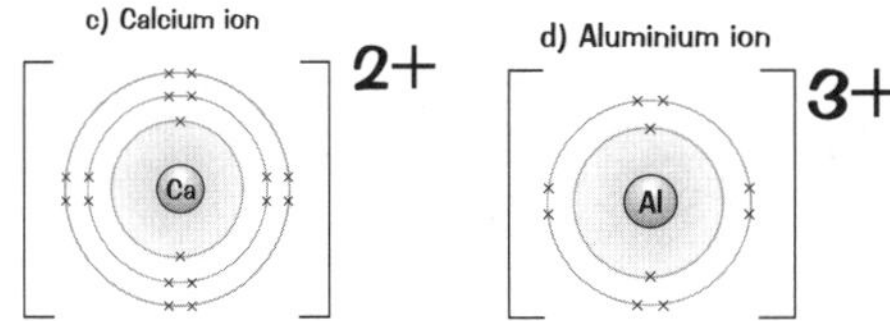

Q3

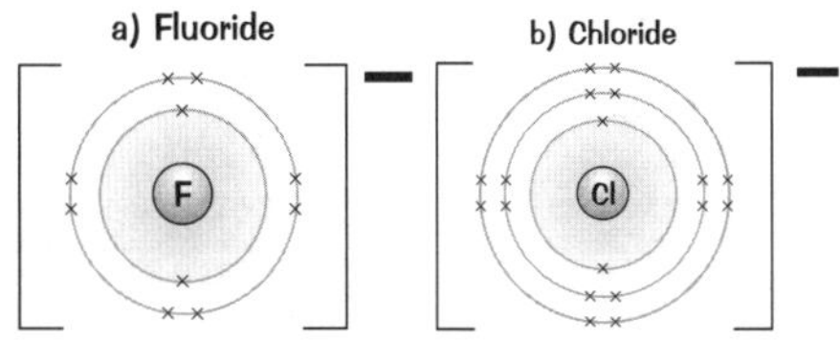

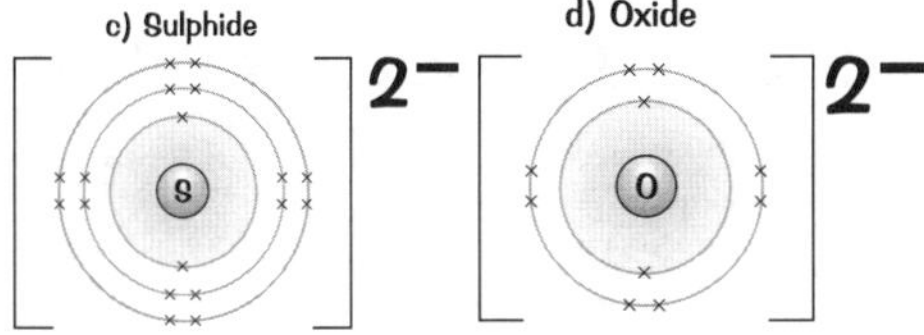

Q4 Positive.

Q5 Negative.

Page 57 — Ions

Q1 a) The electrostatic attraction between oppositely charged ions formed by losing or gaining electrons.
b) 1–
c) 1+
d) As they have lost an electron and thus have one more proton than electrons (only needed to lose one electron to have a full outer shell).
e) As they have gained an electron and thus have one more electron than protons (only needed to gain one electron to have a full outer shell).
f) 2+
g) 2–
h) To form a C^{4+} ion would take a massive amount of energy as four electrons are removed, so carbon normally bonds covalently.
i) A cation is a positively charged ion and an anion is a negatively charged ion.

Q2 a) Lithium chloride formed.

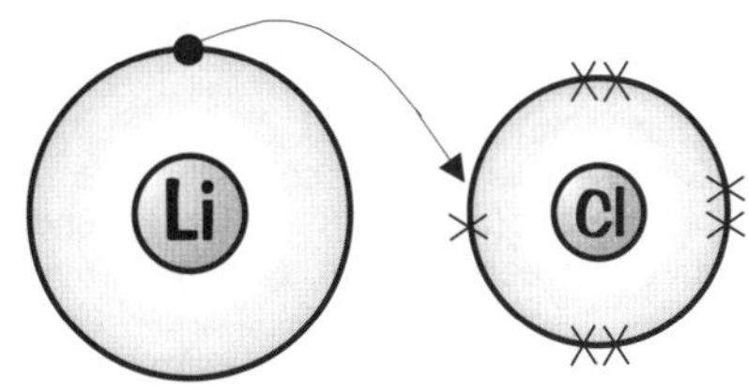

b)

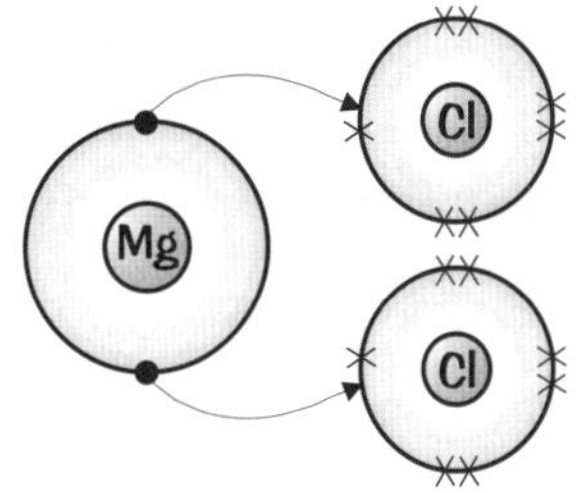

Q3 Equal number of positive and negative charges.

Q4

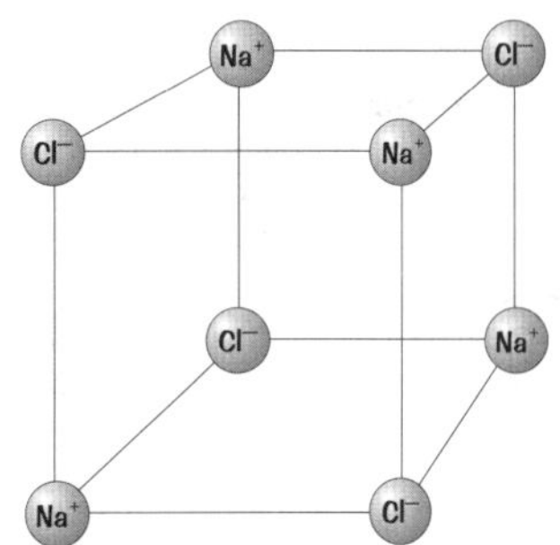

Q5
a) Sodium
b) Chloride
c) Sulphide
d) Nitrate
e) Sulphate
f) Iodide
g) Fluoride
h) Potassium
i) Calcium
j) Magnesium
k) Phosphate
l) Hydrogen
m) Barium

Q6 MgO, NaF, Na_2O, $MgSO_4$, Na_2SO_4.

Q7 a) Kr **b)** MgO **c)** CO_2 **d)** MgO or CO_2
e) SO_4^{2-} or Mg^{2+} **f)** SO_4^{2-}

Q8 a, b

Page 58 — Structures

Q1

Bonding	Structure	Melting point	Boiing point	Conductivity		
				Solid	Liquid	Aqueous solution
Ionic	Giant	HIGH	HIGH	Poor	Good	Good
Covalent	Giant	HIGH	HIGH	Poor	Poor	Poor
Covalent	Molecular	LOW	LOW	Poor	Poor	Poor
Metallic	Giant	HIGH	HIGH	Good	Good	Not applicable

Q2 It is the electrons that govern the chemical properties of substances and this effects the physical properties. **Agree** – use examples like molecular substances having low melting points. **Disagree** – use examples like diamond and graphite — same atoms but different physical properties of the different forms of carbon.

Module Eight — Structures and Bonding

Q3 Because applying a force to them (e.g. hitting a crystal with a hammer) will disrupt the ionic lattice and bring together like charges which repel, thus the crystal lattice will split.

Q4 Because when they are solid there are no free moving ions (they are all involved in bonding), but they are free to move in liquid form or in solution.

Q5 The water molecules split apart the ionic lattice (because of their dipole) and surround the separated ions, holding them in solution.

Q6 The atoms are held together by free moving electrons which fix the metal ions into a regular arrangement.

Q7 All the atoms in the structure are linked together in a large crystal lattice.

Q8 They are electrons from metal atoms in the lattice originating from the outer shells of electrons of each metal.

Q9 1) They allow it to conduct electricity
2) They allow the atoms to slide over each other, making the metal malleable.
3) They hold the atoms together in a regular structure.

Q10a) Energy
b) Vibrate more violently
c) The particles vibrate so violently that they separate from each other and become free to move.
d) The temperature at which the solid melts.
e) Move around more quickly.
f) When the temperature is high enough the particles have enough energy to overcome the attractive forces and escape from the liquid. The water turns into steam.

17.2 — Different Types of Substance

Page 59 — How Structure Affects Properties

Q1 a) Gases, liquids or solids which have relatively low melting points and boiling points and do not conduct electricity.
b) Water, oxygen, methane, nitrogen, hydrogen, chlorine or similar.
c) Low.
d) No.
e) Low boiling/melting points due to weak intermolecular forces. Don't conduct electricity as the molecules have no overall electrical charge.

Q2 Intermolecular, forces, strong, weak, easy, low, atoms, large, high, diamond, graphite, carbon, four, rigid, slip, no, one, graphite, diamond.

Q3 a) A substance consisting of many atoms covalently bonded together.
b) High.
c) The large number of covalent bonds in their structure.
d) Carbon.
e) Atoms in diamond have four bonds, atoms in graphite have three.
f) Graphite.
g) Silicon dioxide (silica).

17.3 — Periodic Table

Page 60 — The Periodic Table

Q1 a) Vertical column.
b) Horizontal row.
c) ~ 100.
d) Order of atomic number / proton number.
e) Same number of electrons in outer shell hence similar chemical properties, form similarly charged ions etc.
f) The number of shells of electrons that they have, regularly changing chemical properties, similar atomic mass.
g) Mendeleyev.
h) 1.
i) Group II.
j) Group VII.

Q2 a) H, I; **h)** F;
b) D; **i)** A, E;
c) B; **j)** H, I, C;
d) B; **k)** G;
e) C; **l)** A;
f) A; **m)** H,I.
g) C,D,G,H,I.

Q3 Na - 2,8,1 Al - 2,8,3
Be - 2,2 F - 2,7
Mg - 2,8,2 Cl - 2,8,7
B - 2,3 Ne - 2,8

Period	Group 1	Group 2	Group 3	Group 7	Group 0
2	Li 2, 1	Be 2, 2	B 2, 3	F 2, 7	Ne 2, 8
3	Na 2, 8, 1	Mg 2, 8, 2	Al 2, 8, 3	Cl 2, 8, 7	Ar 2, 8, 8

Page 61 — Group 0: The Noble Gases

Q1 a) They have 8 electrons in the outer shell (except for helium).
b) Non-reactive.
c) They have a full outer shell of electrons, making them stable so they have no need to react.
d) In order: Noble, 0, Periodic, full, shell, electrons, inert, low, increase, radon, helium, individual, diatomic, 1%.

Q2 a) Increase down the group.
b)

Noble Gas	Atomic Number	Density g/cm^3	Melting Point °C	Boiling Point °C
Helium	2	0.00017	-272	-269
Neon	10	0.00084	-248	-246
Argon	18	0.0016	-189	-186
Krypton	36	0.0034	-157	-153
Xenon	54	0.006	-112	-107
Radon	86	0.01	-71	-62

c) Increase in atomic radius

Q3 It gives out a bright light when a current is passed through it.

Q4 Light bulbs. Gives an inert atmosphere and stops burning of the filament.

Q5 Argon is denser than air, helium is less dense so the balloon rises rather than falls.

Module Eight — Structures and Bonding

Q6 a)

Noble Gas	Symbol	Atomic Number	Mass Number	No. of Protons	No. of Electrons	No. of Neutrons
Helium	He	2	4	2	2	2
Neon	Ne	10	20	10	10	10
Argon	Ar	18	40	18	18	22
Krypton	Kr	36	84	36	36	48
Xenon	Xe	54	131	54	54	77
Radon	Rn	86	222	86	86	136

b) **i)** neon **ii)** helium **iii)** argon, neon.

Page 62 — Group I: The Alkali Metals

Q1 a) Symbols: Li, Na, K, Rb.
b) i) Around 669°C.
ii) Around 29°C.
iii) Around 1.8g/cm^3 (any reasonable answer, following a pattern).
c) As you go down the group the atoms have more shells to accommodate more electrons.
d) Rubidium
e) The metallic bonds.
f) i) Rb between 39 and 688°C.
ii) K between 63 and 760°C.

Q2

Alkali Metal	No. P^+	No. N^0	No. E^-	Z	A
Lithium	3	4	3	3	7
Sodium	11	12	11	11	23
Potassium	19	20	19	19	39
Rubidium	37	48	37	37	85
Caesium	55	78	55	55	133

a)

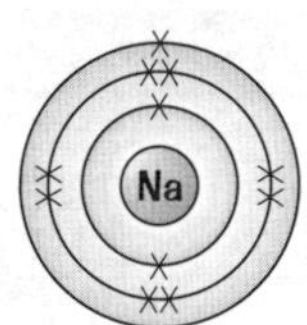

b) 1.
c) Easy to lose its outer electron.
d) Needs to lose an electron.
e) +1; there is now one more positive charge than negative charge in the atom overall.
f) It is an atom or group of atoms which has gained or lost electron(s) and so carries a negative or positive charge.

Q3 Cs, Rb, K, Na, Li. Reactivity increases down the group because the outermost electron moves further away from the nucleus, so is lost more easily.

Q4 A → 3, B → 1, C → 2.

Q5 a) Hydrogen.
Burning splint pops (ignites).
b) Sodium hydroxide + Hydrogen,
Lithium hydroxide + Hydrogen.
c) **i)** $2K_{(s)} + 2H_2O_{(l)} \rightarrow 2KOH_{(aq)} + H_{2\,(g)}$
ii) s; solid, l; liquid, aq; aqueous, g; gas.

Page 63 — Group VII: The Halogens

Q1 They all have 7 electrons in the outer shell.

Q2 a) Mpt 114°C or a sensible value close to this.
b) Melting point increases down the group, boiling point increases down the group.

Q3 a) Molecules contain two atoms each – Cl_2, Br_2, etc.
b) **i)** Cl_2 **ii)** I_2.

Q4 a)

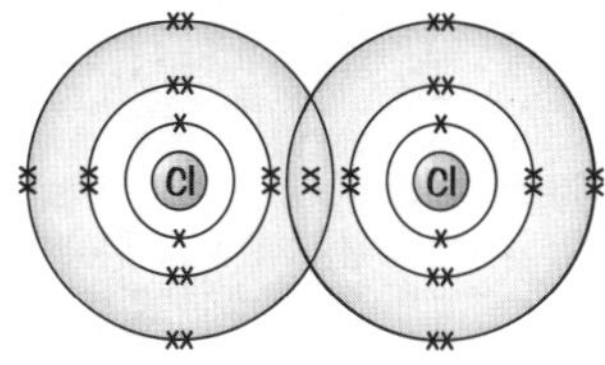

b) Covalent.

Q5 a) Ionic bond
b) 1–
c) A salt.
d) eg. CCl_4 (tetrachloromethane).

Q6 It becomes increasingly harder for the halogens to gain an electron (due to increased electron repulsion by inner shells), whereas it becomes increasingly easier for the alkali metals to lose an electron, as you go down the groups.

Q7 a) A compound containing a positive metal ion and a negative non-metal ion.
b) In the fume cupboard.
c) Iron chloride, aluminium bromide, tin chloride.
d) The salts are ionic compounds. The metal atoms lose electrons and from positive ions, the halogen atoms gain electrons and form negative ions. These attract each other and form an ionic bond.

Q8 a) Bromine (orange/brown) forming in the tube.
b) Chlorine.
c) Chlorine is more reactive than bromine, so displaces the bromine from the sodium bromide.
d) Chlorine + sodium bromide → sodium chloride + bromine.
e) **i)** $F_2 + 2NaI \rightarrow 2NaF + I_2$
ii) $Cl_2 + 2NaBr \rightarrow 2NaCl + I_2$
iii) No reaction
iv) $Br_2 + 2KI \rightarrow 2KBr + I_2$

17.4 — Groups of Elements

Page 64 — Electron Arrangement

Q1 a) The electrons orbit around the nucleus with the nucleus taking the part of the sun, and the electrons playing the role of the planets.
b) The negative charge of the electrons keeps them attracted to the positively charged nucleus.
c) Shell

Q2

Electron shell	Maximum number of electrons in the shell
1st	2
2nd	8
3rd	8

Module Eleven — Forces

Q3

Element	Symbol	Atomic Number	Mass Number	Number of Protons	Number of Electrons	Number of Neutrons	Electronic Configuration	Group Number
Hydrogen	H	1	1	1	1	0	1	—
Helium	He	2	4	2	2	2	2	0
Lithium	Li	3	7	3	3	4	2, 1	1
Beryllium	Be	4	9	4	4	5	2, 2	2
Boron	B	5	11	5	5	6	2, 3	3
Carbon	C	6	12	6	6	6	2, 4	4
Nitrogen	N	7	14	7	7	7	2, 5	5
Oxygen	O	8	16	8	8	8	2, 6	6
Fluorine	F	9	19	9	9	10	2, 7	7
Neon	Ne	10	20	10	10	10	2, 8	0
Sodium	Na	11	23	11	11	12	2, 8, 1	1
Magnesium	Mg	12	24	12	12	12	2, 8, 2	2
Aluminium	Al	13	27	13	13	14	2, 8, 3	3
Silicon	Si	14	28	14	14	14	2, 8, 4	4
Phosphorus	P	15	31	15	15	16	2, 8, 5	5
Sulphur	S	16	32	16	16	16	2, 8, 6	6
Chlorine	Cl	17	35	17	17	18	2, 8, 7	7
Argon	Ar	18	40	18	18	22	2, 8, 8	0
Potassium	K	19	39	19	19	20	2, 8, 8, 1	1
Calcium	Ca	20	40	20	20	20	2, 8, 8, 2	2

Q4 a) The number of outer electrons determines the group that the element is in.
b) All noble gases have a full outer shell / Every element with a full outer shell in its atoms is a noble gas.
c) 7
d) 8
e) Properties.

Q5 a) It's in group 2 — alkaline Earth metals.
b) Metal
c) Any group 2 element, e.g. magnesium, calcium.

17.5 — Compounds of Halogens

Page 65 — Industrial Salt

Q1 Put on the roads to stop them icing over.

Q2 In the sea and in underground deposits.

Q3 Washed out of deposits using high pressure water.

Q4 Brine

Q5 Decomposition of a salt using electricity.

Q6 a) Brine
b) Electrolysis can only happen when there are ions free to move – this occurs in solution (or when molten).

Q7 Industrial, rock salt, brine, electrolysis, $Na^+ + Cl^-$, chloride, lose, chlorine, chlorine atoms, chlorine molecule, H^+, gain, hydrogen, hydrogen atoms, hydrogen molecule, sodium hydroxide.

Q8 Cl_2 — bleaches damp litmus, H_2 — lighted splint "pops".

Page 66 — Uses of Halogens and Salt Products

Q1 $Cl_{2\,(g)} + 2NaOH_{(aq)} \rightarrow NaOCl_{(aq)} + NaCl_{(aq)} + H_2O_{(l)}$.

Q2 Disinfectant, plastics (first gas used as weapon in WWI).

Q3 Soap manufacture, oven cleaner, organic chemical production.

Q4 Sodium hydroxide, hydrogen, chlorine, chlorine, hydrogen chloride, hydrocarbon, fats, margarine, sodium hydroxide, oven cleaners, textiles.

Q5 $2Cl^- + 2e^- — Cl_2$

Q6 Light, X-rays and radiation from radioactive substances.

Q7 Making photographic film and paper.

Q8 You would get an acidic solution.

17.6 — Symbols, Formulae and Equations

Page 67 — Symbols, Formulae and Equations

Q1 Hydrogen (H), Helium (He), Lithium (Li), Beryllium (Be), Boron (B), Carbon (C), Nitrogen (N), Oxygen (O), Fluorine (F), Neon (Ne), Sodium (Na), Magnesium (Mg), Aluminium (Al), Silicon (Si), Phosphorus (P), Sulphur (S), Chlorine (Cl), Argon (Ar), Potassium (K), Calcium (Ca).

Q2 Fe, Pb, Zn, Sn, Cu.

Q3

Name	Formula	Proportion of each element present in substance
Zinc oxide	ZnO	1 zinc 1 oxygen
Magnesium oxide	MgO	1 magnesium 1 oxygen
Sodium chloride	$NaCl$	1 sodium 1 chlorine
Hydrochloric acid	HCl	1 hydrogen 1 chlorine
Sulphur dioxide	SO_2	1 sulphur 2 oxygen
Carbon dioxide	CO_2	1 carbon 2 oxygen
Sodium hydroxide	$NaOH$	1 sodium 1 oxygen 1 hydrogen
Potassium hydroxide	KOH	1 potassium 1 oxygen 1 hydrogen
Calcium carbonate	$CaCO_3$	1 calcium 1 carbon 3 oxygen
Copper sulphate	$CuSO_4$	1 copper 1 sulphur 4 oxygen
Sulphuric acid	H_2SO_4	2 hydrogen 1 sulphur 4 oxygen
Iron(III) oxide	Fe_2O_3	2 Iron 3 oxygen
Magnesium chloride	$MgCl_2$	1 magnesium 2 chlorine
Hydrogen	H_2	2 hydrogen
Chlorine	Cl_2	2 chlorine

Q4 Chloride; Oxide; Sulphide

Q5 a) Sodium bromide
b) Sodium fluoride
c) Oxygen
d) Oxygen (less than when end is -ate)
e) Sodium, fluorine, phosphorus, oxygen.

Q6 a) Sodium + chlorine → sodium chloride
b) Carbon + oxygen → carbon dioxide
c) Sulphur + oxygen → sulphur dioxide
d) Zinc + oxygen → zinc oxide
e) Iron + sulphur → iron sulphide
f) Potassium + chlorine → potassium chloride
g) Lead + oxygen → lead oxide
h) Calcium + oxygen → calcium oxide

Module Eleven — Forces

Page 68 — Equations

Q1 a) Iron sulphide.
b) Iron oxide.
c) Magnesium oxide.
d) Sulphur dioxide.
e) Water.
f) Magnesium sulphide.
g) Aluminium chloride.
h) Hydrogen iodide.
i) Carbon dioxide.

Q2 a) Gas, aqueous, solid. (l) might be used, for liquid.
b) The 2 shows that 2 moles of HCl are used for every mole of Mg.
c) Because Mg is a 2+ ion, and Cl is a 1- ion. 2 Cl^- ions are needed to balance out the 2+ charge of the Mg^{2+} ion.
d) Because hydrogen molecules contain two hydrogen atoms.
e) **i)** $2KI + Cl_2 \rightarrow 2KCl + I_2$ **ii)** $2Na + Cl_2 \rightarrow 2NaCl$
iii) $4Li + O_2 \rightarrow 2Li_2O$ **iv)** $2Li + 2H_2O \rightarrow 2LiOH + H_2$
v) $MgCO_3 + 2HCl \rightarrow MgCl_2 + H_2O + CO_2$

Page 69 — Equations

Q1 a) $C + O_2 \rightarrow CO_2$
b) $Zn + H_2SO_4 \rightarrow ZnSO_4 + H_2$
c) $Cu + 2Cl \rightarrow CuCl_2$
d) $H_2 + CuO \rightarrow Cu + H_2O$
e) $Mg + H_2SO_4 \rightarrow MgSO_4 + H_2$

Q2 a) $N_2 + 3H_2 \rightarrow 2NH_3$
b) $CaCO_3 + H_2SO_4 \rightarrow CaSO_4 + H_2O + CO_2$
c) $2H_2 + O_2 \rightarrow 2H_2O$
d) $2Mg + O_2 \rightarrow 2MgO$
e) $Mg + H_2SO_4 \rightarrow MgSO_4 + H_2$
f) $H_2SO_4 + 2NaOH \rightarrow Na_2SO_4 + 2H_2O$
g) $Ca + H_2SO_4 \rightarrow CaSO_4 + H_2$
h) $H_2SO_4 + 2KOH \rightarrow K_2SO_4 + 2H_2O$
i) $Fe_2O_3 + 3CO \rightarrow 2Fe + 3CO_2$
j) $C_6H_{12}O_6 + 6O_2 \rightarrow 6CO_2 + 6H_2O$
k) $6CO_2 + 6H_2O \rightarrow C_6H_{12}O_6 + 6O_2$
l) $2C_4H_{10} + 13O_2 \rightarrow 8CO_2 + 10H_2O$
m) $C_2H_4 + 3O_2 \rightarrow 2CO_2 + 2H_2O$
n) $C_3H_8 + 5O_2 \rightarrow 3CO_2 + 4H_2O$
o) $C_5H_{12} + 8O_2 \rightarrow 5CO_2 + 6H_2O$
p) $2C_3H_6 + 9O_2 \rightarrow 6CO_2 + 6H_2O$
q) $2C_2H_6 + 7O_2 \rightarrow 4CO_2 + 6H_2O$

20.1 — Describing Motion

Page 70 — Speed, Distance and Time

Q1 a) 10 m/s **b)** 20 m/s
c) 2.5 m/s **d)** 0.1 m/s

Q2 a) 17.14 m/s — he is probably right.
b) 10s
c) 30s

Q3 a) 2700m **b)** 16250m
c) 15000m **d)** 17500m

Q4 How, fast, direction, direction.

Q5 a) 20 m/s
b) The car will be speeding up and slowing down in traffic. It will take corners slowly, etc
c) 30 km

Q6 a) 42 m/s **b)** 1.3 m/s

Q7 a) 36 km **b)** 125 km

Q8 20 m/s North

Page 71 — Velocity and Acceleration

Q1 a) 8 hr **b)** 8 mins. 20 secs.

Q2 2 m/s East

Q3 90 m/s South East.

Q4 a) 1.4 m/s North-East
b) 1.7 m/s South-West
c) 1.2 m/s including rest
1.5 m/s excluding rest

Q5 a) a is the acceleration, ΔV is the change in velocity and Δt is the time taken.
b) m/s^2, m/s and s.
c) Acceleration is used to describe the **rate** of change in velocity. Its units are m/s^2. Velocity is used to describe the rate of change of position in m/s.

Q6 Acceleration, second, velocity, 3 m/s, acceleration, second, velocity, 4 m/s.

Q7 a) 54 km.
b) 128 km/h, 35.6 m/s.
c) 25 seconds.
d) 7.2 km.
e) 1.87 m/s^2

Page 72 — Describing Motion Graphically

Q1 a) 225 metres.
b) The car continues to move at a steady velocity of 15 m/s.
c)

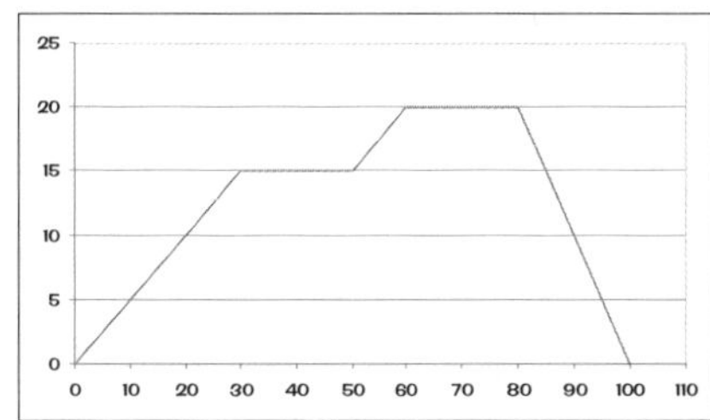

d) 0.5 m/s^2.
e) 1 m/s^2.
f) 600 m.

Module Eleven — Forces

Q2 a) 800m
b) $1.5 m/s^2$
c) 500m
d) Riding at constant speed 10m/s
e) 1.5 km.

Q3 a) Steady speed then stationary, then steady speed in opposite direction.

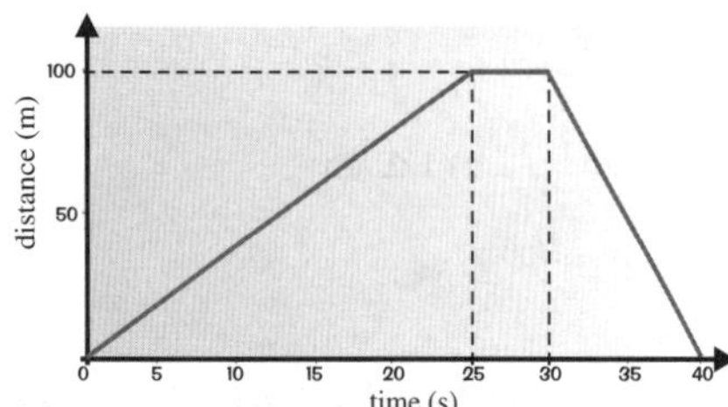

b) 4m/s
c) 5s
d) 10m/s.
e) 200m

20.2 — Speeding Up or Slowing Down

Page 73 — Mass, Weight and Gravity

Q1 Attraction, bodies, weak, large, strong, field, weight, newtons, centre

Q2 **Mass:** amount of matter; measured by a balance; not a force; same anywhere in the universe; measured in kilograms.
Weight: measured in Newtons; is a force; measured by a spring balance (newton meter); caused by the pull of gravity; is lower on the moon than on the earth.

Q3 a) "Weighs" refers to weight, whereas 1kg is its mass. You ought to say,
b) **"**This bag of flour weighs 10N, and it has a mass of 1kg.**"**
c)

Mass (g)	Mass (kg)	Weight (N)
5	0.005	0.05
10	0.010	0.10
100	0.1	1
200	0.2	2
500	0.5	5
1000	1.0	10
5000	5.0	50

Q4 a) 50N **b)** 100N
c) 25N **d)** 3kg
e) 15kg **f)** 45kg

Q5 a) 8N **b)** 16N
c) 4N **d)** 10kg
e) 50kg **f)** 600kg

Page 74 — Force, Mass and Acceleration

Q1 a) Gravity or weight.
b) Drag or air resistance or friction.
c) Tension.
d) Lift.
e) Thrust, push or pull.
f) Reaction force.

Q2 a) Weight (down) and reaction (up).
b) The object is not accelerating.
c) It would accelerate in the direction of that force.

Q3 Weight down, tension up (in line).

Q4 a) Weight down, reaction up.
b) Thrust forward, drag backwards (both equal).

Q5 Faster; unbalanced; greater; force; greater; smaller; thrust; drag; weight; reaction; downwards; drag; upwards.

Page 75 — Force, Mass and Acceleration

Q1 a) Greater.
b) Greater.

Q2 a) 5N.
b) Increasing: putting a load on the wood, making the wood/surface rougher
b) Decreasing: making the wood/surface smoother (polish). Use a lubricant

Q3 **(a)**, **(b)** and **(d)** minimise friction. **(c)** maximises friction for better grip.

Q4 Useful: saddle, handlebar grips, pedals, tyres, brakes. Nuisance: air resistance, wheel bearings.

Q5 a) Skidding car, floor polisher, bicycle brakes.
b) Rubbing hands together to keep them warm. Boy Scout method of starting a fire by rubbing two sticks together.
c) Lubricants e.g. oil/grease - careful machining of parts.
d) It will seize up as the extreme heat causes the parts to weld together.
e) Heating and wear greater. The faster the car goes, the greater the energy expended by brakes to slow it down.

Page 76 — Force, Mass and Acceleration

Q1 a) Time taken for the driver to react and start braking; Time taken for car to come to a complete stop once the brakes have been applied.
b) Any of : Travelling at high speed.
Driver's reactions slower (tiredness, drugs, alcohol).
Adverse weather conditions.
Poorly maintained vehicle.
c) Tyres lose their grip and the car can skid.

Module Eleven — Forces

Q2 Force, accelerate, decelerate, direction, starting, stopping, speeding up, slowing down, unequal.

Q3 a) F=ma
b) a=F/m
c) $1m/s^2$.

Q4 a) $10m/s^2$
b) $20m/s^2$
c) $30m/s^2$

Q5 18 m/s

Q6 a) 450N
b) 450N
c) 1 m/s^2 in the opposite direction to Coco.

Page 77 — Force, Mass and Acceleration

Q1 Forces, direction, overall, motion, accelerate, decelerate, steady, adding, subtracting, same, resultant.

Q2 a)

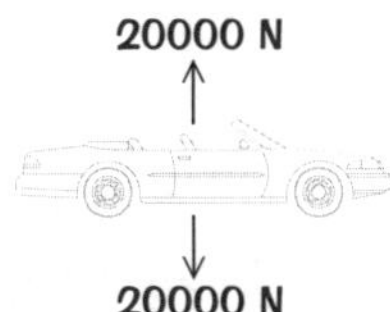

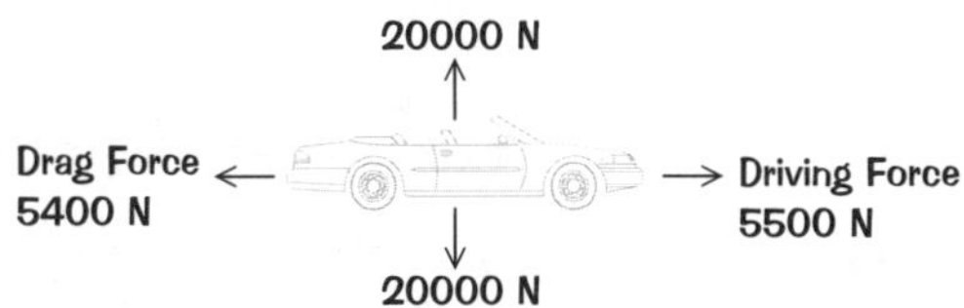

b) $2.75m/s^2$
c) $0.05m/s^2$.

Q3 a) Gravity.
b) Drag.
c) Terminal Velocity.
d) Parachute.
e) Aerodynamic or Streamlined.

Q4 a) 60.0m/s
b) (i) 19.5m/s (ii) 45.0m/s
c) 18s
d) The additional drag of the parachute gives rise to a resultant upward force that decelerates her. As she slows down, the upward drag force decreases until it balances her weight, at which point she reaches a terminal velocity
e) Yes. Speed decreases until drag equals weight.

Q5 a) 50N; right
b) 0.5N; up
c) 15N; up
d) 0.05N; down

20.3 — Energy

Page 78 — Work and Energy

Q1 a) Joules (J).

Work Done
6.72J
4.48J
5.76J
8.26J
4.05J

b) Friction.
c) 2025 J.

Q2 a) 1 050 000 J = 1050 kJ = 1.05 MJ
b) 1170 kJ
c) 955 kJ. Yes, I would save energy, provided that I could push the car up the hill.

Q3 a) Scott - 190 kJ; Sheila - 170 kJ.
b) The motor would not be 100% efficient, and the motor will also be doing work pushing the boat and driver along.
c) 219.4 kJ

20.4 — Orbits

Page 79 — Orbits

Q1 a) False – planets are observed because of the light that they reflect from the sun.
b) True – all the planets in the solar system orbit around the sun, a very massive object.
c) False – all planets follow elliptical orbits with the sun at one focus of the ellipse.

Q2 a)

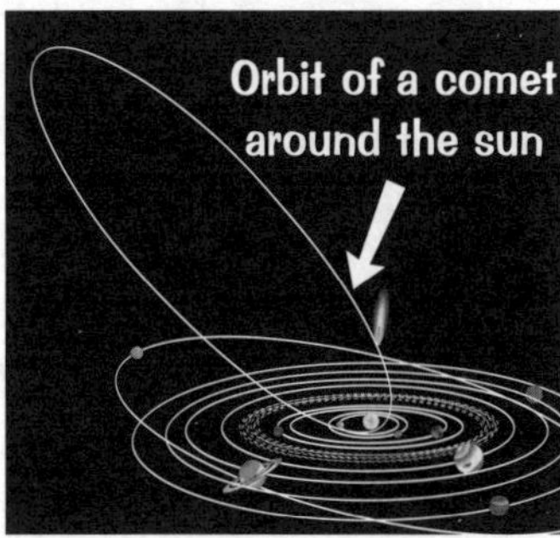

b) Ellipse (elliptical).
c) A comet's orbit is more eccentric (elongated) than a planet's orbit, which is almost circular.

Module Eleven — Forces

Q3 a) **1.** There is no distortion or blurring caused by the atmosphere.
2. Can receive all wavelengths of radiation.
3. 24hr viewing possible, in any direction away from the sun.
b) **1.** It is easier to see much greater detail, and further into space.
2. Many different instruments for detecting the different radiations can be fixed to one telescope.
3. Cost-effective, and viewing not interrupted by the weather.

Q4 a) Ganymede.
b) Callisto.
c) It is further away from Jupiter.
d) Jupiter's moons are attracted to Jupiter due to Jupiter's gravitational force acting upon them. Jupiter's moons also have a gravitational force that acts upon Jupiter however this attraction is smaller as the moons are much smaller. Smaller bodies orbit around larger bodies due to the imbalance in gravitational forces.

Page 80 — Orbits

Q1 a) A, D, F, H.
b) B, C, D, E, G.
c) B, C, E, G.
d) A, D, F, H.

Q2 The shuttle does not orbit the earth in a geostationary orbit, so there is not always a direct-line view of one point on the Earth's surface (where the station would be).

Q3 a) True
b) False, as the distance between two bodies increases the attractive force between them decreases more than in proportion to the increase in distance.
c) False, the nearer an orbiting body is the shorter the time taken to make a complete orbit.
d) False, to stay in orbit at a fixed distance, smaller bodies must travel at a fixed speed.
e) False, comets' orbits are far from circular.
f) True.
g) False, monitoring satellites are usually put in a low polar orbit.

Q4 Increased the amount of oxygen in the Earth's atmosphere.

20.5 — Universe and Stars

Page 81 — The Universe

Q1 a) Astronomers are looking for chemical changes in the atmospheres of planets that could be caused by the presence of living organisms. The Earth's atmosphere has changed greatly due to the presence of life, there is more oxygen and less carbon dioxide than would be present if there were no life. Reflected light from the surface of planets can also give clues to the presence of water.
b) **S**earch for **E**xtra **T**errestrial **I**ntelligence, SETI looks for radio signals from other planets.
c) If the signal was made from a narrow band of wavelengths.
d) Robots can be used to explore other planets, collecting samples and taking photographs.

Q2 Supernova, gas, neutron star, matter, dense, gravitional, light, electromagnetic, black hole, X-rays, stars.

Q3 a) The Milky Way is the galaxy that we are located in.
b) The Milky Way is a spiral, disc shaped galaxy. When viewing the milky band of light stretching across the sky, you are looking into, and across, this disc of stars.

Page 82 — The Universe

Q1 a) True. **b)** False. **m)** True.
c) False. **d)** False.
e) False. **f)** True.
g) True. **h)** True.
i) False. **j)** True.
k) True. **l)** False.
Q2 a) Nuclei of lighter elements gradually fuse together to produce nuclei of heavier elements.
b) Hydrogen and Helium.
c) That the solar system was formed from the material produced when the early stars exploded.

Q3 a) Red-shift.
b) More.
c) That the universe was formed in one place with a huge explosion.
d) The Big Bang Theory.

Page 83 — The Life Cycle of Stars

Q1 a) Gravitational attraction.
b) Heat inside the star gives rise to very high pressures which lead to an outwards force.
c) They are both balanced hence the Sun is stable.
d) It is much denser (tonnes per cm^3).
e) The life span of a typical star is billions of years. Unfortunately, astronomers haven't been around for that long and are unlikely to be so in the future! So they examine many different stars of different ages to get the big picture.

21.1 Light and Sound Waves

Page 84 — Waves — Basic Principles

Q1 a) Longitudinal, transverse.
b) Frequency, hertz (Hz).
c) Period, seconds (s).
d) Amplitude.
e) Crest or peak.
f) Trough.
g) Speed, metres per second (m/s).
h) Refraction.
i) Diffraction.

Q2 Energy.

Q3 a) Oscillation
b) Shake hand faster.
c) Increase distance of hand movement.
d) Insufficient tension in the string means that a wave will not be transmitted effectively.

Module Twelve — Waves and Radiation

Q4 a) 0.2Hz. **b)** 3m.
c) 3m. **d)** 5s.
e) 0.6m. **f)** 0.6m/s.
g) Up and down.

Q5 a) Correct equations are:
Speed = frequency × wavelength, v = fl.
Wavelength = speed / frequency, l = v/f.
Frequency = speed / wavelength, f = v/l.

Page 85 — Reflection and Refraction

Q1 a) Reflect.
b) Clear, Shiny.
c) Diffuse, dull.
d) Reflection, equal, incidence.

Q2 A ray.

Q3 The normal.

Q4

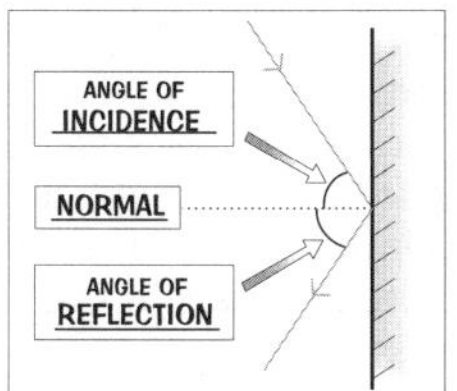

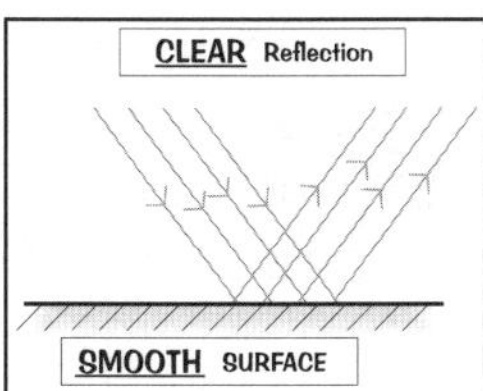

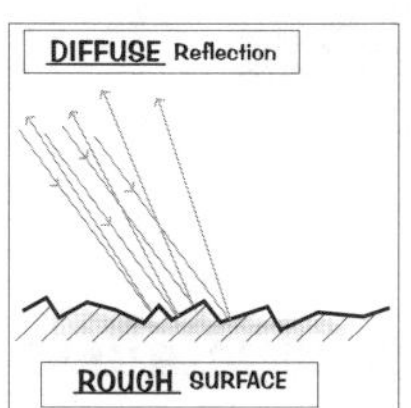

Q5 Person 1 can see statue C and person 2 can see statues A and D.

Q6 a) Speeds.
b) Slow down.
c) Speed up.
d) Boundary.

Q7 It is the line at right-angles to the surface.

Q8 No.

Page 86 — Diffraction

Q1 a) Diagram 1: *X*;
b) Diagram 2: *B*.

Q2 Towards, Away from.

Q3 a) Spread out (or change direction), gap, obstacle.
b) Diffraction.
c) Smaller (narrower).
d) Wavelength, semicircular.

Q4 a) 440Hz. Yes.
b) 6×10^{-7} m.
c) A sound wave has a wavelength similar to the size of the doorway (75cm), so it will be diffracted significantly. But the wavelength of light is about a million times smaller than the gap and there is virtually no diffraction, so we can't see around corners!

Q5 a) Yes, signal will be received behind flats
b) No significant diffraction
c) Some diffraction; this, together with reflection of the sound of the walls will help sound to be heard throughout the room.

Q6 a)

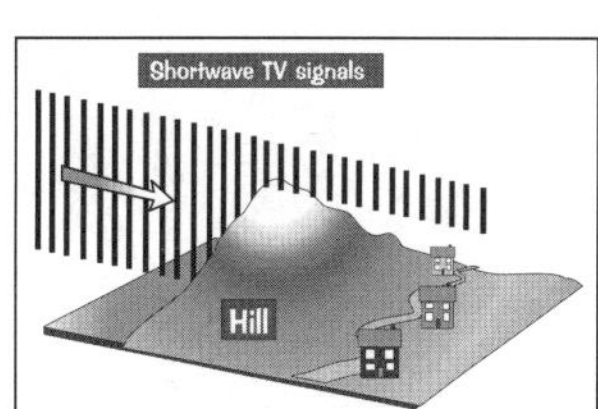

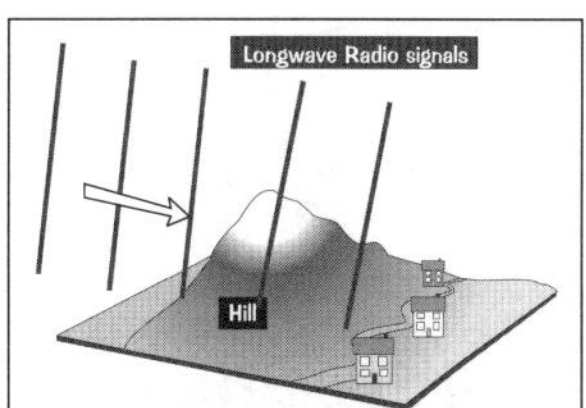

b) Mountains diffract longwave radiowaves more effectively than TV signals, leading to a better reception in mountainous areas.

21.2 — The EM Spectrum

Page 87 — The EM Spectrum

Q1 a) Spectrum, medium, speed, vacuum, speed, seven, radio waves, micro waves, infra red, visible light, ultra violet, x-rays, gamma rays.
b) Radio, longest, gamma rays, shortest, visible light.

Q2 **a**, **c**, **e**, **h**, **i**, and **j** are correct. **f** is debatable as X-rays are *relatively* safe compared with the high risks of investigative surgery including death under anaesthetic, post-operative shock and infection, but are still highly hazardous.
b) Replace microwaves with infra red.
d) Replace visible light with all EM waves.
g) Replace infra red with ultraviolet.
f) Ultrasound might be suggested as an alternative to X-rays for medical imaging but the two techniques give very different results which is why X-rays are still widely used.

Q3 a) Order in the diagram should read:
Gamma rays: 10^{-12} m 3×10^{20} Hz
X-rays: 10^{-10} m 3×10^{18} Hz
Ultra Violet: 10^{-8} m 3×10^{16} Hz
Visible Light: 10^{-7} m 3×10^{15} Hz
Infrared: 10^{-5} m 3×10^{13} Hz
Microwaves: 10^{-2} m 3×10^{10} Hz
Radio waves: 10^{0} m 3×10^{8} Hz
b) 300,000,000 m/s.
d) 1000.
e) 100,000.

Module Twelve — Waves and Radiation

Page 88 — The EM Spectrum

Q1 A microwave or quite a short radiowave.

Q2 1×10^{10} Hz (10,000,000,000Hz).

Q3 a) Critical angle;

b) Total internal reflection; periscopes; reflectors (e.g. bicycle).

c) **i)** Boosted/amplified; **ii)** Data/information; **iii)** Tapped into; interference; **iv)** Reflection; boosting/amplifying

d) endoscope

Q4

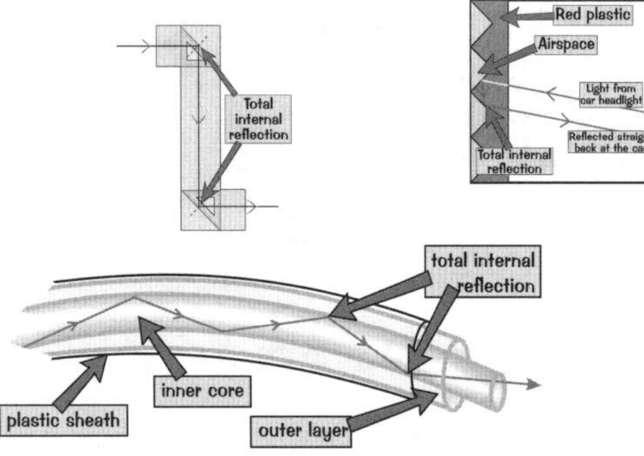

Page 89 — The EM Spectrum

Q1

Type of Radiation	Effects on Living Tissue	Uses
Gamma	• kills living cells in high doses • lower doses can cause cells to become cancerous	• kill bacteria in food • sterilise medical equipment • treat tumours
X-Ray	• kills living cells in high doses • lower doses can cause cells to become cancerous	• imaging internal structures in the body • studying the atomic structure of materials
UV	• kills living cells in high doses • lower doses can cause cells to become cancerous • causes tanning	• fluorescent tubes • tanning • security marking
Visible	• activates sensitive cells in the retina	• seeing • optical fibre communication
IR	• causes burning of tissues	• radiant heaters • grills • remote controls • thermal imaging
Microwave	• heating of water in tissues can cause "burning"	• satellite communication • cooking
Radio	• probably none	• communication • broadcasting • radar

Q2 a) Heat; electricity (alternating current with the same frequency as the radiation itself).

b) More.

c) By covering her skin with a barrier, e.g. clothes, sun lotion, or by reducing the amount of time she spends in the sun.
Infrared radiation can damage cells, Ultra Violet radiation can cause cancer.

d) By using lead screens, and limiting himself to short doses.

Page 90 — Digital and Analogue Signals

Q1 a) Digital and analogue.

b) The amplitude and frequency of analogue signals vary continuously. Digital signals are coded pulses, and have one of only two values.

c) Analogue: mobile phone, watch, dimmer switches;
Digital: mobile phone, watch, computers, on/off switches.

Q2 a) FALSE - analogue varies, not digital.

b) TRUE.

c) TRUE.

d) TRUE.

e) TRUE.

f) FALSE - analogue signals lose quality, not digital.

g) TRUE.

Q3 a) Because as signals travel, they become weaker.

b) They pick up noise (random additions).

c) Digital signals retain their original form exactly; analogue ones are altered by amplification.

d) With analogue signals, different frequencies are weakened to different extents, and noise is added. When this is amplified, the resulting waveform is not true to the original. In digital transmission, even a weak signal is taken to be ON, whereas noise is usually of such low-amplitude that it is taken as OFF. Thus when digital signals are amplified, the signal reverts to the original.

Q4

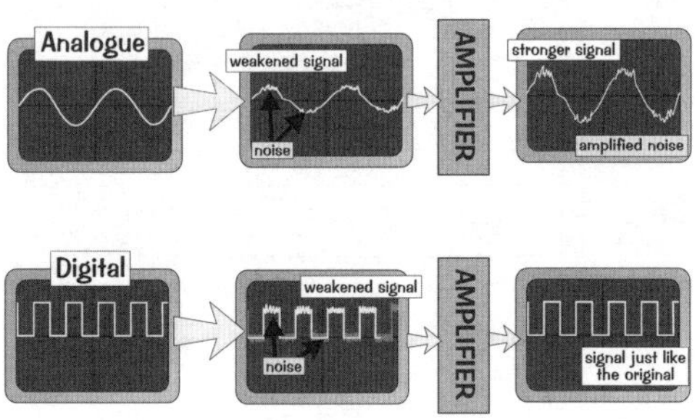

21.3 — Radioactive Substances

Page 91 — Radioactive Substances

Q1 a) Hand stops alpha, thin aluminium stops beta. Thick lead stops gamma.

b) Alpha particles are relatively slow moving and are charged. They also lose energy quickly in collisions (while ionising the atoms of the material).

Q2 a) Ionisation is the process of removing electrons from an atom.

b) Electron, argon ion.

c) The electrons move to the top (+ve) plate and the argon ions move to the (–ve) plate. Electrons travel around the circuit to combine with these argon ions. (Neutral argon atoms are formed at the –ve plate).

d) There can be no ionisation in a vacuum (no atoms to ionise), so there are no moving charges, and therefore no current.

Module Twelve — Waves and Radiation

Q3 a) A tracer is a substance used to follow the movements of a particular chemical. (The tracer should flow in the same way as the chemical of interest and be easily detectable).
b) The thyroid gland. This is where iodine is absorbed in the body.
c) Gamma radiation.
d) **1.** Alpha particles would be absorbed in the neck preventing detection.
2. The radiation would be more harmful.

Q4 a) Gamma rays kill them.
b) The doses of gamma rays kill healthy cells too — destroying a large number of cells can disrupt life processes, like fighting infection, and the patient can become ill.
c) The location(s) of the tumour(s) need to be identified accurately. The minimum dose needed to just kill the tumour(s) and the course of treatment also needs to be worked out.

Page 92 — Effects of Radiation

Q1 a) Alpha, beta and gamma (also X-rays).
b) Ionisation.
c) The nucleus.
d) A mutant cell.
e) They divide uncontrollably (sometimes forming a tumour).
f) Cancer.

Q2 a) Alpha will cause the most damage.
b) Alpha causes the most ionisation owing to its relatively large charge. This means alpha radiation will be totally absorbed in a short distance — the damage is concentrated and so is more likely to kill cells.

Q3 i) The type of radiation.
ii) The energy of the radiation.
iii) The amount of radiation absorbed.
iv) The part of the body exposed.
v) The length of time exposed.
vi) Luck. Damage is random

Q4 Beta and gamma. They have more penetrating power and can get through the skin. Most alpha radiation is stopped by the skin

Q5 Alpha. All its energy is absorbed by the organs inside the body, often in a concentrated area. Beta and gamma generally pass through the body without causing much damage.

Q6 a) Gamma.
b) Kills cells.
c) To prevent killing healthy cells.
d) Not all the cancerous cells are killed.
e) Too many healthy cells may be killed.

Q7 Damage to the nucleus of the cells can mean they cannot repair themselves properly, and the skin will not heal.

Q8 Their cells are reproducing very quickly, so any cancer will develop rapidly.

21.4 — Radioactive Decay & Nuclear Reactors

Page 93 — Atomic Structure

Q1 a) **A** = neutron, **B** = proton, **C** = electron (in orbit).
b) The force of attraction between the electrons and the positively charged nucleus.
c) 8.

Q2 Nucleus, electrons, nucleus, protons, protons, neutrons, mass, volume (or *space*), electrons, nucleus, small, 1/2000. neutron, identical (or *the same*).

Q3

Particle	Mass	Charge
Proton	1	+1
Neutron	1	0
Electron	negligible	-1

Q4 a) Alpha particles.
b) The alpha particles need to be able to travel in straight lines, unhindered by gas molecules.
c) X
d) Most particles pass straight through the atoms without collision (the gold atoms being mostly empty space), but a few alpha particles will come close enough to a gold nucleus to be deflected. (The nucleus and alpha particle are both positively charged so they repel one another.)
e) The nucleus must be very small but heavy. **Small** because a head-on collision is very rare, and **heavy** because the alpha particle bounces off the nucleus.
f) Gold has a heavy nucleus and it is an unreactive element. Some more reactive elements may react with the alpha particle.
g) The molecules would be moving around. The nuclei need to be fixed.

Page 94 — Atomic Structure

Q1 a) "Mass number" is the total number of particles (protons + neutrons) in an atomic nucleus.
b) 126.
c) The unstable atom will have a different number of neutrons in its nucleus (being an isotope).

Q2

	No. e^-	No. p^+	No. n^0	Mass No.	Symbol
oxygen-16	8	8	8	16	$^{16}_{8}O$
aluminium-27	13	13	14	27	$^{27}_{13}Al$
radium-226	88	88	138	226	$^{226}_{88}Ra$
strontium-90	38	38	52	90	$^{90}_{38}Sr$
hydrogen-3	1	1	2	3	$^{3}_{1}H$

Q3 element, protons, electrons, neutrons, atomic, mass, element, three, stable, alpha, beta, element.

Q4 Atoms B, C, F.

Q5 a) Atomic number -2, mass number -4.
b) Atomic number +1, mass number unchanged.
c) Atomic number unchanged, mass number unchanged.

Module Twelve — Waves and Radiation

Page 95 — Radioactive Decay

Q1 a) 15 minutes.
b) 45 minutes.
c) About 31 counts per second.
d) 3 hours.

Q2 a)

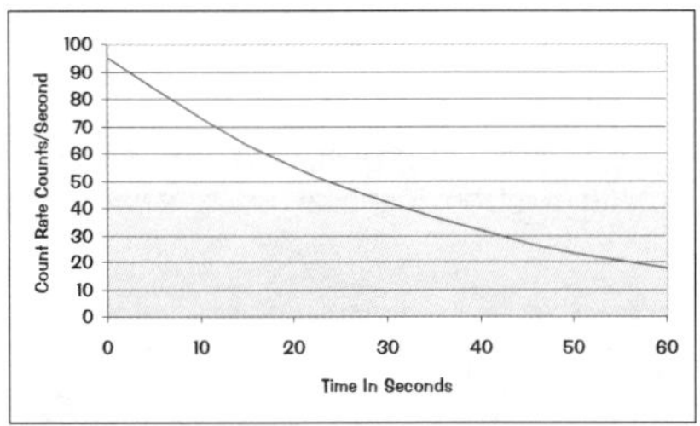

b) 23 ±1 secs.
c) Possible methods: Measure the activity over a long time period; measure a large sample; shield sample and measuring apparatus.

Q3 a) 5,600 years.
b) 16,800 years.
c) 28,000 years.

Q4 Millionth, 12, constant, living, die, decays, activity, long, living, half-life.

Q5 a) $^{210}_{82}\text{Pb} \rightarrow {}^{210}_{83}\text{Bi} + {}^{0}_{-1}\beta \rightarrow {}^{210}_{84}\text{Po} + 2({}^{0}_{-1}\beta)$
b) 5 days (to nearest day).
c) $^{206}_{82}\text{Pb}$ (Mass Number = 206).

21.5 — Ultrasound

Page 96 — Sound Waves

Q1 A vibration.

Q2 Drum skin, violin string, loudspeaker-cone, voice-vocal cords.

Q3 Longitudinal.

Q4 a) 2000Hz, 2kHz.
b) 20Hz.
c) 2Hz.
d) 20kHz.

Q5 a)

Oscilloscope Trace	Frequency (Hz)	Amplitude (V)
E	100	2
C	100	4
B	200	2
D	200	4
A	300	2

b) D is louder than B.

Q6 a) An electrical signal.
b) Converts it into a sound signal.
c) Displays the signal as a visible trace.
d) Turns the sound back into an electrical signal.

Page 97 — Ultrasound

Q1 Frequency, electrical, ultrasound.

Q2 a) 0.0132m = 1.32cm.
b) 0.011m = 1.1cm.
c) 0.0066m = 0.66cm.
d) 0.0033m = 0.33cm.

Q3

Application	Category of use	Ultrasound used to	Basic principles
Removal of kidney stones	Medical	Shatter stones allowing them to be passed out in urine	Use of energy in ultrasound to physically alter material
Quality control	Industrial	Check for cracks in metal castings	Detection of reflected ultrasound to build image
Removal of tartar	Medical	Break up tartar deposits on teeth	Use of energy in ultrasound to physically alter material
Sonar	Military / Scientific	Measure distances to objects or map the sea bed	Detection of reflected ultrasound to build image
Pre-natal screening	Medical	Image the foetus	Detection of reflected ultrasound to build image
Cleaning	Industrial	Cleaning delicate mechanisms without dismantling them	Use of energy in ultrasound to physically alter material

Q4 a) Ultrasound is unlikely to cause any damage to tissues.
b) Ultrasound avoids having to dismantle them and reduces the risk of damage.
c) Surgery is more likely to damage the kidney permanently, and ultrasound will not risk damaging other body parts either.
d) Flaws could cause the material to break. Ultrasound detects tiny cracks, without damage.
e) Tartar encourages the build-up of bacteria, increasing the risk of gum disease. Ultrasound can be used to loosen tartar in difficult-to-reach places.

21.6 — Seismic Waves

Page 98 — Seismic Waves

Q1 a)

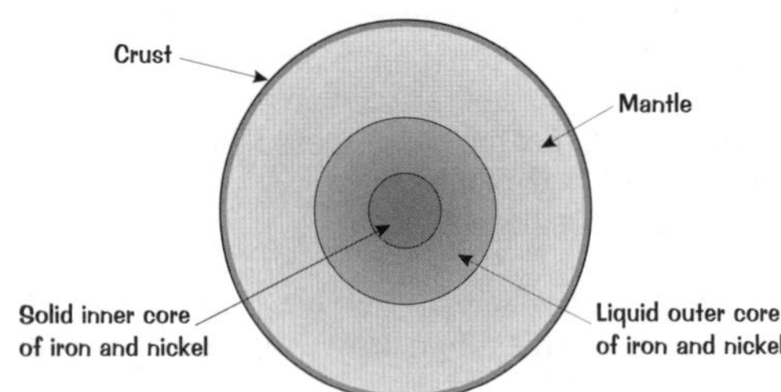

b) Because we can only drill about 10km or so into the crust of the Earth, which is not very far, so seismic waves are really the only way of investigating the inner structure.

Q2 a) A transverse wave that will only travel through solids.
b) Shadow zone.
c) These waves can't travel through the outer core.
d) Solid.

Q3 a) Density
b) The density is continually changing, causing the wave to bend as it slows down or speeds up.

Q4 They are longitudinal, faster than S-waves, and travel through both solids and liquids.

Q5 a) Mantle and the outer core.
b) There is a sudden change of density there.
c) Between points R and S and between points P and Q.
d) They travel through both solids and liquids.

Q6 P-wave; travels faster.

SAV41